ANTONIO DE MENDOZA
FIRST VICEROY OF NEW SPAIN

D, Antonius D Mendoça 1'nouæ Hispanie Pro Rex et dux Generalis
Año. 1535.

V. de Murguia é hijos.

Antonio de Mendoza

First Viceroy of New Spain

BY

ARTHUR SCOTT AITON

NEW YORK / RUSSELL & RUSSELL

FIRST PUBLISHED IN 1927

REISSUED, 1967, BY RUSSELL & RUSSELL

A DIVISION OF ATHENEUM HOUSE, INC.

L. C. CATALOG CARD NO: 66–24664

PRINTED IN THE UNITED STATES OF AMERICA

To

THOMAS MAITLAND MARSHALL
Teacher and Friend

PREFACE

Antonio de Mendoza was the first great administrator in the New World, but despite this fact no adequate study of his labors exists in any language. His work as first Viceroy of New Spain included the establishment of stable government, the completion of "the conquest of Mexico," the organization of social, political, and economic life and the promotion of important discovery and colonization. This study represents an attempt to gather the facts concerning his achievements from widely scattered sources, both printed and manuscript. The great bulk of the new materials used by the writer were found in the Archivo General de Indias in Seville, the most important single find being the complete papers of the first great general *visita* in America made by Francisco Tello de Sandoval, from 1543 to 1547.

The character of the viceroy's task and of the resultant historical materials make this study preëminently institutional. Since the man and his work cannot be divorced, his biography is best written in terms of his most intimate care: the social, political, and economic development of New Spain during his tenure of office. If an excuse for a treatment of this nature is considered necessary, it lies in the fact that the time to examine the projection of institutions from a parent country to an overseas colony is during the critical period of the installation and adjustment of those institutions for New Spain. The epic conquest of Cortés has excited the admiration of historians from Prescott's time to the present to such a degree that not only has the work of his companions been unduly overshadowed, but the whole subsequent movement of conquest and consolidation has been comparatively neglected. The capture of Tenochtitlán was by no means equivalent to the conquest of the vast territory that now goes under the name of Mexico. The last great struggle of the natives to throw off Spanish rule, the Mixton War, and the important work of building up colonial society and government were yet to come. This heavy burden of expansion, completion, and re-casting fell largely on the Viceroy's shoulders and is, in the main, a sober story of institutional beginnings. The thesis is, therefore, the complement to the spectacular initiation of Spanish rule in New Spain by Hernando Cortés, without which the accounts of his last years are relatively unintelligible.

Some of the conclusions reached concerning the introduction of the viceroyalty into New Spain are: (1) that when the audiencia, employed successfully in the West Indies, failed to cope satisfactorily with the problem of a turbulent population, a great area and the control of semi-civilized people in New Spain, vice-regal rule, with its precedents and prestige, was ably superimposed upon it; (2) that the Sandoval *visita* was of greater importance and extent than hitherto has been suspected, and was, in large part, the result of a well-planned attempt on the part of Cortés to oust the viceroy; (3) that the enforcement of the New Laws would have meant the desertion of New Spain by Spanish settlers; (4) that there were noteworthy social and economic developments, such as the elaboration of governmental machinery to protect free Indian labor and to fix just wages; (5) that American history of the sixteenth century is more than a study of conquest and discovery and that the first schools, printing press, mint, mines, ranches, shipyards, cloth factories, and kindred industries should receive greater attention; and (6) that the tremendous output of gold and silver caused the New World to exert an influence on European prices comparable to the effect of the recent output of paper money by the presses of European governments, and should be the object of further study by historians.

The writer's solution of the vexed problems of Spanish terms with no exact English equivalents, of abbreviations in old Spanish texts and of the accentuation of Spanish words will undoubtedly give rise to some criticism. As no generally accepted practice has been adopted, the form which seemed to be best and most reasonable in each case has been used and a special effort to secure consistency has been made. As few modernizations of the old Spanish texts as possible has been the rule, since the faithful reproduction of the original is the accepted ideal of modern scholarship. This has meant the retention of abbreviations as in the original except in cases where the expanded word is not easily discerned in its shortened form.

The preparation of this volume has laid the author under a deep debt to the generous aid and assistance of others. This study was begun in the seminar of Professor H. E. Bolton, of the University of California, to whose knowledge of the entire field, encouragement, and unfailing enthusiasm he owes more than these few words can indicate. Professor H. I. Priestley and Professor C. E. Chapman of the Bancroft Library group also placed their expert knowledge at his disposal and their criticism and assistance beyond the years of graduate study have been greatly appreciated.

A year of research abroad was made possible by the generosity of the Native Sons of the Golden West, a fraternal order which maintains two annual travelling fellowships in history at the University of California. The writer held one of these fellowships during the year 1920-1921 and feels that this excellent phase of the order's activities deserves wider recognition. While in Seville, the writer was extended every courtesy by the officials of the Archivo General de Indias, particularly by the now retired *Jefe* Pedro Torres Lanzas; and, in the early stages of acquaintance with the archives, Miss Irene Wright gave invaluable help from her great store of archive lore. Thanks are also due to the management of the Biblioteca Nacional and the Academia Real de la Historia for permission to use their materials, especially for access to the Muñoz collection of transcripts. In Paris, similar treatment was experienced at the Bibliothèque Nationale, for which the author desires to render grateful acknowledgment.

In this country, the great kindness of Mr. Edward E. Ayer, in granting permission to use materials in the Edward E. Ayer Collection of the Newberry Library, and of Mr. William L. Clements in extending the right to utilize the resources of the William L. Clements Library of the University of Michigan, and the unstinted use of his valuable time accorded by Dr. R. G. Adams, the custodian of the last-named library, are gratefully remembered. In the last phases of composition, Professor R. B. Merriman read and criticized some of the chapters and with a kindliness unusual in this day postponed his treatment of the later phases of the Viceroy's activities to the next volume of his great survey of Spain's rise to world empire. His student, Mr. Salmon, was also generous in providing information concerning the genealogy of the Mendoza family.

In conclusion the writer wishes to express his gratitude to the Duke University Press for their patience and coöperation in the trying days of transformation from manuscript to book. The usual labor of proof-reading was greatly lightened by assistance from his wife.

A. S. A.

Ann Arbor, 1926.

TABLE OF CONTENTS

PLATES

ANTONIO DE MENDOZA
First Viceroy of New Spain

BIOGRAPHICAL FOREWORD

Environment and heredity are the two determining forces whose interplay on man decides the march of events we term history. Where the life and character of a single individual are concerned, their influence is almost irresistible; and no clear comprehension of the meaning of his actions can be gained without reference to his ancestry and a portrayal of the surroundings that molded his character in early youth. This foreword represents an attempt to reconstruct the family and environmental background for Antonio de Mendoza, the first viceroy in the long line that ruled over the destinies of North America for Imperial Spain. His greatness, his limitations, and the qualities that made him respected and revered by his subjects are only understandable in the light of these data and in an appreciation of the age that produced him. His century was the child of past history in Spain and he is only differentiated from it by the forebears from whom he sprang and the world of his associations as a young man.

Two years before the discovery of America, within the grim walls of a mountain outpost on the Granada border, Antonio de Mendoza first saw the light of day.[1] His father, Iñigo López de Mendoza, second Conde de Tendilla

---

[1] "Aviendo sesenta y dos años que murió"—"Mémoire" in *L'Espagne au XVIe et au XVIIe Siècle,* ed. Albert Morel-Fatio, Heilbronn, 1878, p. 59. This would seem to fix 1490 as the date of his birth since he died July 21, 1552, but there is other evidence which points to the early part of 1491. His father met his mother for the first time in two years sometime after the month of April, 1490, when he greeted her in Álcala la Real on his return from a successful raid. Cf. Hernando del Pulgar, "Crónica de los señores reyes católicos," in *Biblioteca de Autores Españoles,* LXX. 508. This reunion must have been a few months later than April, as Antonio's father was not made captain-general of the frontier of Jaén until Ferdinand had come to Córdoba after the festivities held that month in Seville to celebrate the betrothal of the Infanta Isabel and Prince Alonzo of Portugal, and in all likelihood, after the exploits against Alhendin, Marchena, and Albolodny.

and captain-general of the Christian forces before the doomed Moslem stronghold, made this fastness, Álcala la Real, his headquarters.[2] Born on the frontier, the future arbiter of Spanish polity and policy overseas was a scion of the rich and powerful Mendoza family celebrated for its warriors in the annals of the Christian reconquest of Spain. It belonged to the haughtiest Castilian aristocracy, tracing a long lineage back to Roman patricians and the Gothic dukes of Cantabria. It claimed descent from the Cid and the lords of Biscay; the original seat of the main branch of the house being Lodio in Álava, one of the Basque provinces in the north of Spain.[3] Spanish royalty was related to the line through the Catholic monarchs and the dukes of Infantado, who took precedence over all other Spanish grandees. Over seventy titles of nobility were distributed through the family and it ranked not only with the first houses in Spain but had also achieved fame beyond the limits of the Iberian Peninsula.[4]

Distinguished personages adorn the name prior to the viceroy's appearance. His great-grandfather, Iñigo López de

[2] Pablo Beaumont in his *Crónica de Michoacan*, IV. 425 ff., alleges that Antonio de Mendoza named Patzcuaro (modern Morelia) in Michuacán, Valladolid in honor of his birthplace, but the statement is unsupported by any proof save the fact that the city was founded during the viceroy's reign in New Spain. That he had any direct connection with its establishment is exceedingly doubtful. Cf. De la Torre, *Bosquejo histórico y estadístico de la ciudad de Morelia*, Mexico, 1883, pp. 1 ff. Granada itself has been named as his natal city by a number of authorities, notably the *Cartas de Indias*, Ministerio de Fomento, Madrid, 1877, p. 798, and the *Diccionario Universal de historia y de geografía*, but this is impossible since this place was in Moslem hands until January 2, 1492. Álcala la Real has a better claim since the future viceroy's father conducted his operations from it during the period in which he was born and his mother in all probability remained there in 1490, after the journey thither from Guadalajara to join her husband after a separation of two years. Cf. Pulgar, "Crónica," in *Biblioteca de Autores Españoles*, LXX. 508; Medina y Mendoza, "Vida del Cardenas," in *Memorial Histórico Español*, VI. 285.

[3] Medina y Mendoza, *op. cit.*, in *M. H. E.*, VI. 155.

[4] S. P. Scott, *History of the Moorish Empire in Europe*, Philadelphia, 1904, III. 234.

Mendoza, the illustrious Marqués de Santillana, second son of Diego Hurtado de Mendoza, grand-admiral of Spain and its wealthiest nobleman,[5] was one of the outstanding figures of his age. Born in 1398, he became known to the Europe of his day as a poet, statesman, warrior, and scholar. As a mere youth, after the death of his father and his eldest brother, he was compelled to fight to hold his estates together and to recover those lost to rapacious neighbors. He showed himself to be a skilled and determined soldier and earned the respect of his Christian compeers and the fear of the followers of the prophet. He shone both in the courtly circles of his sovereign, Juan II of Castile, and in the knightly accomplishments of the age, once holding the lists all day against any challenger. In short, as Ticknor says, ". . . his name and position were so great that all who discuss his times must notice the important part he played in them."[6] His fiefs lay principally in the Asturias and in Castile and his favorite residence was Guadalajara, which continued to be the chief seat of the Mendozas down to modern times.[7] His title was the direct outcome of gallant action in the battle of Olmedo, in 1445, when a grateful sovereign created him Marquis with a grant of Santillana near Santander. This doughty ancestor was devoted to Our Lady of Guadalupe and remembered her in his motto "Dios Y Vos," used by the viceroy a full century later in the New World.

[5] M. Schiff, *La Bibliothèque du Marquis de Santillane*, Paris, 1905, Introduction, p. xxiv.

[6] G. Ticknor, *History of Spanish Literature*, Boston, 1882, I. 389, footnote B.

[7] "Los Mendozas venían ya con tradición analoga desde mucho antes. D. Gonzalo Yáñez de Mendoza, Montero Mayor de Alonso XI., Casó en Guadalajara con Da. María de Orozco, hija de Iñigo López de Orozco, señor de Santa Olalla, vecino de Quadalajara, tuvieron por hijo a D. Pedro González de Mendoza, señor de Hita y Buitrago."—Quadrado y La Fuente, *Castilla la Nueva*, in *España sus Monumentos Y Artes*, II. 110, footnote A. This last named person became famous in Spanish song for saving the life of Juan I of Castile at the cost of his own in the battle of Aljubarrota in 1385. Cf. Ticknor, *History of Spanish Literature*, I. 387, note 2.

Antonio de Mendoza's grandfather, Iñigo López de
Mendoza, third son[8] of the Marqués and the Marquesa
Catalina de Figueroa,[9] gave his attention from early
youth to the study of letters and the profession of arms.
He distinguished himself by brilliant exploits in the wars
against the Moors and is best known through his inheritance
of Tendilla, a small town near his native city of Guadalajara, honored by Henry IV with the rank of *Conde* in 1468.[10]
His genealogical record is as follows: "Don Iñigo,
the first Conde de Tendilla . . . by grace of his Majesty, Juan
II, caballero of the Order of Santiago, Commendador de Socuellanos, third of the said Order, member of the Council of

[8] The Marqués de Santillana had seven sons and four daughters. The
sons in the order of their birth were: Deigo, Duque de Infantado; Lorenzo, Conde de Coruña; Iñigo López, Conde de Tendilla; Pedro Lasso,
señor de Mondéjar; Pedro González, Grand Cardinal of Spain; Juan
Hurtado señor de Fresno y del Colmenar el Cardoso; Pedro Hurtado,
adelantado de Cazorla for Pedro González.—Medina y Mendoza, *op. cit,.*
in *M. H. E.,* VI. 155. Vilar y Pascual, *Diccionario histórico genealógico
y heráldico de las familias ilustres de la monarquia española,* V. 320,
states that Iñigo López is the second son.

[9] "El solar de la casa de Mendoza es en Alava, donde por linea paterna
deçiende de los señores della. Sus pasados fueron Iñigo López de Mendoza, Marqués de Sanctillana, de cuya felice memoria estan las historias
llenas; el qual fué hijo del Almirante de Castilla Don Diego Hurtado y
de Doña Leonor de la Vega y de Dona María (Mencia) de Cisneros,
. . . y el Almirante su abuelo fué hijo de Pedro Gonzalez de Mendoza,
Mayor domo del Rey, que murió en la de Aljuba Rota, y de Doña
Aldonça de Ayala, camarera de la Reyna Doña Juana Manuel, hijo del
Maestre Don Lorençio de Figueroa y de Doña María de Orozco su
muger, que fué hija de Iñigo López de Orozco, señor de Santa Olalla y
de Doña María de Valdes su muger, y fué el Maestre su abuelo, hijo de
Don Gomez Suarez de Figueroa, que fué eleto Maestre, y murió en la
batalla de Araviana, y de Doña Teresa de Quadros, su muger. De
manera que por parte de su padre tenia Mendoça y Ayala, Lasso de la
Vega y Cisneros; y por parte de su madre era Figueroa, Quadros y
Orozco y Valdes. . . ."—Medina y Mendoza, *op. cit.,* in *M. H. E.,* VI.
154, 155. This is written of his brother Pedro González but applies
equally to him.

[10] The privilege of this *pueblo* was first given to his grandfather
Diego Hurtado de Mendoza for loyalty and service, November 20, 1395.
It passed from him to the first Marqués de Santillana and on his death
to his son, Iñigo López de Mendoza, the viceroy's grandfather. During
his life it was favored by Henry IV of Castile, who raised it from a
señorio to a *condado* and granted the royal rents to the *Conde.*—Catalina García, *Aumentes y notas* to *Relaciones de pueblos que pertenesen
hoy á la provincia de Guadalajara,* in *M. H. E.,* pp. 90 ff.

Henry IV, twice ambassador to Rome, . . . also captain-general against the Moors of Granada on three occasions as well as against Aragon and Navarre; aid in Seville and adelantado of Andalucia, in which charges and others he comported himself with valor."[11] He died February 17, 1479, in Guadalajara, after a life of useful activity on the border marches of Castile. By his wife, Elvira de Quiñones, he left a numerous posterity. One of the sons, Diego Hurtado de Mendoza, sought and found success within the church, rising to be Bishop of Sigienza and Palencia, Patriarch of Antioch, and finally, Cardinal, Archbishop of Seville.[12]

The eldest son, Iñigo López de Mendoza, the viceroy's father, succeeded to the title of Conde de Tendilla and added to it the estate of Mondéjar through his marriage with Marina Lasso de Mendoza.[13] He was a seasoned border fighter and earned an enviable reputation by his matchless ability in the expedients demanded in that harsh school of warfare. So great did his fame become that he was selected

---

[11] *Resumén genealógico de la casa de Mondéjar,* quoted in Quadrado, *op. cit.,* II. 66.

[12] *Relaciones de pueblos,* in *M. H. E.,* XLIII. 96, note 2.

[13] Mondéjar was given to Juan Carillo de Toledo, *caballerizo mayor* of the king's household. He married María (Juana?) de Sandoval and their only daughter, Juana Carillo, brought it into the Mendoza family when she married Pedro Lasso de la Vega, son of the Marqués de Santillana, October 14, 1435. Two daughters resulted from this union, Catalina and Marina. The first married the first duke of Medinaceli and styled herself "Señora de Mondéjar" and the second married the viceroy's father, Iñigo López de Mendoza, and brought him Mondéjar as her dot. Her death in 1477 led to quarrels between Catalina and the Conde de Tendilla over ownership. The dispute was finally settled by a sale to the crown of Castile in 1486, with the understanding that it could be bought back by the *Conde.* From that time it was definitely united to Tendilla and in recognition of the distinguished services rendered by its lord, King Ferdinand made it a marquisate on September 25, 1512. Despite the greater antiquity of the Tendilla title, Mondéjar became the preferred rank and the estate the favorite place of retirement.—*Relaciones de pueblos,* in *M. H. E.,* XLII. 323 ff. Lúcas Alamán, in his *Disertaciones sobre la historia de la República Mexicana,* Mexico, 1844-1849, Apendice 10, and a number of other writers have confused the viceroy's father and grandfather, making one character out of the two quite distinct persons. From this error many of the mistakes in the viceroy's genealogy have arisen.

to aid Pope Innocent VIII, in 1486, against King Ferdinand
of Naples and acquitted himself of this task in such fashion
as to win the admiration of the Holy See.[14] In the last cam-
paigns on the Granada frontier he held important posts and
made his name a terror to those who fought under the cres-
cent. His work, particularly as Captain of Alhama, Álcala
la Real and in the siege of Baeza, was so outstanding that the
Catholic Monarchs made him captain-general of the captured
province and *alcalde* of the Alhambra.[15] For eight years he
ruled over the city and province with unexampled tolerance
and firmness, a remarkable feat in view of the discordant
elements of the population: Jews, Moslems, renegades and
Christians, conquerors and conquered. His able administration and sympathetic attitude kept the peace and promoted
prosperity until the intrusion of Cardinal Ximénez, whose
intolerant and forceful methods of conversion to Christianity led to disorders and revolt. On one occasion during this
tumultuous period, the Spaniards were only saved from disaster by the coolness of the captain-general and by the esteem
in which he was held by the Moslems. He appeared unarmed
among the enraged populace, promised reform, and left his
wife and two children in the insurgent quarter as a pledge
of good faith. The effect of this bold move was instantane-
ous and the tumult subsided. We can well believe that the

[14] During his stay in Rome he negotiated the bull of July 13, 1486,
granting the Catholic Monarchs the patronage of all the churches of the
kingdom of Granada, and because of his efforts Peter Martyr, famous as a
man of letters and historian of the discovery of America, was induced to
come to Spain, where he died, prior of the Granada Cathedral, in 1526.—
La Fuente y Alcántara, *Historia de Granada,* Paris, 1852, II. 353. By
the license of Innocent VIII, he added a star of eight points and the
legend "Buena Guia" to the coat of arms of his house. "Buena Guia,"
it will be recalled, was the name first applied to the Colorado river by
Alarcón in honor of the viceroy, Antonio de Mendoza, the son.—*Relaciones de pueblo,* in *M. H. E.,* XLIII. 98.

[15] *Relaciones de Pueblos,* in *M. H. E.,* XLIII. 98; "Mémoire," in
Morel-Fatio, *L'Espagne au XVIe et au XVIIe Siècle,* p. 58.

future viceroy was one of the children.[16] In 1512,[17] weighed down by the burden of seventy-seven years, he retired from active service, and his death, July 16, 1515,[18] was mourned by both Christian and unbeliever. His sons and the nobility of the city attended the funeral and his remains were placed in the Chapel of St. Francis within the Alhambra.[19]

The oldest son, Luís Hurtado de Mendoza, third Conde de Tendilla and second Marqués de Mondéjar, had been acting as captain-general of Granada for his father since 1512 and continued to occupy this post, which was to descend from father to son in this family for one hundred and four years.[20] His record includes leadership in Granada against the Communeros; command of the cavalry in the capture of Tunis in 1535, where he killed the notorious Cidececia in single combat; the presidency of the Councils of the Indies, of Castile, and of War; and honorable retirement in 1564. His father had married twice, first his cousin, Marina Lasso de Mendoza, who had brought him Mondéjar, and three years after her death without issue, in 1477, he had wedded his third cousin Francisca Pacheco, daughter of Juan Pacheco, Marqués de Villena. Antonio, with whom this work is chiefly concerned, was the second son by this union.[21] He was a caballero in the Order of Santiago and his official life was spent as royal chamberlain, ambassador to Hungary, and viceroy of New Spain and Peru. The younger brothers were Francisco, vicar-general of the army, Abbot of Medina del Campo and Valladolid, bishop of Jaén, ambassador to the

[16] Prescott, *History of the Reign of Ferdinand and Isabella the Catholic*, Philadelphia, 1864, II. 419.

[17] "Mémoire," in Morel-Fatio, *L'Espagne au XVIe et au XVIIe Siècle*, p. 58.

[18] *Relaciones de Pueblos*, in *M. H. E.*, XLIII. 98, note 2.

[19] La Fuente y Alcántara, *Historia de Granada*, II. 352.

[20] "Mémoire," in Morel-Fatio, *L'Espagne au XVIe et au XVIIe Siécle*, p. 63.

[21] *Ibid.*, 58.

Council of Trent, and finally Cardinal; Bernardino, Governor of Goleta, lieutenant-general of the Spanish galleys, and viceroy of Naples; and Diego Hurtado, ambassador to Venice, England, and Rome, representative at the Council of Trent, and possible author of *La Guerra de Granada* and the early picaresque novel *Lazarillo de Tormes*. The sisters were María, Condesa de Monteagudo and María de Pacheco, who achieved fame as the wife of Juan de Padilla, the leader of the communeros of Castile. After her husband's death she carried on the revolt and was the heroine of the siege of Toledo that finally crushed it.[22]   Another sister, the illegitimate Leonor Beltrán, came to New Spain with her half-brother, the viceroy, and married a conquistador. Still another sister, María de Mendoza, remains to be accounted for by the historian. She was, apparently, another illegitimate daughter and came to the Indies, where she married a mine owner of noble birth, Martín de Ircio, and reared a family.[23]

[22] This María fled to Portugal on a mule carrying geese, in the guise of a laboring woman, and there nursed a hope that some day she would be made Queen of Spain in accordance with the prophecy of Granada witches.—Gómara, *Annals of the Emperor Charles V*, Oxford, 1912, p. 66. She died there, March, 1531, and was buried in the Cathedral in Oporto.—Manuel Danvila, *Historia Crítica y documentada de las communidades de Castilla*, V, in *M. H. E.*, XXXIX. 584.

[23] Vilar, *Diccionario Histórico*, V. 360. The record of her appearance in the New World is quite voluminous, as alleged ill treatment of her was one of the charges brought against the viceroy when his administration was undergoing a *visita*. The tenth charge placed against the viceroy, June, 1546, was ". . . que aviendose casado por palabras de presente Martin dircio con mi hermana por su procurador en los reynos de Castilla y como a tal muger suya el dicho Martin dircio ynbio mucha plata con que viniese y venida que fue como su muger a esta nueva españa y ciudad de Mexico yo la tuve en mi casa. mas de dos años que no la di al dicho Martin dircio" A. G. I., 48-1-2/24, Descargos del virrey, Mexico, October 30, 1546. She had taken a vow before coming to New Spain which might prevent her marriage, and, while consulting *letrados* and churchmen, lodged with the viceroy. After her doubts had been dispelled, she married and in 1546 she was living with her husband and children at Zumpango. A. G. I., 48-1-5/27, Interrogatorio de Mendoza, preguntas 26, 27. Coronado testifies that on his return from his journey she was installed in a separate quarter of the viceroy's palace and enjoyed complete liberty and that he attended her wedding with Martín de Ircio.

We know very little about the early career of the future viceroy. It is fairly certain that he spent his youth in and about Granada, where his father ruled, and that he received an education in the knightly accomplishments of the time as befitted his rank. In later years he spoke of *letrados* with contempt,[24] and gave proof of military training by leading troops in the field with marked success. Indeed, the warlike surroundings of Granada and the traditions of his family could only have led toward one other profession than that of arms—the Church. In 1515 we catch our first certain glimpse of him as a mourner at his father's funeral in Granada. Five years later we sight him again during the course of the uprisings in the province caused by the war of the communeros. With one hundred horse and five hundred foot soldiers, he marched to Huescar and defeated the revolutionaries in that vicinity and, together with his brother Bernardino, was of greatest assistance to the Marqués de Mondéjar, his older brother and captain-general of Granada.[25]

Antonio de Mendoza's succeeding activities were in the field of diplomacy and took him abroad in the service of the Emperor, Charles V. In the month of November, 1526, he set out from Spain for Flanders accompanied by another agent, Presinga. While awaiting definite orders at a northern seaport town he was commissioned to undertake a differ-

A. G. I., 48-1-9/31, Testigo de Coronado, pregunta 27. This would fix the date of her arrival as sometime during his absence in 1540 and 1541 and distinguishes her from Leonor Beltrán who came to the New World with Antonio de Mendoza in 1535. Fortunately she testifies in person that she is a sister of the viceroy on the father's side, is thirty years old, and came to New Spain six years prior to the date of her testimony. A. G. I., 48-1-7/29, Testigo de Maria de Mendoza in Probanza hecha en las minas de çumpango, March 28, 1547.

[24] *Carta de D. Antonio de Mendoza á su Magestad,* Mexico, June 20, 1544, in *Instrucciones que los Vireyes de Nueva España dejaron á sus Sucesores,* 240, 241.

[25] La Fuente y Alcántara, *Historia de Granada,* II. 355. Letters of the Marqués de Mondéjar to the Emperor, Granada, December 6, 19, 1520, in *M. H. E.,* XXXVI. 758-763.

ent mission, namely, to carry letters of credit worth 100,000 ducats to Ferdinand, King of Hungary, and the Emperor's brother. Much depended on the safe arrival of the money and there was grave danger of hostile interception. Mendoza discharged this delicate task with speed and discretion. He remained in Hungary as imperial ambassador until the early part of 1528, when he returned to Madrid. In 1529 he was in Zaragoza for a period and in the autumn, in Madrid, he first indicated his willingness to govern New Spain, when an offer was made by the Queen, whom he was attending as chamberlain. His actual appointment as viceroy was delayed, however, until April 17, 1535. Early in 1530 he journeyed to Italy to visit Charles V and inform him concerning his wife and family. On the morning of February 11, 1530, he joined the court at Bologna and elected to remain for the coronation ceremonies. Very shortly thereafter, a threat of renewed war forced him to hasten back to Spain, where he assumed new duties as representative of Hungary at the Queen's Court. Later, in 1530, lawsuits and other interests held him in Spain and prevented the acceptance of a diplomatic errand to Germany, and, finally, in June, 1534, a fortunate absence from the court in Madrid on a visit to Granada precluded an appointment to Hungary which would have shut him out from New World affairs altogether, as a change of government in New Spain became imperative by 1535. The greater part of this year was given over to preparation for a long sojourn overseas, although Mendoza little suspected that the balance of his days were to be given to the consolidation of the Spanish Empire in America. One of his last acts was to entrust the administration of his affairs to one of his brothers.[26]

[26] The above account is based largely on the diplomatic correspondence of King Ferdinand's Ambassador to the Spanish Court, Martín de Salinas, to be found in A. R. Villa, *El Emperador Carlos V y su corte,* Madrid, 1903, pp. 336-735, *passim.* Additional materials are to be found

Some months after Mendoza's appointment to the office of viceroy of New Spain, he sailed from San Lúcar for the land of his life work, Mexico, where he arrived in October, 1535. After a rule of fifteen eventful years, marked by great success, he was transferred to Peru. An official of such proved value could not be spared even for a well-earned furlough. He arrived in Lima, his new capital, broken in health but hopeful that the change of scene and of climate would restore his waning physical powers. But no respite was granted him, as Peru was in the throes of a controversy over the enforcement of the New Laws prohibiting personal service by the natives. He became involved in the controversy through his office and his counsel of moderation created a breach between himself and the audiencia there. His enfeebled health proved unequal to the strain and he died on July 21, 1552, struggling from his deathbed against the unwise action of his audiencia. His body was buried with great pomp and ceremony in the Cathedral of Lima next to the swine-herd of Trujillo, Francisco de Pizarro. Thus by the irony of history, the aristocratic first viceroy and the lowborn conqueror slept side by side.

Concerning the immediate family of Mendoza, we know that he married Catalina de Vargas, one of the ladies-in-waiting to the Catholic Queen, some time before he was appointed viceroy of New Spain.[27] One son from this union, Iñigo de Mendoza, surnamed "el largo," remained in Europe and served in the imperial armies. He met his death

in Great Britain: Public Record Office, *Calendar of Letters, Despatches, and State Papers, Relating to the Negotiations between England and Spain,* London, 1862-1916, III. 1035, 1058, pt. ii, 1, 14, 25, 72, 106, 148, 150, 246, 660, 680; IV. 472, 479, 528, 714. A visit to England, where he was presented to Henry VIII at Greenwich early in 1527, while en route to Ferdinand's court at Prague, is the most significant additional information concerning Mendoza's movement afforded by these despatches.

[27] According to the *Cartas de Indias,* pp. 798, 799, her name was Catalina de Carvajal. Probably the full name was Catalina de Vargas y Carvajal.

in the siege of San Quentin by Prince Philip, where his illustrious uncle Bernardino died from fatigue, exposure, and
worry due to the vacillation of the over-cautious Philip.[28]
Another son, Francisco, was the trusted coadjutor of
his father in New Spain and accompanied him to Peru.[29]
After his father's death he returned to Spain, where he was
styled "el Indio" by reason of his American antecedents.[30]
He became captain-general of the galleys of Spain, Governor of the mines of Guadalcanal, and bore the titles of
Commendador de Socuellanos in the Order of Santiago and
Lord of the Villas of Extremadura and Valdaracete. He
died without heirs in 1563.[31]

Supposedly contemporary portraits of the viceroy, which
have come down to us, show him to have had a commanding
presence.[32] Dark, somewhat portly in his viceregal robes,
he appears to have been of average height. Keen eyes set in
a long face, a determined chin and a firm mouth, not too
effectively concealed by a well-kept beard and moustache, an
aquiline nose and high forehead, give an impression of as-

[28] Morel-Fatio, *L'Espagne au XVIe et au XVIIe Siècle*, p. 59.

[29] In 1549, when the viceroy was so ill that his recovery was doubtful,
Francisco discharged the duties of viceroy and the home government
was besieged with letters urging that he be officially recognized as his
father's coadjutor and in case of the latter's death he be appointed as
viceroy. This entire movement was rebuked in a letter from the King,
Peñafiel, May 8, 1550. A. G. I., 87-6-2, Oficio y parte, 231.

[30] Morel-Fatio, *L'Espagne au XVIe et au XVIIe Siècle*, p. 59.

[31] *Cartas de Indias,* p. 800.

[32] There are two pictures of note which were copied faithfully from
the contemporary portrait now in the possession of the Museo Nacional
in Mexico City; one in M. Rivera-Cambas, *Los Gobernantes de Mexico,*
Mexico, 1872, 1873, I. 28, the other in *El Liceo Mexicano,* I. 166.
Rivera-Cambas insists on the authenticity of the portrait reproduced in
his work, *op. cit.,* 4, but differences in the other likeness suggest that it
might be taken from another portrait painted later or else that it is
the product of less skillful artistry. In both pictures the Mendoza coat
of arms appears. It is the old shield of the Mendoza and Vega families
consisting of an ". . . eau parti en chef et en pointe de sinople à la
bande de goules bordée d'or (Mendoza) à dextre et à senestre d'or, à
la dévisse de 'Ave María' (Vega)."—Schiff, *La bibliothèque du Marquis
de Santillane,* in *École des Hautes Études,* CLIII, LIV.

tuteness, decision, and high ideals in keeping with the record of his accomplishments. Yet the likeness is not devoid of a suggestion of underlying kindness and human sympathy, which is in accord with contemporary accounts of his life, particularly with respect to his policy toward the subject native population in New Spain, for he so tempered strict justice with mercy that they revered him as their protector against wanton inhumanity.[33] The general conclusion concerning his character drawn from his deeds and writings and from the opinion of his age is that he was resolute, amiable, and just toward all in his public dealings. He was hospitable to a fault, entertaining needy caballeros in his palace at his own expense, and on one occasion providing freely for the 300 survivors of the Hernando de Soto expedition.[34] Coronado says of him, "He was such a zealous Christian and was so rigorous in obeying the commands of God" that he "knew no churchman even of good reputation and life who was as conscientious as the viceroy"; and Baltasar de Obregón, looking back on his reign, remarks that when Mendoza left New Spain all the inhabitants were saddened "because in him they were losing a courageous Catholic man of prudence and principle, who governed this kingdom in peace, love, and concord, a father to all in this land, which he protected, favored, and rendered prosperous by praiseworthy and prudent means."[35]

[33] In 1540, the natives set aside a *cazadero* between Xilotepec and San Juan del Río, near Mexico, as a memorial for his kindness to them. —*El Liceo Mexicana*, I. 169.

[34] *Gentleman of Elvas Narrative* in *Spanish Explorers in the Southern United States*, p. 269.

[35] A. G. I., 1-1-3/22. n. 7, Baltasar de Obregón, *Crónica*, from M.S copy in the Bolton Collection, University of California.

CHAPTER I.

THE APPOINTMENT OF A VICEROY

A new period in Spanish colonization in the New World was inaugurated by the epic conquest of Hernando Cortés.[1] Over a quarter of a century elapsed after the landing of Columbus before this great success produced the rich profits which were the aim of Spain's exploring activity. Her navigators had run the coastline of the continents seeking a strait to the East and a share in its lucrative trade. Her adventurers had been lured to the mainland at various points by rumors of gold and pearls. In the larger islands of the West Indies settlement and exploitation merely served to teach the first lessons in successful imperialism, the fruits of which were to appear later on the mainland. But no solid pecuniary reward had come from these efforts to offset Portuguese triumphs "beyond the line." It remained for the obscure Estremaduran to transmute failure into a dazzling triumph. Following in the footsteps of two earlier expeditions, he instituted the conquest of the semi-civilized Mayas and Nahuas of Mexico, Yucatán, and Central America. These natives lived in substantial towns, possessed a

[1] A recapitulation of early Spanish discovery and exploration is omitted for obvious reasons, nor is it deemed necessary to recount the spectacular conquest of Tenochtitlán by Cortés and his companions. W. H. Prescott and his successors have accomplished this last task so well as to make more than an allusion to it in a work of this character supererogatory. It should be pointed out, however, that the fall of the city, or even the subjection of the area under its control, was not equivalent to the conquest of the vastly greater area which was to bear the name of New Spain. What is usually termed "the Conquest of Mexico" should be more properly designated as "the Conquest of the Nahua Confederation." A study of the page-space devoted to Cortés and particularly his career up to 1521, as compared with that given to general Mexican history, reveals a decidedly faulty emphasis in most of the writers. The story of the completion of the conquest merits a more extended treatment.

considerable supply of the precious metals, and their fixed population, inured to toil, offered a tremendous labor supply for Spanish exploitation. Spain was at last in contact with the most highly developed New World civilizations and the first great store of accumulated wealth aroused men's passions and hopes to the high pitch of the succeeding "Age of the Conquistadores."

As soon as the magnitude of the achievement of the original conqueror was realized in Spain, Charles V and his advisors took steps to make Imperial control over the new possessions more secure. This involved the gradual removal of power over the colony from the hands of Cortés. To encourage new conquests without undue expense to the Crown, Spain was willing to grant extensive rights and privileges to persons who would fit out exploring expeditions at their own cost, but when these ventures proved successful the interests of the home country were best safeguarded by agents more dependent on the government in Spain. Cortés, in the case of New Spain, was regarded as no better than an extraordinarily fortunate adventurer whose control over the Indians and influence with the conquistadores constituted a menace to direct government through representatives who owed their power and office to the King alone. Very early was appreciated the danger of leaving him undisputed authority in the lands he had won. He was an obstacle to be removed, but the necessity of placating him, while his military services were needed and promises of continued accomplishments were held out, slowed up the process by which his wide powers were curtailed and his position made intolerable.

In keeping with this purpose the Spanish Government supplanted Cortés very gradually by officials of its own. Expediency dictated the series of steps by which his presence in New Spain was rendered unnecessary: a program which ultimately forced the establishment of a viceroyalty. Nothing less could have exerted the same measure of prestige or have wielded an equal amount of authority. The very day that his rather nebulous claims to legal authority for his acts were confirmed by an appointment as governor and captain-general of New Spain, October 15, 1522, the central government took over the management of its most vital concern, finance. Royal officers, contador, treasurer, veedor, and assessor, were appointed.[2] These officials arrived in Mexico in 1524 and displaced the appointees of Cortés in the administration of real hacienda. Two years later a more serious blow was struck when the licentiate Luís Ponce de León arrived. He proclaimed the residencia of Cortés, suspended him from the exercise of judicial functions, and assumed the governorship for the duration of the legal process. Cortés was left with only the management of the Indians and military leadership as captain-general. The subsequent deaths, in rapid succession, of the judge of residence and his successor, Marcos de Aguilar, brought the royal treasurer Alonso de Estrada into power. Numerous affronts, which culminated in orders to desist from exercising his office as captain-general, finally drove Cortés to Spain to seek the restitution of his former commands and proper reward for his great services.[3]

In the meantime the Emperor and his advisors, partly influenced by the complaints of the enemies of Cortés, had determined to remedy the situation by the establishment of an audiencia in Mexico similar to the one set up in Santo Domingo in 1524, but clothed with greater powers.[4] They feared that the presence of Cortés might hamper the activities

[2] A. G. I., 48-1-2/24, Merced del oficio de contador al Rodrigo de Albornoz, Valladolid, October 15, 1522.—Bancroft, *History of Mexico* San Francisco, 1883-87, II. 92, 142-145.

[3] Bancroft, *History of Mexico,* II, Chapters xii and xiii, contain a detailed account of the events leading up to his departure for Spain.

[4] *Ibid.,* II. 274; Bancroft, *History of Central America,* San Francisco, 1882-1887, I. 269-70; Riva Palacio, ed., *México á través de los Siglos,* Barcelona, 1888, 1889, II. 147.

of this body, and so requested his presence in Spain, an invitation which accorded exactly with his own plans. His arrival was too late to affect the new government, however, as the first audiencia was appointed December 13, 1527, and he set foot on Spanish soil toward the end of 1528.[5] This body was composed of four licentiates, Francisco Maldonado of Salamanca, Alonso de Parada, who had resided in Cuba, Diego Delgadillo of Granada, and Juan Ortiz de Matienzo, a Biscayan. Nuño de Guzmán, the governor of Pánuco, was appointed president and as the first two died soon after they reached Mexico he was left with only two oidores to aid him in managing the affairs of New Spain.

The oidores arrived in New Spain in December, 1528, and Guzmán assumed his duties as president the first day of the next year. His rule has been described as an orgy of extortion, misgovernment, and cruelty, but a more complete study of the documents in his case may show him to have been no worse than a number of the more successful impresarios of his age with whom history has dealt less harshly.[6]

[5] Bancroft, *History of Mexico*, II. 304, note 26, collates the authorities as to the exact date of the landing in Palos. Herrera, followed by Prescott and others, fixes it at the end of May. Bancroft prefers to follow Gómara and Sandoval, who indicate a date near the close of the year.

[6] The great mass of unutilized Guzmán material existent in the Archivo General de Indias may shed further light on this question when it is thoroughly investigated. The general tenor of the royal orders addressed to Cortés and to the president and oidores of the second audiencia certainly indicate that Guzmán was in good standing at court despite the failure of his government, and that a successful conquest in New Galicia would have brought complete exoneration. Belief in his integrity caused an order to be issued that his residencia be taken without recalling him from his conquest. In addition it was ordered that only fines of less than 10,000 maravedís be assessed against him, and that the balance be placed in deposit for a subsequent appeal. A. G. I., 87-6-1, Oficio y parte, libro 2, XV; Madrid, September 26, 1530, XLV; Ocaña, January 13, 1535, XLVI; Carta, January 25, 1531, LVI; Ocaña, February 17, 1531, libro 3, XXVII; Medina del Campo, March 20, 1532, XXXII-XLVII; Medina del Campo, March 20, 1532, CIX; Medino del Campo, June 5, 1532. Even as late as December 10, 1532, an order to Guzmán to appear before the Council of the Indies within one year to answer certain charges in his residencia was suspended in order not to interrupt the conquest of New Galicia.—*Ibid.*, CLXIX, Madrid, December 10, 1532. The journey of Bishop Zumárraga to

Whatever the truth may be, the activities of the audiencia greatly dissatisfied the Spanish colonists, particularly the influential representatives of the Church. On one occasion, while the oidores, Matienzo and Delgadillo, were in the jail of the audiencia in Mexico City examining the prisoners, the bishop-elect, Juan de Zumárraga, went so far in his opposition as to lead a procession of Dominican and Franciscan friars to its gate, where they held aloft two crosses draped in black, while he proclaimed the oidores to be impostors who held no true power from the King, and whose commands should not be obeyed.[7]

The open quarrel between Church and audiencia finally forced the resolute Zumárraga, when the right of sanctuary was violated, to employ the most effective weapon in his spiritual armory, and he placed the latter under a solemn ban of excommunication in March, 1530. The chief failings of the audiencia, as detailed in the complaints, were peculation in office, the granting of excessive license to brand Indian slaves, the sale of justice, harsh treatment of the friends of Cortés, and failure to coöperate with the Church in its efforts to secure better treatment of the natives. The oidores were also accused of neglect of duty. In the words of the bluff old veteran, Bernal Díaz, "They did not reside in their offices, nor take their seats in court every day as they were bound to do, but went about to banquets and indulged in love making and gambling, and some of them were embarrassed by it."[8]

Spain to discuss the difference of opinion evident in his reports and those of the second audiencia as to methods of converting the Indians, in response to royal order of January 25, 1531, probably marked the turning point in Guzmán's favor at court.—*Ibid.*, libro 2, XLIX. Displeasure with his rule over New Spain was expressed much earlier than this, however, and in a number of statements, of which the following from Fuenleal's appointment to succeed him is typical ". . . q no an guardado nras ynstruciones y q an entendido mas en sus intereses particulares q en lo q conbenia a la buena gobernacion de aquella tierra. . . ."— *Ibid.*, libro 1, CCXVI, Madrid, April 11, 1530.

[7] A. G. I., 144-1-10, Información, Mexico, March 5, 1530.

[8] Bernal Díaz, *True History of the Conquest of New Spain*, London, 1916, V. 161.

Soon the rumors of discontent in New Spain grew into such a flood of demands for relief "with proofs and even letters from bishops and ecclesiastics, that when his Majesty and the Lords of the Royàl Council of the Indies saw the reports and letters which were brought against them, his majesty promptly ordered that the whole Royal Audiencia should be completely removed without delay, and that they should be punished and another President and Oidores be appointed, who would be learned and honorable and fair in doing justice."[9]

As the Emperor Charles V was on the point of departure from Spain when the problem of providing a more suitable government for New Spain became acute, he charged his wife, Isabel of Portugal, with the task. Feeling the importance of a proper settlement of the affairs of such a valuable revenue-producing province, he also took care to see that she was given competent advice.[10]   The president and certain members of the Council of Castile, the Council of the Indies headed by the Conde de Osorno, and the Council of Finance, were called together to consider what should be done in New Spain to further the spread of the faith and to provide good government.[11] The decision of this junta was that the remedy for all the ills of New Spain lay in the appointment of some

[9] *Ibid.,* V. 163.   This, of course, is the expression of the extreme view of a Cortés partizan.

[10] " . . . el Emperador y Rey mi Señor teniendo por tan grande y principal cosa las provincias de la Nueba españa y tan ymportante a la Coruña real destos reynos enbio a mandar q se juntasen el muy Rev^{do} y Xpo padre arcob^{po} de Santa Dm^o presydente del consejo y con el algunos del consejo y asymismo el conde de Osorno presydente del consejo de las yndias y los del dho consejo y los del consejo de la hazienda y que platicasen en lo que debenian proveer. . . ." A. G. I., 87-6-1, Oficio y parte, libro 1, CII, November 9, 1529.

[11] " . . . para el servicio de dios Nro Sr y . . . Nro Santa Fe Católica y para el buen governacion de los dichas provincias . . ." *Ibid.* It was probably during these meetings of the several councils under the direction of the Empress that the decision against the retention of encomiendas, alluded to by Bancroft, was reached. Cf. Bancroft, *History of Mexico,* II. 328.

great personage near the throne to rule over it.[12]   The
Queen immediately sent out letters to a number of persons
who were qualified to accept such an appointment. The
Conde de Oropeso declined the honor on a plea of poor
health.[13] Identical letters were then despatched to the
Marescal de Fromesta and to Antonio de Mendoza, November 9, 1529, urging them to assume the duty.[14] The Marescal de Fromesta made what were considered to be excessive
demands in salary and preferment, but Mendoza's reply was
not only both favorable and satisfactory but it also expressed
a desire to come to court immediately to discuss the new
obligation.[15] As Mendoza would need time to set his
affairs in order and to make necessary preparations for an
indefinite absence from Spain and as the affairs of New
Spain required immediate attention, it was decided that a
new audiencia be appointed forthwith.[16]

The selection of the membership of the second audiencia
was intrusted to the Bishop of Badajoz.   By April 5, 1530,
he had secured acceptance by four new oidores, the licentiate

[12] " . . . ha parecido q el remedio de todo consyste en enviar una
principal persona. . . ." A. G. I., 87-6-1, Oficio y parte, libro 1, CII,
November 9, 1529.

[13] " . . . que por sus enfermedades no tenia dispusycion para ello
. . . . " Ibid.

[14] " . . . . para saber de vos sy teneys despusycion de yr este viaje
donde tanto Nro Sr y S. M. y yo seremos servidos . . ." Ibid. The word
viceroy is not employed in this document but the intention to appoint
such an officer is evident.

[15] " . . . y de la voluntad q mostrais para serbir al empor my Señor
etn este negocio estoy yo bien cierta por que es confomre a lo q syempre
vros pasados hizieron en servicio de nra Corona Real yo vos agradezco
y tengo en servicio lo q en ella dezis la licencia q pedis para venir aca
quando sea tpo yo os lo mandare enbiar y avisar de lo q en ello debeis
hazer. . . " Ibid., CXVI, Madrid, November 19, 1529.

[16] This decision was reached before January 6, 1530, since the nominations of Vasco de Quiroga, Francisco Ceynos, and Alonso Maldonado
as oidores of the new audiencia bear that date. A. G. I., 87-6-1, Oficio
y parte, libro 1, CXLV. Bancroft, History of Mexico, II. 321, is led into
accepting a date early in March as the time of this action by Pacheco y
Cárdenas, XII. 404. The numerous orders which supplemented the
original nominations are probably the cause of the existing confusion
with respect to this date.

Vasco de Quiroga to replace Alonso de Parada deceased, the licentiate Alonso Maldonado to replace Francisco Maldonado deceased, the licentiate Francisco de Ceynos to replace Juan Ortiz de Matienzo, and the licentiate Juan de Salmerón to replace Diego Delgadillo.[17] Quiroga had served the King well in Spain as a juéz de residencia and was to achieve enduring fame in New Spain as a churchman and friend of the Indians; Maldonado came directly from the colegio in Salamanca; Ceynos was a former fiscal of the Council of the Indies; and Salmerón had had New World experience as alcalde mayor of Castilla del Oro. Salaries for the office were fixed at 6,000 maravedís annually, supplemented by 150,000 maravedís for expenses and an equal sum to defray the cost of the journey to Mexico.[18]

The selection of a president to head the second audiencia proved to be more difficult, as it was essential that a person of proved integrity and ability be secured. Several possible appointees were solicited without avail before the bishop of Santo Domingo, Sebastián Ramírez de Fuenleal, president of the audiencia on Española, was persuaded to undertake the burden. This "persuasion" took the form of an order from the Queen, Madrid, April 11, 1530, in which the bishop was informed that the affairs of New Spain had not been properly handled by the first audiencia and that he had been selected, in view of his experience and good record, as president of a second audiencia. On the completion of his work of reforming the government on the mainland it was promised that he could return to his former charge and bishopric

[17] A. G. I., 87-6-1, Oficio y parte, libro 1, CCXXIII, Madrid, April 5, 1530. Bancroft, following Puga (*Cédulas,* I. 37) states that they were not officially named until July 12, 1530 (*History of Mexico,* II. 321, note 1).

[18] *Ibid.,* CCXXV, Madrid, April 5, 1530. The maravedí is equivalent to about a sixth of a cent in present-day United States money, but its actual value, or purchasing power, was then certainly many times greater than this.

and that a president would be appointed in his stead.[19] The newly appointed oidores sailed from Spain September 16, 1530, and arrived at Vera Cruz near the end of the year, but Fuenleal, already an old man, was loath to undertake the heavy task assigned him in this arbitrary manner. He lingered in Santo Domingo so long that his arrival in Mexico was postponed until September of the following year and only the most peremptory orders accomplished this tardy obedience.[20]

Cortés had been disappointed in his great ambition to be made governor of New Spain once more. While he was in the apparent heyday of his influence at court, the Queen was seeking a great personage, quite unrelated to the conquest, for viceroy, and a new government in which he had but a relatively small share was appointed. His commission to explore in the South Sea, his continuance as captain-general of New Spain, a grant of twenty-three thousand Indians in encomienda, and the title of Marqués del Valle de Oaxaca were the greatest favors he could induce the Crown to concede.[21] Nuño de Guzmán likewise saw the end of his brief day of authority. When he heard that he was to be deprived of the presidency and his audiencia was to be removed from office, he adopted a bold course. Using his position he collected all the soldiers he could find, "both horsemen and musketeers and crossbowmen," and departed for Jalisco on the West Coast. The conquest of the province of New Galicia was the result of this expedition.

[19] *Ibid.*, CCXVI, Madrid, April 11, 1530.

[20] A good example of the numerous orders urging Fuenleal to hasten to his new duties is that of the queen dated in Ocaña, February 27, 1531; *ibid.*, libro 2, LXVI.

[21] His commission of October 27, and the confirmatory cédula of November 5, 1529, are printed in Pacheco y Cárdenas, XII. 490-496. Additional indications of his true situation were orders to stay until the new audiencia departed and subsequent commands to keep ten leagues between himself and the Capital City: A. G. I., 87-6-1, Oficio y parte, libro 1, CCXX, Laguna, March 22, 1530, printed in Pacheco y Cárdenas, XII. 403-5; Bancroft, *History of Mexico*, II. 318.

Unfortunately for Guzmán, no New Mexico existed there and, despite an Amazon Queen, he looked in vain for the plunder that would earn forgiveness for his deeds of misrule. For a time he was able to maintain a precarious position based on the hope of gain his conquest and letters aroused in the Crown. Active rivalry with Cortés, whose plans he had anticipated, and defiance of the new audiencia, which had been instructed to conduct his residencia, mark the period down to the establishment of the viceroyalty in 1535. His promises of success brought him appointment as governor over New Galicia,[22] instructions to the second audiencia to advise and favor him in every way possible,[23] the payment of his salary in his old position up to the date of the arrival of the new government,[24] a loan of money on security,[25] permission to undergo residencia *in absentia,*[26] and instructions to Cortés to stay out of New Galicia and confine his discoveries to the South Sea.[27]

Guzmán's endeavors were not utterly sterile. With the help of his able lieutenant, Cristóbal de Oñate, the permanent

[22] Bancroft (*History of Mexico,* II. 365, note 56) says that the document containing the confirmation of Guzmán as governor is not extant. He collates the printed authorities and finds no earlier mention than February 17, 1531. A letter of the queen from Ocaña to the President and oidores of the audiencia of New Spain of January 25, 1531, informs them of the confirmation as already accomplished. "Por las relaciones q Nuño de Guzmán ha enbiado del descubrimiᵒ y conquista que fue a hazer he sydo informada del succeso q dios enello le ha dado y asy por . . . tan bien començo como por la buena ynformacion q tengo de la persona del dho nuño de Guzmán habemos acordado de le Nombrar por nro gobernador de la trra q ha conquistado y pacificado a la qual habemos mando Nombrar Galicia de la Nueva Espana . . . " A. G. I., 87-6-1, Oficio y parte, libro 2, XLVI.

[23] *Ibid.,* libro 2 (misnumbered 3 in the original), XXVII-XXXII, Medina del Campo, March 20, 1532.

[24] *Ibid.*

[25] *Ibid.,* CIX, Medina del Campo, June 5, 1532.

[26] *Ibid.,* XV, Madrid, September 26, 1530.

[27] *Ibid.,* LVI, Ocaña, February 17, 1531. The boundaries of the new province were indeterminate at the outset, but, as worked out, made it include territory lying to the north and west of the kingdom of New Spain comprising modern Jalisco, Aguas Calientes, Zacatecas, and parts of San Luís Potosí.—H. I. Priestley, *José de Gálvez, Visitor-General of New Spain,* Berkeley, 1916, p. 48.

Spanish settlement of New Galicia was begun. Several Spanish towns, among them the *villas* of Santiago de Compostela, Espiritú Santo (Guadalajara), and La Purificación were founded. But since the results were not commensurate with his predictions, the King gave ear to present and past accusations against his rule and appointed the licentiate Diego Pérez de la Torre governor of New Galicia with power to act as Guzmán's judge of residencia, March 17, 1536. Torre arrived very suddenly in Mexico City where he surprised Guzmán, effected his arrest, and threw the luckless adventurer into the public jail. After two years of this disgrace and punishment, Guzmán was permitted to go to Spain to appeal his case before the Council of the Indies. By that time his cause was hopeless and only the intercession of influential friends kept him from a more serious sentence. His death there, in 1544, in the midst of poverty and obscurity ended a stormy and ill-starred career. He had been cruel, rapacious, and self-seeking, but, worse than that, had failed to discover new stores of ready-made wealth, and this failure extinguished any hope of hiding his short-comings.

The second audiencia was faced by a tremendous task of organization and reform. The burden so weighed on Fuenleal and his associates that they petitioned the government for assistance. More oidores were necessary, they asserted. The audiencia, what with the residencia of the former body, the administration of justice, the government of New Spain, and the inauguration of reforms, found that even twelve working hours a day, not excepting feast days, were insufficient for the discharge of its duties.[28] The royal instructions to the new administration encompassed a wide range of ac-

[28] Bancroft, *History of Mexico*, II. 328. These recommendations advocated retention of two oidores in Mexico City while the remainder went on circuit, each to his specified district, to watch over the execution of laws, the collection of revenue, and the general welfare of the people. A formal request for the appointment of a relator and a fiscal was also made at this time.

tivities. Of outstanding importance were the proclamation and conduct of the residencia of its predecessors, the prompt despatch of justice, the regulation of relations with the Church, the promotion of the conversion of the natives, the correction of abuses caused by the encomienda and slave system, and, lastly, the formulation of a report on the resources of the subjugated provinces.[29]

Bishop Fuenleal and his companions strove valiantly to carry out these instructions. The two oidores of the first audiencia, Matienzo and Delgadillo, were brought to trial and convicted, and ultimately left for "their homes in Castile very poor men and with not the best reputation,"[30] where they died in disfavor and misery. The condition of the native population especially absorbed the audiencia's interest inasmuch as Fuenleal bore a secret commission to modify the system whereby encomiendas were granted to conquistadores in return for their aid in controlling the Indian population.[31] The entire matter was left to the bishop's discretion but he failed to find a convenient solution and the problem was passed on to the viceroy. The system fostered to replace the encomenderos in control was part of the general movement toward centralization and royal control. Corregidores were to be placed over the Indians, aided in each area by an alguacil and a priest.[32] The Indians were to be granted almost equal rights with the Spaniards as tributary vassals and they were to be trained in Spanish methods of government.[33] The

[29] Puga, *Cédulas,* Mexico, 1878, I. 38 ff., gives the instructions in their entirety.

[30] Bernal Díaz, *True History,* V. 172.

[31] A. G. I., Oficio y parte, libro 2, CXVII, Medina del Campo, July 15, 1532.

[32] Each corregidor was to have civil and criminal jurisdiction in his district and was to exercise political and economic supervision over the same. They were to be of three classes, letrados, those versed in the law, políticos ó de capa y espada, and políticos y militares. These last two were required to consult the alcaldes mayores in legal cases.—Bancroft, *History of Mexico,* II. 329, note 29.

[33] Two Indian regidores and an alguacil were to sit in cabildo with the regular Spanish town officials.—Puga, *Cédulas,* I. 38 ff.

system was gradually introduced but proved to be unsatisfactory. The corregidores were often worse than the encomenderos in their treatment of the natives, and, as they had
to be paid a salary, the royal revenues suffered a diminution.

The work of the audiencia and its assertion of royal supremacy was felt everywhere in New Spain. The repatria-
tion of natives who had been rudely torn from their localities to labor elsewhere was attempted and the extension of
royal justice made the office of Protector of the Indians, held
by Bishop Zumárraga, unnecessary.[34] The cities of Puebla de
los Ángeles and Santa Fé, near Mexico City, were founded,
with hospitals and colleges for the converted Indians. Quiroga's great visitation to the Tarascan Indians of Michoacán
was undertaken and a humane Indian policy was introduced.
This last was a progressive step, even if the results were comparatively slight. Energetic measures were also taken to
revive and enforce law, in particular the unpopular sumptuary
legislation which forbade the wearing of rich silks. Regulation and reform extended to such matters as the common
ownership of forest, pasture, and stream,[35] and even such a
minor affair as an excessive tariff collected by the notaries
of the capital was not neglected. Credit for expansion into
the Querétaro country must also be given the audiencia.
The supervision of Pánuco as a separate unit and its incorporation into New Spain, and aid to Francisco de Montejo
in his conquest of Yucatán deserve mention. The second
audiencia did more than assert and maintain royal supremacy.[36] It started the Mexicans on the long and thorny path
of white civilization.

[34] Pacheco y Cárdenas, XIII. 219; Puga, Cédulas, I. 300.

[35] Puga, Cédulas, I. 298.

[36] Even Cortés was forced to recognize his inferior position and the
Bishop of Tlascala was obliged to pray for the King "regem nostrum
cum prole regia" rather than for Cortés "et ducem exercitus nostri."—
Riva Palacio, México, II. 196.

The majority of the reforms initiated by the second audiencia were extremely unpopular with the Spanish population of New Spain, which did not extend its cordial support to the program.[37] The creation of corregimientos was especially disliked as it seemed to threaten the labor supply and to be therefore most inimical to the economic well-being of the colony. Relations with the Church were greatly improved, but the lesser clergy, encomenderos themselves, sided with the laity in their opposition to the new Indian program.[38] Cortés was another source of weakness. Returned from Spain, where he had been treated with great consideration, and given great grants and the title of Marqués del Valle de Oaxaca, he could not work in harmony with the audiencia. In New Spain he could never be a subordinate. Even in his capacity as captain-general he was irritated when he found himself obliged to obey a group of civilian lawyers, who distressed the conqueror by their constant balking of his grandiose schemes for new enterprises. The attempts to verify the count of the 23,000 Indians granted to Cortés in encomienda were another persistent source of bickerings. In addition, Nuño de Guzmán was abroad during the entire period of the second audiencia, defying both Cortés and it.

The great weakness of the second audiencia, however, did not lie in the problems confronting it. The feeling that the president and the oidores had of the temporary character of their work, and the constant expectation of release which they entertained, contributed most to the weakness of their position. Two of the oidores and the president were well advanced in years and did not relish the thought that their tenure of office might be prolonged and that Quiroga was more interested in the Church than in administration. They

[37] More than 150 Spanish residents of Mexico City left to follow Guzmán rather than submit to a will other than their own. *Ibid.*, II. 194.

[38] Bancroft, *History of Mexico*, II. 337.

importuned the crown with requests for relief as early as 1532,[39] but, as faithful subjects of his majesty, they performed their duties and waited with impatience for the promised replacements. History must accord them the honor of being the precursors of stable Spanish government in North America.

The conditions in New Spain had demonstrated the inability of audiencia government, unaided, to cope successfully with the new problems of a wide area, a numerous and semi-civilized subject race, and an unruly Spanish population —the by-product of recent conquest and continued expansion. Successful in a moderate way in the West Indies, this body, when transplanted to New Spain, had shown its limitations. And, as has been shown, even before the second audiencia was appointed the home government had projected a viceroyalty.

A strong leader, a great nobleman drawn from the personal following of the Emperor, who could act as his personal representative, alone would suffice to overawe the turbulent factions in New Spain. A military man, versed in the arts of governing a conquered people, was also needed if Cortés were to be supplanted, and, more than anything else, a great administrator was necessary if the beginnings of a society, already made, were to be conserved and increased and if a stable Spanish system of government was to be built up overseas. A man of large calibre and exceptional qualities could expect success, but the size of the undertaking presaged failure for anyone else, and it was all important that the first incumbent do well since he would create the office of viceroy in America. The second audiencia, then, was merely a temporary makeshift until the propitious moment and the right man would permit Spain to transplant this added institution, the viceroyalty, and to superimpose it on the audiencia.

The title of viceroy was not a new one in Spain nor was the use of similar officials to govern outlying possessions peculiar to Spanish administration. In Spain itself, during the course of the wars of the Christian reconquest, particularly when a number of kingdoms were united under one sovereign, either by conquest or for dynastic reasons, it became customary to appoint a viceroy to govern such provinces in the King's stead. The title was held by the governors of Galicia, Navarre, Aragon, Catalonia, Valencia, and Majorca, and survived in Navarre to the close of the eighteenth century.[40]

When the kingdoms of Spain acquired territory outside the peninsula, as Aragon did in Sardinia, Sicily, and Naples, control was secured by placing viceroys, clothed in almost plenary powers, over the local machinery of government.[41] In sending a viceroy to America there is also reason to believe that the Spanish were influenced by Italian and Portuguese examples. Both the Spanish and the Portuguese evinced great eagerness to adopt the Italian system, particularly the methods by which Venice had risen to power and affluence.[42] Since Portugal was in the colonial field first, Spain had the examples of Almeida and Alboquerque before

---

[40] Desdevises du Desert, *L'Espagne de l'Ancien régime: Les institutions*, Paris, 1899, pp. 126-133.

[41] Merriman, *The Rise of the Spanish Empire*, I. 505, and *passim*.

[42] A. J. Keller, *Colonization*, Boston, 1908, pp. 65-71. There are many striking resemblances between the Venetian and Spanish colonial systems. The great number of Italians in Spanish and Portuguese service in the early days of discovery makes it not an untenable belief that these likenesses were not altogether accidental. In the case of the viceroy we find a parallel in the vice-comites (later the baili) who were sent out by the Doge of Venice to bear his name and commission over their fondachi or trade areas. When the Venetians held the more important colony of Constantinople, an official of similar functions called a podestà was placed over it. These officials were chosen for a limited time, were responsible to a home board, the Consoli dei mercanti (comparable to the India House), and were checked by councils resident in the colonies.

her as well. Properly viewed, then, the viceroyalty, like the
audiencia, was simply another well-developed Spanish institution selected for service in America when the novel conditions of colonial expansion and administration in New
Spain seemed to make its projection overseas imperative.

The correct understanding of the entire story of Spain's
expansion into America must begin with a view of that movement as being, at the outset, an extension of the old Moslem
frontier where the existing officials, institutions, and policies,
evolved during a long period of conflict with the infidel, were
used and modified as circumstances of distance, climate,
country, and race dictated. The character of the Spanish
conquest, the rapidity of its spread, and the nature of the
institutions established can only be understood in the light
of this background of the Christian frontier in Spain. The
trained frontier official of Spain, with his knowledge of the
principles common to all frontier policy, was naturally very
successful in his new environment and the institutions he
brought with him were well adapted to the rule of subject
peoples.[43] To picture the fabrication *de novo* of the entire
Spanish policy in the New World, when the conquistadores
were confronted with new and perplexing conditions, is to
commit the mistake of explaining the past as a succession
of miracles rather than an organic whole modified by movements and adjustments to new conditions. Moreover, such a
view is not only untrue but it is unfair to the Spaniards,
whose conduct, in the light of the happenings in America
alone, is reprehensible and worthy of just condemnation, but,
examined with past and contemporary history in Spain in
mind, is quite natural and not to be dismissed with a phrase
or two of conventional horror and self-righteousness. The
policy of Spain in America was, therefore, in its main out-

[43] For a discussion of the evolution of these offices and institutions
see C. H. Cunningham, "The Institutional Background of Spanish American History," in *Hisp. Am. Hist. Rev.,* I. 24.

lines, determined by the forces that had made a united Spain. In this sense the Moslems must bear a share in the responsibility for Spanish tactics in the New World, for they were the opponents against whom they were developed.

Spain herself, at the time of the discovery by Columbus, had just emerged from a period of religious, political, and racial strife. No part of the country was as yet free from signs of its recent border conditions. Indeed, when Charles V entered the country, in 1517, the Castilian towns still preserved much of their original character of military colonies with large territories about them.[44] Charles could do but little to alter this situation. The war of the comuneros with its resultant enhancement of the royal position was an accidental triumph. Charles was busy with European problems and could devote only part of his time to Spain. His widely scattered possessions in Germany, Italy, the Low Countries, and Africa, together with distracting wars with the Sultan Soliman, the Protestant princes, Francis I of France, the Pope, and the Barbary Corsairs, left little leisure for Spain and her expanding colonial empire. Spain and America were important in his European designs in so far as they provided soldiers and the means of replenishing his ever empty war chest and paid the interest due his German bankers.[45] In addition to finance, Charles V manifested a considerable personal concern in the conversion and humane treatment of the natives. He had to depend, therefore, on the good work of his subordinates. The Council of the Indies governed the colonial empire for him. Charles V merely checked the results obtained and approved the larger policies. His reign, notwithstanding this lack of imperial supervision, was to witness the establishment of the military, political,

---

[44] E. Armstrong, *The Emperor Charles V*, London, 1902; I. 19.

[45] Charles left a debt of 4,319,435 ducats.—M. E. Hume, *Spain, its Greatness and its Decay*, p. 89.

and religious government of the colonies, and, because of this lack, they were to represent Spanish ideas.

Over five years after Queen Isabella's original overtures to Antonio de Mendoza with respect to the government of New Spain, his definite appointment as the first viceroy to serve overseas was made public. By royal commissions issued in Barcelona April 17, 1535, he was named viceroy and governor of New Spain and president of the audiencia of Mexico, and as is not generally noted, Cortés was continued in the office of captain-general at the viceroy's pleasure.[46] Mendoza's qualifications are immediately apparent. He came from an ancient and influential Spanish family and would command respect as a member of the older nobility. His family had been distinguished for generations on the Spanish frontiers and he had grown up exposed to frontier conditions in the conquered province of Granada where his father and brother ruled. He was drawn from the immediate circle of the Empress and his personality, ability, and loyalty were well known at court. Above all, he had no interest in the factional disputes which were raging in New Spain and could be trusted to place imperial concerns before his own. The office of viceroy could not be confided to any other than such a person. The viceroy would stand in the King's place as his personal representative in every branch of government, hence no one but a nobleman who could be depended on to impersonate the King in a worthy manner could be appointed.

The Emperor was in Barcelona in the midst of his preparations for an expedition against Tunis when the royal commissions conferring supreme power on Mendoza in all the departments of the government of New Spain were

[46] Puga, *Cédulas,* I. 351-357, prints the commissions. Cavo's unsupported statement ". . . Conforme al nombremiento hecho cinco años atrás por las Emperatriz . . ." (*Los trés siglos de México,* I. 114) is nearly correct since the actual date was November 19, 1529.

signed. Of far-reaching importance, they drew but little attention in the warlike rush and bustle of what seemed at the time to be a much greater enterprise.

As the functions of viceroy, governor, and president of the audiencia were to be exercised by one man in these various capacities, it is almost impossible to point out clearly which office was legislative, which judicial, and which executive. This mixture of powers is a characteristic feature of most Spanish offices throughout the colonial régime.[47]   As viceroy, Mendoza was the highest colonial official in both the Americas, but his influence was only felt in the regions from Panama northward.[48]   He was sent "to represent the person of the King, administer equal justice to all his subjects and vassals, and to be active in everything relating to the peace, quiet, prosperity, and extension of the Indies."[49]   In his commission he was charged to aid in the conversion of the natives to the Catholic faith, to promote the welfare of New Spain, and to govern it according to his best understanding. As viceroy he was also vice-patron and exercised a vague general authority over appointments to ecclesiastical office and approved the publication of papal bulls and briefs.   His salary was fixed at 3000 ducados as viceroy and governor, which, with 3000 as president of the audiencia, brought the total emolument to 6000 ducados a year.[50]   In addition, to enhance the prestige of his person, he received 2000 ducados yearly for the upkeep of a body-guard.   Certain aids in the

[47] D. E. Smith, *The Viceroy of New Spain*, Berkeley, 1913, p. 179.

[48] Effective viceregal government was not to be established in Peru until after Mendoza's death in that office in Lima in 1552.

[49] J. M. Antequera, *Historia de la Legislación Española*, Madrid, 1884, p. 478.

[50] The ducado is given as roughly equal to 2 pesos 25 centavos in modern Mexican money (Riva Palacio, *México*, II. 242). Bancroft estimates Mendoza's salary as equivalent to 48,750 American dollars annually with a purchasing power in certain directions five or ten times greater than the dollar of Bancroft's day.—Bancroft, *History of Mexico*, II. 376, note 3.

form of grants of land, of wood, feed, water, and the customary service rendered by the Indians in his household completed his income.[51]

As governor his duties were mainly civil and concerned with the collection of taxes and their expenditure. The general supervision of the mines and the fostering of local improvements, such as the building of roads, bridges, and harbor improvements, ordinarily fell to his lot in this capacity. Mendoza's most important office, aside from the viceroyalty, was the presidency of the audiencia and chancellory of New Spain. He was sworn to observe its preëminence, prerogatives, and immunities faithfully and to fulfill this office as was the custom in the King's other chancellories and audiencias. Granada and Valladolid were the models indicated and the laws of Toro were prescribed as the basis for decisions.[52] His duties in this body were mainly judicial, but, as he was not a letrado (one versed in the law), he could merely advise and possessed no vote in the decisions in legal cases coming before this tribunal. As its president, however, his signature was necessary to make its provisions, sentences, and decisions binding. Mendoza was also given the power to assume or delegate the supreme military office of captain-general, which was left to Cortés for the time being.[53]

[51] At the time of the Sandoval visita Mendoza was served in his palace by 120 natives from Mexico and Santiago who worked in five-day shifts of 60. The Indians carried his wheat to the mill, hewed wood for his kitchen, and carried water from Chapultepec and from the canal which brought water to the city.—A. G. I., 48-1-2/24, Cargos que resultan de la visita, 33.

[52] This legislative publication of 1505 marked a triumph of Roman principles in Castilian jurisprudence.

[53] ". . . the captain-general had to see to the enforcement of the imperial navigation laws, the running down of smugglers, and the preservation of order on the frontiers and the navigable waters. As head of the armed forces he was chief justice for all cases involving a *fuero militar,* and also the one person in the viceroyalty to whom troops might accord the royal honors."—Smith, *Viceroy,* p. 228. This is a description of what the captain-general came to be in the eighteenth century, but the greater part of it is also applicable to the office in the sixteenth century.

Besides his commissions Mendoza was given two sets of instructions defining his duties with greater accuracy.[54] Both were issued in Barcelona, the first April 17, 1535, the main instruction being added eight days later. Since they form the basis of all future viceregal instructions, they are worthy of a somewhat extended analysis.

The first letter of instruction is brief and defines the relations between Mendoza and the audiencia. He is ordered to leave matters of justice to the oidores, merely signifying his approval by signing the papers drawn up by that body in its judicial capacity. He is required, however, to see that its procedure conforms with the best Spanish practice. In governmental affairs he is to have sole jurisdiction in accordance with his instructions and provisions. He is advised in decisions of great importance, however, to consult with the audiencia and thus share the responsibility of his actions with its members.

The more lengthy instructions of April 25, 1535, give a more adequate notion of the viceroy's work. By them Mendoza is first ordered to look into the affairs of the Church and to see that the churches necessary for the proper conversion and instruction of the natives in the faith are established. He is also enjoined to consult the churchmen in all ecclesiastical affairs and in matters concerning the welfare of New Spain.

Mendoza is next ordered to visit all the cities, towns, and villages of New Spain possible, after a brief stay in Mexico City. On this tour of inspection he is to gather information from the best sources concerning the towns, the number of native inhabitants, the Spanish merchants resident in them, and the tribute paid to the crown or to the merchants resident in them, and the tributes paid to the crown or to the encomenderos. The Emperor particularly requests that he

[54] Pacheco y Cárdenas, XXIII. 423-425 and 426-445.

be furnished with data concerning the encomiendas and the taxes and decrees of the audiencia concerning them.

The increase of the royal revenue derived from New Spain is urged throughout the instructions. The Emperor finds the business of the defense of his realms and the Holy Faith to be an exceedingly costly affair, so he mentions various methods of revenue promotion for the viceroy's examination and opinion. The gradual increase of the proportion of gold and silver over local products in the payment of tributes by the natives, the general payment of the tithe so that any amount over and above the needs of the Church will go to the Crown, and the resumption of the alcabala sales tax and other special taxes for a period of time are suggested. Mendoza is strictly instructed to inquire merely and to report on these schemes, lest precipitate action endanger the settlement or security of New Spain. Orders for a census of the towns and of the conquistadores occupy another section of the instructions. This information is an essential preliminary to any system of intelligent taxation and reward of these soldiers. All properties thus definitely granted to individuals are ordered appraised so that the King's due in acknowledgement of fiefdom will be paid regularly into the royal coffers.[55] His Majesty's imagination has also been aroused by rumors of hidden treasures in the temples of the Indian "devil-worshippers," so, for the sake of the true faith and the replenishment of the treasury, these are to be sought out and confiscated. Government operation of gold and silver mines is another important device for swelling revenues suggested to Mendoza. An investigation is ordered of the feasibility

[55] " . . . como Nuestros fuedatarios de toda la dicha renta y aprovechamiento del tal lugar, abemos Nos de haber y llevar, perpetuamente una cierta parte . . . y poneis en el dicho, vuestro parescer, la cantidad que debeis llevar por bia de feudo, de las rentas y provechos de los lugares que se dieron á los dichos pobladores." Pacheco y Cardenas, XXIII. 434.

of working mines on the crown lands, using Negro and Indian slaves, in addition to those mines exploited by private
enterprise and subject to payment of the royal fifth.

The question of the treatment of the natives is called
to the viceroy's attention in a number of connections in these
instructions. The vexed problem of service in the mines
is to be examined but no action is to be taken without the
advice of the audiencia, the Church, treasury officials, and
prominent citizens. The employment of lazy Indians on
royal farms as a remedy for their idleness is rather ingen-
uously recommended, with profit to the real hacienda in mind.
The viceroy is also requested to investigate the important
subject of Indian slavery. Abuses of the right to make slaves
of Indians in rebellion and their treatment at the hands of
their owners, both native and Spanish, are to be probed.
Generalizations on the theme of good treatment of the natives occupy another section; and the new cities founded for
their benefit, Puebla de los Angeles and Santa Fé de Michoacán, are confided to the viceroy's personal care. The duties
of the viceroy as vice-patron are dwelt upon at some length
and his supremacy in ecclesiastical matters is set forth. Part
of his duties in this capacity are to delimit accurately the
boundaries of the various bishoprics, to prevent abuses of
the right of sanctuary, to assert the superiority of the civil
courts, to see that the clergy lead good lives, and to guard
against undue harshness to the natives in the collection of
the tithe.

On the important subject of defense the instructions are
thorough. The viceroy is asked to canvass the general situation and to report on the number of forts constructed or in
process of construction, to seek out good harbors on the
coast, and to make a report on the amount of artillery and
munitions needed for the proper defense of New Spain. The
protection of Mexico City is recommended for particular

study. The question of a citadel on the Tacubaya causeway, as perhaps the best site, is broached and the viceroy is requested to carry out the royal provision that every Spaniard possess and bear arms. To prevent surprises it is advised that the Spaniards be concentrated in one quarter of the city, which could be defended in case of an uprising of the natives.

Another item of note in the instructions deals with the utter lack of money in New Spain and efforts of the shop-keepers to use slugs of gold as media of exchange. To remedy this awkward condition Mendoza is ordered to examine into the feasibility of founding a mint in Mexico City for the coining of copper and silver money.[56] A last and quite interesting charge asks the viceroy to foster and give aid to the project of two German merchants, Enrique and Alberto Guon (Kuhn?) who wish to set up a New World monopoly in the manufacture of blue and saffron dyes.

These instructions to the first viceroy show the conception of the office entertained by Charles V and his advisors. It still remained for Mendoza to make their numerous suggestions real by actual deeds. His function was to adapt them to the actual conditions of life in New Spain as he found them, and, in so doing, he was to create the colonial viceroy as an official and to lay down a definite imperial policy with respect to the various problems dealt with in the above analysis. This he could do by amplifying his orders in certain directions, by curtailing them in others, and, in some cases, by absolutely disregarding them. Such a course was expected of him and only great confidence in his judgment and integrity warranted the trust. In any case Spain was so distant from the scene of his activities that immediate interference or punishment was impossible. Theoretically, the supreme authority in American affairs was vested in the Council of the Indies, resident in Spain and definitely or-

[56] Final authorization for the establishment of the mint was contained in the royal cédula of May 11, 1535.

ganized in 1524. Actually, however, since the viceroy was permitted to use his own discretion in the conduct of affairs and could adhere to or depart from the Council's edicts, within reasonable limits, it could only check and guide rather than actually direct. The selection of the proper man, a good set of instructions, and consistent support of good policies was the limit of the Council's capabilities. The great task of evolving a stable social and political order out of the discordant elements in New Spain devolved upon the viceroy. A proper use of his powers and a sane deviation from his instructions were to characterize his early government.

The newly appointed viceroy was treated with great distinction and respect in Spain before he sailed from the port of San Lúcar en route for his distant kingdom. At Seville, where he stopped, he was lodged in the king's residence, the Alcázar, and the costs of the transportation of his family and numerous retinue were borne by the government.[57] The fleet conveying the viceroy reached Vera Cruz early in October, 1535.[58] After an inspection of the harbor and the official reception were over he set out for Mexico City, the seat of the new government. One of his last acts before starting inland was the appointment of Martín de Peralta as justice, to see to the enforcement of discipline and the proper treatment of the natives by his party in the districts traversed in his progress toward the Capital City.[59]

[57] Moses, *The Establishment of Spanish Rule in America*, New York, 1898, p. 88.

[58] August 20, 1535, the Town Council of Mexico City, in view of the notice of the coming of Mendoza and his expected arrival at Vera Cruz, appointed the regidores, Gonzalo Ruyz and Francisco Manrique, as a reception committee to proceed to the port with the official greetings of the city. At the meeting of August 25, two additional regidores, Bernardino Vázquez de Tapia and Juan de Mansilla, were named to represent the capital. News of his arrival at San Juan de Uloa, the port of Vera Cruz, reached the city fathers at their deliberations of October 2, and the committee armed with credentials set forth to kiss the hands of his majesty's representative.—*Actos de Cabildo*, libro 3, 121, 123, 129.

[59] A. G. I., 48-1-5/27, Interrogatorio de los descargos del señor vissorey, pregunta 2.

His march was signalized by demonstrations and celebrations along the route, and sometime between the 12th and the 17th of November, probably on the 14th, he entered Mexico City in great state and ceremony.[60] Trumpeters with gaily colored cloaks and the roll of kettle drums greeted his arrival as the city dignitaries, knights and commoners, went out to meet him arrayed in fiesta attire. Games in the plaza and a repast for the viceroy, his gentlemen, and the contestants, following the solemn reading of his commissions by the public crier in the presence of audiencia, cabildo, and citizens, completed the official ceremonies provided at the cost of the city.[61] The day following his entry Mendoza entered into conference with the cabildo and the other governing bodies to inform himself concerning the affairs of New Spain. At two o'clock each afternoon these meetings convened in the viceroy's lodgings.[62] This immediate action was characteristic of the energy and earnestness of Mendoza. The Mexicans knew that viceregal government in New Spain had begun.

[60] Bancroft, *History of Mexico,* II. 378, note 6, collates the printed authorities on the date of his arrival and reaches the conclusion that "his arrival probably took place on the 15th" of October. This is an error, since the acts of the ayuntamiento which he cites fail to reveal any meeting of that body on the 13th and the date of the report of the viceroy's first meeting with it is November 17th, not October 17th. The date set for the fiesta in honor of his arrival by the cabildo is Sunday, November 14th, and three days later the minutes state that Mendoza "a platicado con esta cibdad."—*Actos de Cabildo,* libro 3, 131. The viceroy himself states that he entered the city November 5th. " . . . yo entre en esta ciudad de Mexico y fue Recebido al dicho cargo a cinco de Noviembre. . . ." A. G. I., 48-1-2/24, Los descargos del Virrey, October 30, 1546; descargo 10. It seems, however, that the contemporary record of the cabildo should be accepted for this date.

[61] "Este dia mandaron que por quanto el domingo primero que biene hace esta cibdad fiesta por la buena benida del señor birey e para ello son menester tronpetas mandaron que se le compre sendos capuzes de color para que salgan con la cibdad e se compre a pague de los proprios ue la cibdad y cometieron ai mayordomo para que lo compre, e asi mismo que se aperciban los atabaleros e se les pague."—*Actos de Cabildo,* meeting of November 12, 1535. The meeting of the following day added a "colacion" and mentions "los jugadores que jugaron en la plaza."

[62] The cabildo sent a delegation of four members to represent it in this junta. *Ibid.,* 132.

CHAPTER II

THE ADMINISTRATION OF NEW SPAIN UNDER THE VICEROY

In the commission to Cortés as governor and captain-general of New Spain, October 15, 1522, his territorial jurisdiction was defined in vague and indefinite language.[1] As the conquest by Cortés and his companions progressed, the region became better known and its legal extent was gradually more clearly delimited. In 1525, with the conquest of Tabasco, it reached its greatest size under the conqueror. At this date it stretched from Colima to Salvador on the South Sea and from Pánuco to Honduras on the Atlantic.[2] In this same year the home government, tired of the jealous attitude of the conquistadores, began to create independent territorial units on the mainland. Pánuco and Vitoria Garayana were granted as a separate governorship to Nuño de Guzmán as successor to Francisco Garay; Honduras, despite conflicting claims, was placed under an independent royal governor, Diego López de Salcado, and Yucatán and Cozumel were granted to Francisco de Montejo as governor and captain-general for life. The last named region was to be of little importance down to 1549, however, as the New Empire of the Mayas fought the invader valiantly. The last great blow to a single jurisdiction before the arrival of Mendoza was the royal recognition of Guatemala as a separate entity under its intrepid conqueror, Pedro de Alvarado, in 1527.

[1] The complex story of the evolution of New Spain as a political unit down to 1535 is admirably set forth by C. W. Hackett in "The Delimitation of Political Jurisdictions in Spanish North America," in *Hisp. Am. Hist. Rev.*, I. 40-70.

[2] *Op. cit.* p. 57.

The next step in the territorial evolution of New Spain, the appointment of the first audiencia, was in the direction of closer royal control.   The cédula of December 13, 1527, creating this body, placed "New Spain and its provinces, Cabo de Honduras and Las Ygueras, Guatemala, Yucatán, Cozumel, La Florida, Río de las Palmas, and all other provinces between the Cape of Honduras and the Cape of Florida on both the South Sea and the coasts of the north,"[3] under its immediate jurisdiction.   Thus the grants of Cortés, Nuño de Guzmán, and Pánfilo de Narváez were considered to be under the authority of the audiencia of New Spain.[4]   The second audiencia had almost identical powers and jurisdiction with those of its unsuccessful predecessor.[5]

When Mendoza arrived, in 1535, New Spain as a viceroyalty was already identified as a political division, although it was modified later.   To the northeast was Florida, an immense and unexplored area, whose contacts were with the nearer audiencia of Santo Domingo.   To the south Hibueras and Guatemala were the extreme limits of the territories over which he held sway.[6]   In the north the distant

[3] *Op. cit.* p. 61.   Footnote 102 points out that the political jurisdiction of the audiencia only extended to the land conquered by Cortés and his agents with the exception of Honduras, Guatemala, and Pánuco.

[4] *Op. cit.* pp. 64-67.   Narváez' attempt to settle his grant was a dismal failure, but both Cortés and Guzmán, whose grants were later in date, made discoveries and planted settlements within their territories.   New Galicia, despite the pretensions of Guzmán, was never recognized as a separate and independent Mayor España, while the colony of the former in Lower California was short-lived.

[5] *Op. cit.* p. 64.

[6] Under Alvarado, Hibueras was united in practice to Guatemala, as he ignored the claims of the Montejos to its inclusion in Yucatán.   In 1543, with the creation of the Audiencia de los Confines, Yucatán, Cozumel, Tabasco, Chiapas, and Guatemala became virtually independent of New Spain, although the viceroy had financial and military authority over the area of the new audiencia on occasion.   For the audiencias at the close of the period of Charles V, see R. B. Merriman, *Rise of the Spanish Empire*, III. 643-645.   The line of demarcation drawn between Guatemala and New Spain in 1549 would seem to change this combination, and to leave all but Guatemala within the jurisdiction of New Spain. Cf. H. I. Priestley, *The Mexican Nation*, New York, 1923, pp. 1-3.

conquests of Guzmán invited a further advance along a frontier which stretched from Culiacán along the western boundary of modern Jalisco, including parts of the present-day states of Aguascalientes and Zacatecas, and which dipped south below Querétaro and beckoned into the unknown north again at the eastern outpost of Pánuco. Behind these lines, even, there lay great areas still unexplored, still unconquered, and Hibueras, Guatemala, New Galicia, Yucatán, and Florida were semi-independent border marches in 1535.[7] New Spain proper was divided, in February, 1534, into four provinces, Mexico, Michoacán, Goazacoála, and Meztecapan, and the limits of each were properly defined by royal cédula. The bishoprics, which were intended to follow the same boundaries, were known as Mexico, Michoacán, Tlascala, and Oajaca.[8] Nuño de Guzmán's conquest, New Galicia, was added to New Spain February 3, 1537, and its governor and other authorities were placed under the jurisdiction of the audiencia of Mexico.[9]

In addition, Mendoza's position as viceroy over New Spain was to mean that the Kingdom of New Spain in a wider sense included everything north of the second viceregal area of Peru, that is, supremacy over the area comprised in the older audiencia of Santo Domingo and the audiencia of Guatemala as well as the region of the audiencias of Mexico and New Galicia. It will be seen, therefore, that the first viceroy had a vast and not too well-defined area within which he must make the influence of his administration effective.

[7] Pánuco had been suppressed as a separate unit in 1528 and had been incorporated into New Spain. Recognition of the remoteness of New Galicia from the governmental seat, Mexico City, was yet to come in the establishment of a separate audiencia there in 1548. New Spain proper some years later was defined as "the district confined by the audiencias of Guatemala and New Galicia—from a line drawn between the gulfs of Tehuantepec and Honduras and from the southern border of New Galicia to Florida."—Bancroft, *History of Mexico,* II. 278, note 11.

[8] Vasco de Puga, *Cédulas,* pp. 90-91.

[9] Bancroft, *History of Mexico,* II. 391.

When Mendoza relieved the second audiencia of its duties, he found that New Spain was in a very unsettled condition. Partial reforms had been instituted in many directions, and the more flagrant abuses of the first audiencia had
been checked, such as the open enslavement and branding of
Indians and the forcible removal of them from their native
localities. The Bishop and his colleagues had ruled wisely,
but they left a legacy of discord. For a time Guzmán and
Cortés were in the land with numerous followers, and the
attempt to supplant the encomenderos by royal corregidores
had given rise to two discontented elements; first, the encomenderos, including many friars and the powerful conquistador group, who resented this move to favor the Indian
at their expense, and second, the corregidores, whose salaries
were too small. Mendoza was confronted with a real task.
The number of unorganized provinces, the opposing factions,
and the different conditions prevailing in the various sections
made it difficult to apply general remedies, and sectional
variations in his rulings would lay the viceroy open to charges
of favoritism.

First of all, Mendoza turned his attention to the building
up of the instruments of government through which his
desires were to find expression. Incompetent officials and
cumbersome methods of procedure had to be got rid of,
and unrelated departments of government had to be unified,
before he could begin his constructive work. To stop the
excessive and unnecessary litigation, involving great expense,
between the various town councils, he placed their suits on the
same basis as those between private parties, a move calculated to promote greater harmony, as it made these law suits
less attractive.[10] In order to extend his influence over those
distant portions of his jurisdiction over which the audiencia

[10] Mendoza, Carta, Mexico, December 10, 1537, in *Coleción de Documentos Inéditos,* ed., Pacheco y Cárdenas, Madrid, 1864-1884, II. 180.

had exercised little authority, he urged the king to place alcaldes mayores there. Their absence, he pointed out, permitted ill-treatment of the natives in the more remote regions without fear of governmental retribution.[11] He was greatly handicapped in these early endeavors by the small number of oidores at his disposal and could not take advantage of a proposal that one of them leave his bench and go on a mission in the provinces whenever it was believed that the natives were being mistreated. Later, with a more complete complement of judges, he was able to make good use of them and of his household officials on such inspections.[12]

Mendoza even found that the fiscal of the audiencia and the corregidores, with which he had been saddled by inheritance from the second audiencia, were quite incompetent. He informed the King that the former was valueless and, in rather blunt language, declared that worthy to be possessed of the intelligence of a block of wood.[13] To rid himself of the latter group he proposed to substitute alcaldes mayores, who, if appointed by him, would be more responsive to control and more trustworthy in character. He proposed to make these officers responsible to the treasury for the collection of all the tributes in their territories and thus to save the cost of tax-gatherers. He planned to appoint them for life on good behavior and believed it would improve the collection of the royal revenues by concentrating it in a few

---

[11] *Ibid.*, II. 183: ". . . en las provincias y partes que no llegaria el calor desta audiencia."

[12] For example, the visita conducted by the oidor Lorenzo de Tejada in Nueva Galicia in 1544 (A. G. I., 48-3-3/30, Residencia de Franco de Coronado y Xpoval de Oñate y demas oficiales, August to September, 1544) and the visita of the village of Tutepeque by Luís de Castilla, who was sent there without salary by the viceroy to see what harm passing Spaniards were doing to the natives, and to hold trials (A. G. I., 48-1-5/27, Interrogatorio del señor vissorey, pregunta 227).

[13] Mendoza, Carta, Mexico, December 10, 1537, in Pacheco y Cárdenas, II. 181.

responsible hands.[14] In the city and district of Mexico he assumed the chief civil and military functions as viceroy and governor, a right which was bestowed on later viceroys with the special title of corregidor.[15]

The center of the viceroy's public life was the capital city, Mexico, where he maintained a large household. Sixty Indian servants were always in attendance on him and his guests in his palace, where he maintained a miniature court.[16] From thirty to forty gentlemen, foot and horse, composed a bodyguard which was always about him and formed an escort when he went abroad.[17] Agostín de Guerrero, majordomo to the viceroy and captain of the guard, with the aid of Luís de Castilla, saw that his orders were carried out. For the upkeep of this establishment Mendoza had his salary, the produce of his ranches, and the customary service of the Indians in the work of supplying free fuel, food, and water. The ranches were located, one in the valley of Matalcingo, eleven leagues from Mexico; five in the vicinity of Marabatio, in Michoacán, twenty-six leagues from Mexico, named respectively Del Paso, Del Carrizal, Del Ancon, Baquiçuata, and Ocoraritarco; others near Vera Cruz; two near the pueblo of Tecamachalco, thirty-seven leagues away, named Ozumba and Astapa; and lastly, two days journey beyond these last two, the entire valley of Ulizabal, which was used as a horse-ranch.[18] These ranches were acquired by grant and by purchase.[19] In the main they were stocked with sheep

[14] *Ibid.,* II. 184. For the final solution of the question of the relations between these officials, see Smith, *The Viceroy of New Spain,* Berkeley, 1913, p. 116.

[15] *Ibid.,* p. 164.

[16] A. G. I., 48-1-5/27, Interrogatorio del señor vissorey, preguntas 119, 120.

[17] *Ibid.,* preguntas, 66, 67. A. G. I., 48-1-2/24, Fees de la guarda de su señoría desde el año de 37 hasta el de 46.

[18] A. G. I., 48-1-2/24, Relacion del Licenciado Tejada, in Descargos del señor vissorey, Mexico, October 30, 1546.

[19] *Ibid.,* Cédula, Madrid, April 24, 1540. Tradition asserts that the viceroy introduced Merino sheep into Mexico, but in all cases in which he

and supplied the viceroy's household and his expeditions with meat, while the wool was sold or made into cloth in factories likewise owned by him.[20]   An idea of the size of the viceroy's official and unofficial family is to be gained from the amount of provisions necessary for its upkeep.   His service of supply consisted of one hundred and twenty natives, half the quota being furnished by Mexico, the rest by Santiago.   These contingents relieved each other every five days and during their period of service brought eighty large loads of hay for Mendoza's horses daily, besides twenty-one loads of wood, five of which were for his guests.   Ten or twelve of them took his wheat to mill every third day and sometimes daily.[21]

In the midst of this crowd of retainers and vassals, and with his own family, represented by his son Francisco and his sister María, Mendoza lived in almost regal splendor, giving daily audience and despatching the business of state.   According to Francisco Vásquez de Coronado, the viceroy rose early in the morning, as he slept little, to hear and to act on the affairs of state which required attention, and, in cases of extreme urgency, such as the arrival of a messenger after he had retired or very early in the morning, would sit up in bed and listen to the petitioner or bearer of news.   In all his

acquired ranch land by purchase, he bought the sheep and had the owners turn over to him their rights in the land the sheep were on.   By a royal order of 1550 viceroys and oidores were forbidden to transact anything but official business and to own property or engage in business.

[20] Without the aid these sheep afforded in supplying his house the viceroy's salary would not have sufficed, and before his ranches were developed he was forced to borrow money to pay his debts.—A. G. I., 48-1-5/27, Testigo de Coronado, Mexico, January 18, 1547, pregunta 54.

[21] A. G. I., 48-1-2/24, Cargos que resultan de la visita secreta contra el muy illustre Señor don Antº de Mendoza, Mexico, June 21, 1546, cargo 33. The viceroy claimed that only thirty Indians served him gratis, fifteen from Mexico and fifteen from Santiago, which was the same number that had served Fuenleal, President of the second audiencia.   The rest came because they wished to, not by command, and in return he had given these towns 1500 *fanegas* of wheat and fifteen loads of clothes.   Even the carping critic Tello de Sandoval was served in like manner during his visitation.—A. G. I., 48-1-2/24, Descargos del señor vissorey, Mexico, October 30, 1546, descargo 33.

dealings he was affable but brief, and listened to high and low with equal attention. He was very accessible and no porters or other officials barred the way if an audience were desired. He listened attentively to everyone, and when he spoke he was grave in his manner and temperate in speech.[22] He did not stay in his palace all of the time, however, but was abroad almost daily examining the ejidos of the City of Mexico, the condition of the roads, the lands that were to be divided, or some kindred matter about which he wanted information. He was frequently absent on extended inspections in the provinces also, and during his fifteen years of rule in New Spain, visited parts of Mexico which had never been seen by former governors.[23] During his sojourn in Mexico City, his household was not lacking in pomp and even gaiety at times. He was accompanied in public by his bodyguard of well-appointed gentlemen armed with halberds, and on more important occasions, by both horse and foot fully armored and equipped. These gentlemen and the numerous guests of the hospitable viceroy spent their time fencing, tilting, and singing or bull-fighting, and banquets of great splendor were not unknown. Indeed, even the Indians who served him were instructed in music, trumpeting, and the art of minstrelsy, and those talented in the arts were trained as painters and silversmiths. The generous viceroy gave needy guests over three hundred horses in the period from 1535 to 1546, and fed and clothed scores of indigent cavaliers.

When Mendoza was about to turn over his work to a successor he wrote a list of instructions for the guidance of the incoming official. In this document we find the distilled

---

[22] A. G. I., 48-1-9/31, Testigo de Franco de Coronado, Mexico, January 18, 1547, pregunta 9.

[23] A. G. I., 48-1-5/27, Testigo de Miguel de Ibarra, Compostela, January 28, 1547, pregunta 125. Ibarra mentions particularly the viceroy's visits to Colima and remarks that reform and order followed in their wake.

wisdom of his long career as a public servant, and from its amazingly frank utterance, for he spoke as one who had run his race, much can be learned concerning what he actually thought about the rôle of the viceroy in the administration of New Spain. He warned Velasco that in New Spain, as elsewhere, men were more interested in other people's concerns than in their own and that this was especially true with respect to the government. Everyone wished the government to conform to his fantasy, and the diversity of counsel was beyond belief. If the viceroy in an ill-advised moment ventured to put anyone right or to contradict him, he merely stirred up a hornet's nest of juntas and letters, and soon found himself quite alone in the controversy, accused of being opinionated and uninformed. To avoid this Mendoza had listened to all manner of advice and had informed his counselors that their plans were very good and that he would adopt them. As a result he had been able to act at his own discretion without arousing great antagonism, and he remarked that New Spain would have been turned upside down twenty times if he had attempted to put in effect what he had said was so excellent. His principal intent, he assured Velasco, had been to oppose sudden changes, especially where the natives were concerned, as there had been so many changes, so many experiments made with them already, that he wondered they had not become insane. He showed that he had grown with the passing years when he said he had spent his long tenure of office making changes and still found the government more confused and newer to him than when he first took over control, and things to be done that he had not seen before. The ruler stood alone, he told Velasco, and although many gave advice, few gave aid when things went contrary to their desires. The secret of good government, he especially wrote, was to do little and to do that slowly, "since most affairs lend themselves to being handled in that

way and in that way alone can one avoid being deceived."[24]
At the very outset of his reign he had adopted this maxim
and still found it good when he relinquished office.[25]

The viceroy exercised the general powers assigned to him
in his commissions and instructions, but in the actual operations of government certain special powers and limitations
were added. He was in direct communication with the supreme home agency of government, the Council of the Indies,
which sought to govern the Indies as a royal monopoly, and
was supposed to carry out its decrees as a responsible but
subordinate official. The distance of that body from the
scene of action and the slowness of communication gave
Mendoza great latitude in his obedience to these orders,
which in some cases amounted to power of veto.[26] Delay
in the execution of undesirable laws, on one pretext or
another, until the conditions for which they were framed
ceased to exist, was one of the methods by which this was
accomplished. His right to frame laws, subject to the confirmation of the Council of the Indies, was another great
source of strength, enabling him to steer the course of legislation for the viceroyalty in Spain. As he was not a letrado,
Mendoza sought the coöperation of the audiencia in all cases
of that character.

[24] Mendoza, "Relacion, apuntamientos y avisos que por mandado de
S. M. di al Sr. D. Luís de Velasco," in *Instrucciones que los Vireyes de
Nueva España dejaron á sus Sucesores,* p. 238.

[25] When he arrived in New Spain and found the local laws differing
from those of Castile, he accepted the lack of system of his predecessor
until experience taught him what to do: surely extraordinary restraint in
any age.—A. G. I., 48-1-2/24, Descargos del señor vissorey, Mexico,
October 30, 1546, descargo 21.

[26] For instance, when oidor Gómez de Santillán was ordered to Yucatán to act as visitor, in 1549, we find him writing to the Council, in 1551,
explaining the fact that he did not go because the viceroy could not dis-
pense with his services and had ordered him to remain in Mexico, but
that he would send someone else.—A. G. I., 58-5-8, Carta del oidor el
Lic^{do} Gómez de Santillán, Mexico, February 29, 1551.

In New Spain he was empowered to grant corregimientos, lands (pedazcos and cavallerías),[27] and Indians to any worthy person on presentation of a royal cédula, but also had the power to withhold the grant in case he thought the applicant was well enough provided for or unworthy.[28] This entrenched him securely as a source of patronage, for these were the things Spaniards were dependent on for a livelihood. Nothing could be proclaimed by the town-criers of New Spain without his consent, nor could any act of the cabildo of Mexico have legal character until his confirmation had been obtained.[29] The titles to all encomiendas were granted by him up to the time of the New Laws, and even inheritance of an encomienda was illegal without this viceregal título.[30]

The viceroy's relations with the cabildo resident in Mexico City were of an especial character owing to the fact that the City was the seat of his government. He was interested in everything which concerned the city fathers, issued ordinances to be obeyed in the city, and confirmed all local ordinances passed by the cabildo before they became law.[31] He was petitioned to inspect all its projects[32] and, although as

[27] A pedazco was the amount of land given a foot-soldier; it was the amount of land on which one hundred hills of potatoes could be planted. A cavallería was twice as large and represented the grant to a horseman.

[28] A. G. I., 58-1-5/27, Interrogatorio del señor visorrey, preguntas 45 et seq.

[29] Actas de cabildo, Mexico, May 29, 1536, Libro 4, 19, 20. The minutes of almost every meeting of this body furnish examples of this confirmatory power.

[30] A. G. I., 58-5-8, Carta al rey, Mexico. March 17, 1545.

[31] Actas de cabildo, Mexico, December 12, 1536, Libro 4, 56: "En treze de diziembre del dicho año el yllustrisimo señor birrey abiendo visto esta hordenanza dixo que la confirmaba e confirmo segun y como en ellase contiene e mandaba e mando que se efectue y cumpla como en ella se contiene." This statement in the form of a marginal note with the proper rúbrica and notice of proclamation accompanied every local ordinance of the town council that became effective as law.

[32] This custom became firmly established before the arrival of the second viceroy, Luís de Velasco, and in numerous instances, such as the selection of a site for the Cathedral, he acted with the aid of a committee from the cabildo. Ibid., Mexico, September 9, 1552, Libro 6, 65.

viceroy he was not represented in its body[33] and did not interfere with its privileges, to correspond with the Council of the Indies and to have representatives at court.[34] As president of the audiencia, however, the viceroy did acquire representation in the cabildo of Mexico City. By royal cédula dated at Madrid, May 26, 1536, Mendoza was empowered to appoint an oidor of the audiencia of Mexico to have voice and vote in the cabildo to prevent discord in the election of the alcaldes ordinarios of the city. Oidor Francisco de Loaysa, his appointee, definitely took his seat in the council, October 6, 1536, despite protests against increasing the number of votes beyond the legal limit of twelve.[35] Loaysa was not present as a regidor, but as a justice with vote and the right to participate in all deliberations. In this fashion the number of regidores was not increased beyond the stipulated number, yet an additional voice and vote were added. The right of the viceroy as gobernador over the province of Mexico to be represented in the cabildo by a teniente de gobernador was, by reason of this representation, never exercised.[36] In fact, in this last capacity the viceroy's powers were very extensive in all governmental matters. Beyond the jurisdiction of the city, which was fixed at fifteen leagues

[33] One of the viceroy's first acts on reaching Mexico City was to go into session with a committee of the cabildo to learn the condition of the city's business; and beginning March 21, 1539, the cabildo met regularly with the viceroy for the first meeting of the month in his palace. *Ibid.*, Libro 4, 164.

[34] In the event of quarrels and discord within the cabildo he reserved the right to intervene, as in the case of a proposed letter to the king favoring the new Mercedarian monastic order, fostered by Bernardino Vásquez de Tapia and energetically opposed by the Augustinians and their partizans within the town-council. When he took the matter out of their hands he was later accused of unjust interference. A. G. I., 48-1-2/24, Descargos del señor vissorey, Mexico, October 30, 1546, descargo 4.

[35] *Actas de cabildo*, Libro 4, 35-42. This right had been denied the first audiencia.—*Documentos de Ultramar*, X. 14.

[36] "e Ansi se podria poner aqui un teniente de gobernador por el señor vissorey. . . ." *Actas de cabildo*, Libro 4, 36.

round about,[37] he was supreme, and even within these limits the cabildo possessed complete and final rights only in such matters as the granting of citizenship and town-lots (solares).[38] In addition, the free Indians within this area, as elsewhere in New Spain, had their officials, like Don Diego, Indian governor of Mexico City, appointed by and responsible to the viceroy. The cabildo was, in brief, overshadowed in authority by the viceroy.

Mendoza's power of appointment to lesser offices was a powerful factor in his work of building up an effective political machine, as it enabled him to place men responsive to his will where he most wished to have them. In addition to this, he could, in a certain sense, create extra offices for those already serving in other capacities. An example of this is his appointment of his captain of the guards, Agostín Guerrero, and the oidor Ceynos as accountants to check over the books of the treasurer, Juan Alonso de Sosa, and the factors (fatores), Antonio de la Cadena and Juan de la Peña Vallejo, by a commission dated in Mexico, July 25, 1536.[39]

The authority of the viceroy was in theory checked by the audiencia, which could also correspond directly with the Council of the Indies.[40] Since Mendoza was in perfect accord with his audiencia, the check was never utilized; and indeed, in the presence of the viceroy's power, this counteracting force was too feeble to offer great opposition to his

[37] *Ibid.*, Mexico, September 3, 1540, Libro 4, 207-209, còntains a copy of royal cédula, dated Madrid, October 24, 1539.

[38] A. G. I., 48-1-2/24, Descargos del señor vissorey, October 30, 1546, descargo 3.

[39] A. G. I., 58-6-9, Carta de Aranda al rey, Mexico, May 30, 1544.

[40] This did not mean so much in Mendoza's time as it might have later, as he permitted letters to pass freely in both directions. Coronado tells of sending personal letters to the Council of the Indies and of even having the courtesy of the viceroy's pliego extended to him. Mendoza refused to read such letters and said to Coronado on one occasion, "You know very well that I never see, know about, or read what others write nor what is written to them."—A. G. I., 48-1-9/31, Testigo de Franco de Coronado, Mexico, January 18, 1547, pregunta 15.

will. There were, however, certain specific things which the viceroy could not do. He could not grant town-lots (solares), licenses for churches or convents, titles of nobility, titles to cities or villas, or confer citizenship on any individual.[41] Finally, he could not increase salaries beyond the point fixed by law, nor could any viceroy extend the term of his office beyond the legal limit.[42] Mendoza's term of office was indeterminate; and, despite a fixed legal term of three years, most of his successors in reality held office at the king's pleasure.

The audiencia of Mexico was created in 1527, with a basis of organization of four oidores who heard civil cases, and before whom criminal cases were to be tried. There were, in addition, a prosecuting attorney (fiscal), a court bailiff (alguacil mayor), and a number of other officers provided in the law.[43] In actual practice, however, the audiencia rarely had its full complement of oidores, in the case of the first audiencia four being appointed. Before the arrival of Mendoza it was the highest judicial and administrative body in New Spain, but the presence of a viceroy restricted its activities greatly. Its functions became largely judicial thereafter, although a considerable amount of civil government was transacted through this body and orders for the construction of such works as a custom-house at Vera Cruz and light-houses along the coast were addressed to the pres-

---

[41] Solórzano, *Política Indiana*, Madrid, 1776, libro V, cap. II, contains a discussion of the viceroy's powers and tells particularly what he could not do. Mendoza enjoyed three things denied later rulers, the right to bring members of his family (we know of two who were with him in Mexico City) with him, to own property, and to engage in discovery.

[42] Smith, *Viceroy of New Spain*, p. 127.

[43] Merriman (*Rise of the Spanish Empire*, III. 642) corrects the mistake made by many historians in attributing to it a larger organization on the basis of eight oidores. In actual practice, only four oidores or fewer were present; cf. *Recopilación* lib. 2, tit. 15, ley 3.

ident and oidores of the audiencia, not to the viceroy.[44] This condition existed despite the viceroy's sweeping claim that justice could only be dispensed by the audiencia through its scribes, and matters of civil government through the viceroy's instruments.[45] The latter as president of this body, with the prestige of his other appointments, wielded a tremendous if not a preponderant influence. During his absence on tours or in case of illness, it worked out during Mendoza's régime that the audiencia ruled in his place, although, in the former case, he kept in touch with it by means of messengers. Later on the *ad interim* rule of the audiencia was also developed. Since, however, when Mendoza left New Spain for Peru his successor in office was already in the country, this question did not arise immediately.

Soon after the arrival of Mendoza the residencias of the president of the audiencia, Fuenleal, and of the oidores, Salmerón, Ceynos, and Quiroga, were taken.[46] Mendoza, among his letters, commissions, and instructions, brought one of thanks to Fuenleal for his meritorious services and was instructed to honor him and to take counsel with him concerning the government of New Spain.[47] The retiring president, on his return to Spain, was rewarded with the bishoprics of Tuy, Leon, and Cuenca in succession, and served as president

[44] Cédulas so addressed are extant on such widely varied subjects as slavery, water rights, boundary disputes, the tithing of sugar-mills, salting of mines, Indian carriers, and a question of Real Patronato involving the authorized circulation of a book of confession.

[45] "Es preminencia de visorrey despachar cosas de governacion con la persona que a el bien le pareciere . . . . " and the balance of the assertion.—A. G. I., 48-1-2/24, Descargos del señor vissorey, October 30, 1546, cargo 11.

[46] It seems that an attempt was made to permit the bishop to retire without the formality of a residencia. The cabildo of Mexico, early in January, 1536, petitioned the viceroy to have it taken and he replied "que su señoria no trae probicion para tomar la dicha residencia." Not satisfied, they consulted the city attorney (letrado) to determine upon further action as no office involving justice could be vacated without a residencia. *Actas de Cabildo,* Libro 4, 5-11 *passim.*

[47] Herrera, *Historia General,* Madrid, 1601-1615, dec. V, lib. IX, cap. I. 202.

of the audiencias of Valladolid and Granada, and ultimately his knowledge of New World affairs gained him the presidency of the Council of the Indies. The residencias were taken by the new oidor, Francisco de Loaysa,[48] and Quiroga was the only one against whom charges were brought. He was accused of having erected two hospitals, one in Santa Fé and the other in Michoacán, with materials torn from the homes of Indians. Proof of the great benefit of the hospitals earned him exoneration in March, 1536. Quiroga's interest in the Church and the conversion of the natives led him to relinquish service under the new administration, and in 1537 he was consecrated first bishop of Michoacán, in which charge he died in 1565 at the ripe age of ninety-five, leaving a memory of saintly devotion which the Indians revere to the present day. Alonso Maldonado also remained in the New World, but was drawn to Yucatán to assume charge of the interests of his wife, Catalina Montejo, daughter of the adelantado Montejo. In March, 1542, he was appointed provisional governor of Guatemala and assumed his duties on May 17th following.[49] In 1543, he was made president of the newly created Audiencia de los Confines and removed to its seat, Comayagua and later Gracias á Dios, in Guatemala. Fuenleal and Salmerón returned to Spain, where the latter eventually became a member of the Council of the Indies.[50]

---

[48] Puga, *Cédulas*, I. 377.

[49] Bancroft, *History of Central America*, II. 323.

[50] Bancroft is mistaken in sending Ceynos back to Spain with these two (*History of Mexico*, II. 380). Ceynos was still in New Spain as an oidor in 1546 and did not sail for Spain until February of that year and then only by special permission granted by reason of his years of absence from his family, the condition of his affairs, and with the express understanding that he leave a substitute to stand residencia for him.—A. G. I., 48-1-3/25, Cargos y descargos que resultaron de la visita contra el lic^do Franco Ceinos, Mexico, July 13, 1546. He returned later and was present in Mexico down to 1565.

The audiencia as constituted under Mendoza had a limited personnel. Francisco Ceynos was the only permanent hold-over member from the previous régime, while Alonso Maldonado gave limited service until he was relieved by Gómez de Santillán; and the new members arriving with the viceroy were Francisco Loaysa and Alonso de Tejada. The four-man strength of the body was insured, following the departure of Ceynos in 1546, by the appointment of Doctor Antonio Rodríquez Quesada.[51] Their salaries were fixed at 500,000 maravedís a year,[52] and the territory over which they held sway in a judicial capacity included the southern and eastern region of modern Mexico excluding Tabasco, Chiapas, and Yucatán but including the gulf coast around to the tip of Florida.[53] Into the north and west its jurisdiction extended indefinitely over an unknown region. In 1548 this domain was narrowed by the creation of the subordinate audiencia of New Galicia controlling the region west of a line run north from Zacatula and inclined slightly in an easterly direction. This same year, however, saw a widening of its authority to the south when Yucatán, Cozumel, and Tabasco were brought under its sway.[54] The audiencia was primarily a judicial body, but transference to the New World had added all the other duties of government, including military affairs. Even the coming of the viceroy failed to force a return to complete absorption in legal matters, since its secondary capacity was to serve as a check on this official and to aid him as an advisory body in governmental matters of a political character. Meetings of this sort were termed

[51] A. G. I., 2-2-1/1, No. 57, Relacion de Bartolomé de Zárate.
[52] Pacheco y Cárdenas, XXIII. 426-445.
[53] Merriman, *Rise of the Spanish Empire*, III. 643, with notes and map opposite page 644.
[54] In 1547 Merida petitioned that this change be brought about, as Gracias á Dios was too distant and Vera Cruz within eight days' sailing distance, and a royal order transferred these provinces to the audiencia of Mexico in 1548.—Herrera, *Historia General*, dec. VIII, lib. V, cap. V; Bancroft, *History of Mexico*, II. 450, note 40.

acuerdos, and the decisions of the president and audiencia became law as autos acordados. In this manner independent laws were framed for New Spain by reason of which the audiencia might be said to have enjoyed legislative functions. In its judicial capacity the audiencia served as a supreme court with appelate jurisdiction in criminal and civil cases from the lesser courts of the corregimientos, alcaldías, and towns. In such cases its decisions were final unless the crime involved a person of sufficient influence and means to secure an appeal to the Council of the Indies as a court of last resort. In civil cases which involved a sum of over 10,000 pesos the case could likewise be carried to the Council of the Indies for final decision. In all cases in which the litigants were towns, its own members, or the viceroy, it served as a court of first instance with original jurisdiction but with the usual possibility of an appeal to the Council of the Indies.[55]

The viceroy as president of the audiencia occupied a strong position even if he were deprived of a vote in legal cases.[56] His wishes bore great weight with the oidores in such cases, and in all other matters they acted much like an advisory council. Mendoza introduced some improvements

[55] For a general account of the audiencia in America in this period see Merriman, *Rise of the Spanish Empire*, III. 640-649, with references. A more extended treatment for the entire colonial period, but with illustrations drawn from the audiencia of Manila, is contained in C. H. Cunningham, *The Audiencia in the Spanish Colonies*, Berkeley, 1919. The story of the inception of New World audiencias is briefly told in Bancroft, *History of Central America*, I. 270-273, footnote 10. Solórzano y Pereira, in his *Política Indiana*, II. 271-282, points out the more extensive powers of the New World audiencias and explains them as necessary because of distance and, in some instances, the absence of any other supreme political authority. Other useful accounts are H. I. Priestley, *José de Gálvez*, Berkeley, 1916, pp. 60-65; *Documentos de Ultramar*, X, V, CXI, *passim;* A. Rivera, *Principios Críticos sobre el Vireinato de la Nueva España*, I, *passim*.

[56] His presence there was viewed by the visitor Valderrama as a distinct menace to good government unless he were a letrado, as the power of the viceroy to bestow patronage on the friends, relatives, and servants of the oidores made them fearful of voting contrary to his desires.— Pacheco y Cárdenas, *Carta del Lic. Valderrama á Filipe II*, Mexico. February 24, 1564, IV. 364.

in the procedure of the audiencia which are worthy of mention. Having found that the records of the transactions of the court, and of the government provisions received by it, were not being properly kept, he provided a book in which all governmental provisions were to be entered,[57] and kept another one in his audience chamber in which the scribes of the audiencia, the cabildo, and any others present in the city of Mexico (del numero desta Cuidad), were to write all the sentences of the respective courts within three days after they were passed. He was particularly solicitous that the fines (penas de cámara) be noted down, so that the money received from this source could be accounted for.[58] In cases involving the natives he gave the oidores new duties and widened the jurisdiction of the court; the first, by ordering that they visit the Indian jails regularly; the second, by empowering the judges of residencia sent to native towns, to transfer important cases to the audiencia, where, owing to the number of cases, three days of each week were given over to suits between Indians and between Indians and Spaniards.[59] For the expedition of business he framed ordinances with the aid of the oidores, and carefully defined the duties of the lesser officials.[60] His great concern, he informed his successor, was to preserve harmony between himself and the oidores and among those officials.[61] This was a particularly difficult feat as the audiencia possessed poorly defined powers while he was supposedly supreme within his domain as executive, and his right to sign its decisions before they became binding

[57] A. G. I., 48-1-5/27, Interrogatorio del señor vissorey, pregunta 28.

[58] Mendoza, *op. cit.*, in *Instrucciones que los Vireyes de Nueva España dejaron á sus Sucesores,* p. 228.

[59] A. G. I., 48-1-5/27, Interrogatorio de señor vissorey, preguntas 295, 300.

[60] These were promulgated in 1548, and are printed in F. M. García Icazbalceta, *Colección,* Mexico, 1858-1866, I. 27 ff.

[61] Mendoza, *op. cit.*, in *Instrucciones que los Vireyes de Nueva España dejaron á sus Sucesores,* p. 227.

enabled him to encroach on its field as presiding officer although he had no vote in judicial matters.

Although, as constituted by law in 1527, the audiencia was a fairly complete institution, it was not until Mendoza's time that it acquired the number of officials and the composition characteristic of it during the viceregal period, and until its reorganization in the eighteenth century. For instance, although by law it was possessed of two prosecuting attorneys (fiscales), we find Fuenleal petitioning the king for two such officers,[62] and we know that a separate criminal court (sala de crímen), was not introduced into Mexico until 1577.[63] Under Mendoza, that important officer, the fiscal, was active for the first time, and such officials as the chancellor of the audiencia, the receptores, the relatores, and the escribano mayor were empowered with clearly defined duties. It would be useless to enumerate the great number of minor officials, but those just mentioned and certain groups of attendant officials like the high clerks (escribanos de cámara) and the counselors (abogados) deserve attention.

The audiencia at this early time had only one fiscal, the licentiate Cristóbal Benavente, whose duty it was to see that justice was executed, to fight public sins, and to bring action against all persons infringing on the rights of the king.[64] The position of chancellor of the audiencia was held by the viceroy's captain of the guard, Agostín de Guerrero, and in his keeping was the official seal which could not be removed from the court room and without which no document possessed legality. He was provided with an assistant, Juan de Salazar, in this office.[65] The receptores were scribes who

[62] Bancroft, *History of Mexico,* II. 325, note 27.

[63] Pacheco y Cárdenas, VIII. 38.

[64] A. G. I., 48-1-1/32, Visita secreta a el fiscal el licenciado Cristóbal de Benavente, Mexico, June 30, 1546.

[65] A. G. I., 48-1-14/36, Visita á Agostín Guerrero Chanciller de la real Abdia de Mexico y a Ju⁰ de Salazar su oficial y teniente, Mexico, November 20, 1546.

made the official transcripts of testimony and who took the depositions of witnesses. They were also the officials who kept state statistics and when a census was taken the work was confided to their care.[66] The business of the relatores was to put cases in order for presentation before the audiencia and to prepare digests of them for the purpose of speeding up justice. Fuenleal, at the beginning of his rule, reported New Spain to be without such officers, and they were ordered provided, February 27, 1531.[67] At the time of the Sandoval visita Hernando de Herrera and Juan Alvarez de Castañeda were serving the audiencia in that capacity.[68] Antonio de Turcios, the chief scribe (escribano mayor) of the audiencia of Mexico was an important personage in the official life of Mexico under the viceroy, and stood high in his esteem and in that of the oidores. Hardly an official act took place without his cognizance or presence and his advice was greatly valued. He was respected for his learning, and nearly every important document that has come down to us from this period is in his handwriting; indeed, one suspects that he was a great aid to the viceroy in the writing of his official despatches.[69] In addition to these officials there were numerous scribes, lawyers, several interpreters, the court bailiff (alguacil mayor), and his assistants (alguaciles), charged to enforce the decrees of the audiencia and to apprehend criminals,

---

[66] As in the case of the census taken by the order of the viceroy Velasco, which was completed in May, 1592. Archivo Nacional, Madrid, 1049, Libro tercero de cartas de la Inqon de la Nueva España, 54-58.

[67] A. G. I., 87-6-1, Oficio y parte, libro 2, Ocaña, February 27, 1531, LXVI.

[68] A. G. I., 48-1-14/36, Visita á Hernando de Herrera, Mexico, November, 9, 1546, Visita á Juo Alvarez de Casteñeda, Mexico, January 19, 1547.

[69] Antonio de Turcios was jailed on a number of charges by the visitor Tello de Sandoval, but such an outcry went up from the viceroy and the oidores that he was permitted to use his home as a jail and to go to his duties with the audiencia. He was preceded in his office by Juan de Samano.—A. G. I., 48-1-14/36, Visita á Antonio de Turcios, Mexico, November 19, 1546-March 26, 1547.

and the jailers (carceleros), who watched over the destinies of the special prison of the audiencia.

The audiencia of Mexico and its individual members had certain special duties and rights, which should be mentioned, in addition to the general attributes already discussed. As an administrative body it acquired the right to interfere in the municipal affairs of the capital city, although forbidden to do so at the beginning of Mendoza's rule.[70] The original plan of the home government was that the audiencia and the town officials (regidores and alcaldes ordinarios) should meet together when local improvements were under consideration,[71] but the audiencia gained an advantage when the oidor Loaysa was empowered to enter the cabildo as a representative of the audiencia, August 7, 1536.[72] All petitions for appointments to office, after the coming of the New Laws, had to be approved first by the president and the oidores before they could be sent to Spain.[73] This gave them power over all office-seekers, and was designed to eliminate the nuisance of indiscriminate appointments from Spain.

The audiencia enjoyed representation at court in Spain, and, until the royal order of April 24, 1549, expressly forbade it, its members could be property owners, work mines, and have private interest in discovery.[74] It also gained the clear right to be the supreme governing body when no viceroy was present, or, during this first administration, when the viceroy in office was incapacitated, which meant a re-

[70] *Real cédula,* Madrid, October 27, 1535, in *Documentos de Ultramar,* X. 299, 300.

[71] *Real cédula,* Madrid, January 22. 1535, *ibid.,* X. 236, 237.

[72] *Actas de Cabildo,* libro 36, 37. He was officially a justice, not a regidor, as only twelve were allowed by law, but he possessed the right to vote.

[73] A. G. I., 91-1-9, Petición de Baltasar de Salto, Mexico, January 18, 1546.

[74] A. G. I., 87-6-2, Oficio y parte, Valladolid, April 29, 1549, LXIX. This order was repeated on a number of occasions, but was evaded on one pretext or another.

sumption of the pristine powers of the years from 1528 to
1535. Its individual members enjoyed wide powers as judges
in local residencias and visitas and after 1545 it was the body
which collected all evidence in cases involving the encomienda system for the Council of the Indies. The oidores
were severely restricted in their freedom of residence, however, for they could not leave their positions, and in their
case a special license for return to Spain was necessary.

From 1537, when Nueva Galicia was placed under the
audiencia of Mexico, down to the formation of a separate
audiencia there, in 1548, this territory was ruled over, first,
by military governors to 1545, when Coronado was deprived
of this office as a result of the Tejada visita of the previous
year, and then, by Baltasar Gallegos in the capacity of alcalde mayor. The new audiencia was subordinate to that of
Mexico and its powers included those of governor and judi-
ciary. Its seat was Compostela, later removed to Guadalajara, and its jurisdiction extended over all the known territory to the north and northeast, and along the South Sea
it included Colima, Zacatula, and the towns of Avalos. The
audiencia of Mexico could revise its decisions when the
oidores and the alcalde mayor disagreed, and, after 1555,
ruled over it in his stead when the viceregal seat was
vacant.[75]

The audiencia of Nueva Galicia was organized with a
president and four oidores who also served as alcaldes del
crímen, one fiscal, alguacil mayor, and a vice-chancellor.[76]
This new body was subordinate to the viceroy, and army and
treasury affairs were completely under his control.

---

[75] Bancroft, *History of Mexico*, II. 547, note 28, collates the printed
authorities. This meant the exercise of political and administrative
power from Mexico and the ordinary viceregal supervision of financial
and military affairs in the province.

[76] *Recopilación*, lib. 2, tit. 15, ley 7, cited by Priestley, *José de Gálvez*,
p. 63.

The outlying provinces of New Spain, like Yucatán, Cozumel, and Tabasco were ruled over by governors or adelantados,[77] who were subordinate to the viceroy, and their judicial officials to the audiencia of Mexico.[78] In New Spain proper, the provinces were ranked as alcaldías mayores under alcaldes mayores, corregimientos ruled over by corregidores, gobiernos under governors, and remote regions, over which adelantados presided. Each of these districts, save perhaps the last named, had its chief town and was in turn divided into partidos, each under an alcalde. In the case of the mining districts they were made separate provinces under alcaldes mayores de minas selected from those who resided at the mines by the viceroy.[79] Culiacán, in Sinaloa, because of its mines and its remoteness from Compostela and Guadalajara, was made an alcaldía mayor in 1545, and its alcalde mayor received a salary of four hundred pesos of common gold annually.[80] The provincial government was therefore of three main types, gobiernos, alcaldías, and corregimientos, each ruled over by a distinct type of official. The most important of the three was the governor. His powers were civil unless, as happened at a later date, the exposed position of his province warranted the additional title of captain-general and the exercise of military duties. These governors were appointed by Mendoza, subject to confirmation by the Council of the Indies, and were responsible to him, although free communication with the home government was permitted. The corregidores were placed over Indian districts ordinarily and were chiefly concerned with the adjustment of relations between the natives and the Spaniards. Their duties were in the main judicial and in-

---

[77] For a study of this official as a frontier governor see Hill, "The Office of Adelantado," in *Political Science Quarterly*, XXVIII. 646-669.

[78] Puga, *Cédulas*, I. 395. Nicaragua was also included under the Audiencia de los Confines erected in 1543.

[79] A. G. I., 48-1-5/27, Interrogatorio del señor vissorey, pregunta 90.

[80] A. G. I., 58-5-8, Carta del audiencia, Mexico, March 17, 1545.

volved cases arising between Spaniards and Indians and Indian litigants, although all the forms of government might be exercised by them within their districts. The alcalde mayor might be more important than the corregidor, as in the case of Baltasar Gallegos, who held sway over all of New Galicia, but ordinarily he ruled over a smaller area and might even be an assistant to a corregidor. The encomenderos with their large holding of Indians were still powerful in Mendoza's period and in provincial matters still overshadowed the rival corregidores.[81] These officials, together with the municipal officials in the towns within their districts, relieved the viceroy of local judicial and administrative matters, although constant visitations and residencias were necessary to prevent laxity.[82]

Local municipal government was transplanted to New Spain while the tradition of the great days before the war of the comuneros still flourished in all its vigor. It must also be remembered that Vera Cruz was founded before the decline of municipal strength in Spain. The cabildo was the center of the only real growth in self-government in the Spanish colonies.[83] The city governments managed their local affairs, with the exception of Mexico, where the viceroy and the oidores interfered, and were in charge of improvements, police, and the municipal revenues. These cabildos or ayuntamientos were composed of a varying number of

[81] Alamán, *Historia de Méjico*, I. 37-40; J. M. Antequera, *Historia de la Legislación Española*, Madrid, 1884, pp. 569-570.

[82] At first, there were fewer competent officials than offices and they went begging, but by the time that Sandoval came to New Spain, there was a great demand for livings, particularly corregimientos, and the viceroy was able to lower and even claim all salaries for the royal treasury. The visitor's salary was paid out of such funds.—A. G. I., 48-1-5/27, Interrogatorio del señor vissorey, preguntas 86, 87, 88.

[83] As early as Mendoza's time this body had ceased to be truly elective, as in all cases the regidores were required to present a título of appointment from the crown and the annual elections included merely the election of members of the cabildo to such posts as that of municipal judge (alcalde ordinario) or judge of the sheep-walk (alcalde de la mesta).

aldermen (regidores) and elected the two alcaldes ordinarios,
who were judges and administrative officials. In Mexico,
which was the seat of a bishopric, twelve regidores were
elected, six every other year, on the first day of the new year.
From 1538 on, the regidores also elected two alcaldes de
mesta (judges of the sheep-walk) each year. The cabildos
regulated local affairs, fixed prices and passed measures with
the consent of the viceroy, granted citizenship and lands to
newcomers, and filled a real place in the administration of
the kingdom. They corresponded freely, under Mendoza,
with the authorities in Spain and kept regular representatives at the court.[84] On certain occasions we even find
the proctors of the various towns meeting together in general
assemblies to promote their common interests, as they did
under Fuenleal when a general complaint was formulated
against the rule of Guzmán. Even Indian caciques and governors were represented in this embryo cortes.[85]

Lastly, there was a local Indian government which was
fostered by Mendoza, who placed Spanish alcaldes, regidores,
and alguaciles in the Indian towns.[86] He also confirmed the
election of Indian alcaldes and other officials in some of the
native towns and obtained good results.[87] On the whole,
however, it was found that the Indian caciques were even
crueler to their subjects than the Spaniards and that white
supervision was necessary. To accomplish this control,
judges of residencia were sent to the native pueblos and
the caciques, alguaziles, alcaldes, governors, and regidores
were questioned as to their use of office and treatment of the
Indians. When Mendoza instituted his work he found great

[84] A. G. I., 48-1-5/27, Interrogatorio del señor vissorey, preguntas,
86, 87, 88.
[85] Bernal Díaz, True History, V. 170.
[86] A. G. I., 48-1-6/28, Testigo de Juan de Arana, Colima, February,
1547, pregunta, 300.
[87] Mendoza, op. cit., in Instrucciones que los Vireyes dejaron á sus
Sucesores, p. 235.

confusion reigning in the elections of these caciques and governors of Indian towns. Some were appointed by encomenderos, others by the religious authorities, and still others inherited their offices from Montezuma's day. He immediately sought out what had been the primitive usage or custom in each locality and, while insisting on the good character of the office-holder, selected his Indian officers on that basis, forbidding the ecclesiastical officials or the encomenderos to interfere. He provided for examinations of these candidates for office before granting title to it. Indian judges of residencia were also employed and, in his instructions to Velasco, he boasted that Indians filled every type of office in their own local government.[88]

[88] *Ibid.,* pp. 234-238.

CHAPTER III

REAL HACIENDA IN NEW SPAIN UNDER THE FIRST VICEROY

In the eyes of the monarchs of Spain colonies existed chiefly for the production of revenue. They were conceived of as the personal possession of the Crown, attached to Spain through the person of the reigning prince. This conception of Castile's colonial acquisitions, once it is grasped, makes clear the broader meaning of the term "real hacienda" (royal estate), as including the colonies in their totality. In its restricted meaning, however, the expression was applied to the special department of government which was organized to supervise the promotion, collection, and expenditure of the King's revenue from all sources. By reason of this intimate relation to what was regarded as the most important reason for the existence of colonies, the greatest solicitude for the welfare of this branch of government was repeatedly expressed in royal instructions to the viceroys and other officials, and every consideration was subordinated to it, even that of the conversion of the Indians and the salvation of their immortal souls.[1]

The ledgers of the royal treasurers in Mexico begin in September, 1521,[2] but the first royal officials (officiales reales) were not appointed until October 15, 1522, when a royal treasurer, contador, factor, veedor, and assessor were commissioned.[3] These officials arrived early in 1524, and supplanted the appointees of Cortés, who had been receiving

---

[1] For an annotated list of works treating this important subject of real hacienda, particularly as it applies to New Spain, see Priestley, *José de Gálvez*, p. 82, note 79.

[2] C. H. Haring, "Ledgers of the Royal Treasurers in Spanish America in the Sixteenth Century," in *Hisp. Amer. Hist. Rev.*, II. 174.

[3] Bancroft, *History of Mexico*, II. 92, 142.

the royal fifth (quinto) and tributes from the natives for the Emperor, through the medium of Cortés.

In general, the duties of these officials were: the treasurer, to collect and expend royal funds; the contador, to keep account books of such transactions and to audit them; the veedor and factor, to oversee disbursements, the collection of royal rents and tributes, and to attend all government finance meetings;[4] and the assessor to act in an advisory capacity. The treasurer received the large salary of 510,000 maravedís for his labors, slightly more than an oidor was paid for his important services; the contador, 500,000 maravedís, an amount equal to the oidor's salary; the veedor, 390,000 maravedís, and the factor 170,000 maravedís. These salaries furnish a basis of comparison for arriving at an idea of the relative value, from the viewpoint of the home government, of these financial officials and the highest judicial and administrative officers in New Spain below the viceroy; they show that the royal treasurer was considered to be next to that dignitary in the eyes of the Council of the Indies.[5] By a law of 1538 they were given preference over all others for the office of regidor in the towns in which they were resident, but it seems that this and other provisions only served to make them arrogant and self-important, as they imagined this recognition was due to superior ability.[6]

When Antonio de Mendoza took charge of New Spain as viceroy in 1535, with special instructions to attempt the increase of royal rents, he discovered little method in the

[4] The office of veedor and the office of factor were ordered joined in one person by royal cédula of November 2, 1549.—A. G. I., 87-6-2, Oficio y parte, 118.

[5] The royal treasurers in New Spain during the early period were: under Cortés: Julian de Alderete, September 25, 1521—May 17, 1522; Diego de Soto, May 20, 1522—March, 1524 (also Deputy under Alderete); Royal: Alonzo de Estrada, August, 1524—February 16, 1530; Jorge de Alvarado (ad interim), February 16, 1530—November 6, 1531; Juan Alonzo de Sosa, November, 1531—March, 1533; Fernando de Portugal, 1553—.

[6] Herrera, Historia general, dec. VI, lib. V, cap. IX, 122.

existing system of collecting the king's due and great confusion in the records of these financial transactions. Vast sums which should have been in the royal coffers (cajas reales) were unrightfully in unknown hands, and practices for evading the payment of tribute, such as substituting personal service for gold, were being carried out quite unchecked. He called a halt to this by instituting regular tribute rolls, based on the original payments made by the natives, and levied and collected tributes from these. To keep a closer control over the royal officials and to prevent peculation, he provided account books, which were placed in all royal coffers, and required that sworn statements of the royal moneys collected be inscribed in them every week. To straighten out the muddled accounts, he appointed two auditors, the licentiate Ceynos and his majordomo, Agostín de Guerrero, July 25, 1536.[7]

The first thorough visita of the work of the royal officials came in 1544, when Gonzalo de Aranda was sent out with the visitor, Tello de Sandoval, equipped with complete instructions for that purpose. In an informing letter to the king, written in Mexico City, May 30, 1544, Aranda reported that he had examined the accounts of the treasurer Juan Alonzo de Sosa and a number of lesser officials and had found them to be correct. He had only heard of rumors of graft in connection with the officials of Vera Cruz, whom he excused, with refreshing humanity, on the grounds that the place was notoriously unhealthy and that the sub-officials there had been forced to serve without salary. The only fault he could find with the oidor Ceynos and Agostín de Guerrero, Mendoza's hard-working auditors, was that they had failed to do the most important thing, namely, check the accounts they had examined with the tribute-rolls (libro

[7] A. G. I., 58-6-9, Carta de Gonzalo de Aranda al rey, Mexico, May 30, 1544.

de las tasaciones), as they showed exactly what should have been paid in by each pueblo every year. The auditors had been engaged in their task for seven years, seven months, and sixteen days, less Sundays and three days a week devoted to their other duties, and the time Guerrero had been absent during the Mixton War, or a total of one hundred and fifty-eight days a year for seven years, and that without pay.[8] That Aranda did not realize the magnitude of the task set these men at this time is evidenced by the fact that, in 1548, we find him striving in vain to complete his own work of checking the accounts of the oficiales reales of New Spain before his commission expired.[9]

In the opening years of the conquest much ready-made wealth in gold, silver, and precious gems was confiscated by Cortés and his followers as the legitimate spoils of war. Of this a fifth (the quinto) was supposed to go to the Crown of Castile. Another source of income was the tributes, which were paid as an acknowledgement of allegiance by the Indian tribes.[10] In 1524, with the advent of royal officials, customs duties (almojarifazo) were levied on goods entering New Spain and during the succeeding seven years fifty thousand pesos were realized from this source alone.[11] Receipts from judicial fines and confiscation were also lucrative, but in large part were spent to support the judges and in donations to the Church and to those favored by the king. These, with the addition of a good revenue derived from the juzgado de

---

[8] *Ibid.*

[9] A. G. I., 87-6-2, Oficio y parte, Burgos, October 4, 1548, 1, 2, 3.

[10] The amount of the tribute was reduced to thirty-two reales during Mendoza's period.—Priestley, *José de Galvez*, p. 322.

[11] Haring, *op. cit.*, "Ledgers of the Royal Treasurers, "in *Hisp. Amer-Hist. Rev.*, II. 177. The peso de minas was an imaginary coin used as a unit of value in America before (and after) the establishment of royal mints there and equaled 1/50 of a marc of 22 carat gold or 4.18 grams of gold. The peso fuerte was a silver coin worth 272 maravedís or eight reals, which was minted in America after 1537 and became famous as the Spanish dollar or "piece of eight." The peso referred to here is the former.

bienes de difuntos, a body created in 1550 to hold decedent's estates in trust,[12] and the gifts to the king (donativos), constituted the chief devices by which the Spanish monarch secured an income from his real hacienda.

The mines were the most important source of supply of the wealth which the Castilian kings required in great quantities. Their failure would have meant the loss of almost all of that revenue for they were the life of the land. In his pressing need of money to keep his grandiose projects going, Charles V could not hamper production just to assure the full payment of his due. For example, the enforcement of the quinto was not strict, particularly in the case of the silver mines, where, to encourage an increased output, amounts varying from a tenth to a fifth of the silver mined were authorized at various times down to 1572, when the king's share was fixed at one tenth.[13]

There were comparatively few mines in active operation in New Spain at the time of the conquest, but the country was one of the richest mineral areas in the world. The conquistadores soon discovered this fact, and the location of native "diggings" and the discovery of mines became one of the most important duties of the pioneers into each new region. The principal areas in which mines were worked in the period of Antonio de Mendoza were in the vicinity of Mexico City, in the districts of Tasco, Zumpango, Zultepeque, and the southeastern portion of the valley of Toluca. These mines were organized as alcaldías de minas and were considered

[12] Bancroft, *History of Mexico,* II. 322, note 7.

[13] An interesting instance of this suspension of the quinto, as it applied to silver, is afforded by the law of September 4, 1540, in which it was declared that all who would lend silver to the Crown in its desperate need would only be required to pay one-eighth on it and on all other silver mined for a period of two years. Luís de Castilla was sent to the individual mines to collect the loan. This was perhaps an attempt to induce mine owners to speed up production, but it is doubtful that the Emperor would ever be in a position to repay what he borrowed.—A. G. I., 88-6-2. Carta del Virrey, Mexico, March 4, 1542.

important enough to be inspected by the visitor Sandoval.[14] Other mines were actively exploited in the sierras of Oaxaca, in Michoacán, and in Nueva Galicia, where the chief towns were for the most part simply mining camps. Near Compostela was the famous mine of Espiritú Santo, discovered in 1543; and, in 1548, Juan de Tolosa and his companions, Cristóbal de Oñate, Diego de Ibarra, and Baltasar Treviño de Bañuelos, found the fabulously rich mines of Zacatecas and established the town of Nuestra Señora de Zacatecas near by. Miners flocked to it from all parts of New Spain and for a time the adjacent regions of Nueva Galicia were threatened with total depopulation as their citizens joined in the "gold-rush."[15]

The excitement and disorder which are the inevitable accompaniment of mining rushes were not absent in New Spain, where the country was soon dotted over with mushroom mining settlements (reales de minas). The consequent disturbances led the viceroy to frame laws to govern questions of claims, discovery, and ownership of mines, and to introduce officials into the mining country to enforce them. As early as July 3, 1536, he promulgated such laws,[16] and, when they failed to secure the desired results, continuous revision of them was undertaken, so that finally, January 14, 1550, a code of mining law[17] was formulated which remained in force in New Spain to the end of 1577 at least.[18]

[14] A. G. I., 48-1-2/24, Probanzas hechas por parte del visitador Sandoval.

[15] Riva Palacio, *México á través de los Siglos,* II. 483 ff., contains an excellent brief account of early mining activity in New Spain.

[16] *Traduccion paleográfica del libro Cuarto de actas de cabildo de la Ciudad de Mexico,* Mexico, 1874, p. 24.

[17] Ordenanças hechas por el Sr Vissorey don Antonio de Mendoça sobre las minas de la Nueva Spaña, Mexico, January 14, 1550 (in the Edward E. Ayer Collection of the Newberry Library).

[18] A. G. I., 58-5-9, Carta del Audiencia, Mexico, December 16, 1577. The writer complains that the laws made by Mendoza concerning the discovery and registration of mines are still in effect in New Spain despite the fact that many of them conflict with the regulations of the Council

These laws of January 14, 1550, were made necessary by the fact that in many parts of New Spain mines had not been registered as the law required and that there had been fraud in registration to such an extent that fear of litigation between rival claimants made miners afraid to work mines from which great quantities of metal had formerly been extracted. This brought about a great loss of royal revenue, so that the viceroy, in order to restore order, rescinded the mining laws of March 13, 1548, which had been in force, and formulated a new, and, as it proved to be, final code of mining law.

The laws of 1550 provided that all mine owners were to appear before the nearest justicias de minas with their titles and certificates of registration, and, in case they were not registered, were to swear to the location and ownership of the mines. To prevent confusion in the matter of ownership, very severe punishment was to be meted out to anyone who failed to comply with this provision of the law. Explicit directions were given as to the exact procedure to be followed. The owners were to register their mines before the juez and escribano in each district, and a copy of the register was to be sent to the viceroy every year, the original being preserved in the royal strongbox (arca á las tres llaves) to prevent alterations.

Mendoza was meticulously careful in providing rules whereby unoccupied mines might be claimed by new proprietors. The person finding such property could go before a justice and enter petition for it as abandoned (despoblada). In this petition the claimant was required to give a clear description of the mine both as to its condition and its location. The law further stipulated that these documents were to be read aloud for four consecutive Sundays at the largest

of the Indies. A full account of the contents of this code will be found in A. S. Aiton, "The first American Mining Code," in *Michigan Law Review*, XXIII. 105-114.

church in the vicinity, immediately after mass, and with at least eight Spaniards present. If no one appeared to dispute the new claim, the petitioner was then permitted to file on the apparently abandoned property. To secure a clear title, however, the new owner was obliged to work the mine for three months, with the understanding that if the original owner appeared during this interval it would revert to him. These careful provisions make it evident that "claim-jumpers" were not unknown in sixteenth-century New Spain and that the viceroy was determined to protect legitimate owners against them.

In the important matter of the discovery of mines Mendoza's laws contain clauses which sound quite modern. They declare that any person discovering gold or any other metal in a place one thousand varas[19] distant from a known mine was the discoverer of it and as such entitled to a claim forty by eighty varas in extent, if, within two weeks after the discovery he registered his mine with the nearest royal officials. Failure to do so within the stated time reduced the claim of the original discoverer to a plot sixty by thirty varas, or, in other words, he lost the benefits of his priority and received no more land than the late-comers. In the event that two persons discovered pay ore within a new area at the same time, the one who first succeeded in filing his claim before a royal official would be the legal discoverer, despite the fact that the other might have extracted ore first.

A fortnight after registry the discoverer was obliged to select his claim and to locate all new arrivals in the time order of their coming. In case two should request claims simultaneously, the law decreed that the question of precedence should be left to the decision of chance and that lots should be drawn. Where one individual asked for a claim and another took possession first and then asked for his location,

---

[19] A vara is a linear measure approximately thirty-three inches long.

the latter would be considered to have the better legal right to the property ("tenga prehemenencia de ser el primero").

Persons were permitted to take possession of mines for others by this law if properly provided with proxies, and when a mine was discovered by a slave it became the property of his owner just as if he had acted in person. The law concluded with minute regulations concerning the construction of mines and forbade all alcaldes de minas and other officials to have any kind of interest in a mine under the heaviest penalties for an infraction of its provisions.

The nerve center of the entire system, whereby the king's share of the products of the mines of New Spain was gathered together from the remotest parts of the viceroyalty, was the smelting house (casa de fundicion) in Mexico City. To it came all the gold and silver to have the king's portion removed, and out of it went the bullion which loaded the fleets at Vera Cruz en route for Spain, where this wealth was ultimately, if not too immediately for the comfort of the Spaniards, broken up and scattered over Europe. The output was tremendous[20] and this sudden influx of gold and silver undoubtedly exerted an influence on Europe comparable to the effect of the recent out-pouring of paper money by the government presses there. At the outset, however, it did supply a keenly felt want of Europe in the fifteenth and sixteenth centuries, namely gold and silver to meet the demands of her expanding commercial activity.

[20] In the first period, 1521-1532, 694,000 pesos were received by the treasury officials in New Spain, of which about 373,000 pesos went to the king. From November, 1531, to August, 1539, the receipts more than doubled and 333,000 pesos were shipped to the king. The increased cost of government in New Spain undoubtedly absorbed a good part of the total which would otherwise have been sent to Spain. The following decade saw the receipts doubled again (2,488,000 pesos) and, including profits from sale of bulas de cruzada, 640,500 pesos were transported from Vera Cruz to Seville as the royal share.—Haring, "Royal Treasurers," in *Hisp. Amer. Hist. Rev.*, II. 177, 178.

Mendoza as viceroy was, with the aid of the treasury officials, directly responsible for the organization of the necessary machinery of government that would insure a steady flow of gold and silver from the mines of New Spain, through the smelting house, and on board the vessels to be conveyed to his liege lord in Europe. To this end he compiled laws for the proper handling of the precious metals brought into the casa de fundicion, dated in Mexico, March 22, 1539.[21] These ordinances covered the work of extracting the royal fifth and for casting it into bars marked by a distinctive stamp in the keeping of the veedor, whose chief duty was to guard this treasure. In addition, the casa de fundicion received gold and silver tributes from the Indians, which served to swell the total shipments to Spain. This establishment was placed under the responsible control of the officials of real hacienda.

The political mechanism which took care of the transportation of the precious metals from the mines to Mexico City and restored the balance to the owners after the casa de fundicion had done its work was likewise constituted by Mendoza. His ordinances of August 30, 1539,[22] ordered that there should be a strongbox in every region in New Spain where silver was mined, with three keys, one in the possession of the Alcalde Mayor or Justicia, one in that of the escribano de minas, and the third in the keeping of a deputy selected from among the miners by the first two. In this chest, placed in the official residence of the alcalde, was the official stamp for the mining area with which all the metal was marked before it was sent to Mexico City. For further identification each owner of mines and slaves (as the labor in the mines was mainly by slaves) or company that operated mines, also had a stamp of unique design, which was likewise deposited

[21] A. G. I., 88-6-2, Ordenanzas, Mexico, March 22, 1539.
[22] A. G. I., 88-6-2, Hordenanzas hechas por el yll mo. Dn Anto de Mendoza, Mexico, August 30, 1539.

in the district strongbox. The escribano de minas kept a
record of these marks and every Sunday of the year at two
in the afternoon, all of the mine proprietors met with the
king's officials in the office of the alcalde for the purpose of
weighing and stamping the week's output of silver. As the
miners gave account of what their mines had produced, the
escribano saw to the proper entry of amounts and persons
into official account books and forwarded a copy to the treasury officers in the Capital City. This was intended to frus-
trate any attempt to evade the sending of the full amount of
metal to the casa de fundicion for the payment of the royal
fifth. All owners were obliged to bring their silver, so
marked and registered, to Mexico within two months, under
penalty of seizure for the king.

All illicit traffic in silver was strictly prohibited, and the
harshness of the punishment provided in the law[23] indicates
that such illegal trade was going on and that the viceroy
wished to put an end to it. The officials responsible for enforcement were paid the small salary of fifty pesos annually,
but were granted a liberal percentage of the fines assessed
violators of the law. This last provision was intended to
intensify their zeal by making their incomes dependent on
the vigor with which they enforced obedience of the viceregal ordinances.

The casa de fundicion in Mexico City was nominally under the control of the treasury officials, but in actual practice
the veedor was in direct charge and had in his keeping the
official metal stamp in New Spain. Under him were the
smelter (apartador), foundryman (fundidor), assayer (ensayador), stamper (marcador), and other officers who did
the work of separating the king's share from the mine-

[23] The penalty consisted of the loss of mines and slaves, one hundred
stripes in public, and banishment.

owner's share and of preparing the metal bars for shipment to Spain.[24]

Not all of the gold and silver collected for the king in New Spain reached the royal coffers in Europe. Of a total of 1,518,340 pesos received by the treasurer of New Spain, Juan Alonso de Sosa, between June, 1544, and December, 1549, the Crown realized only 600,000 pesos; 450,000 pesos were paid to the viceroy's brother, Bernaldino de Mendoza, captain-general of the Spanish galleys, for the pay of his crews, and the balance was spent in New Spain itself.[25] The largest disbursements were for the civil list: viceroy, judges, and treasury and provincial officials; while the bishops of Oajaca and Michoacán, whose tithes were collected by the government, received five hundred thousand maravedis as salary. The regular shipment of the net amount of bullion in New Spain, after all deductions for local expenses had been made, was one of the most important and trying tasks of the department of real hacienda. It was more than a question of dealing with light-fingered Spaniards, as the ocean had to be crossed, and to the perils of the deep was added the menace of swift foreign corsairs.[26]

When a remittance was sent to the king's treasury in Spain, the bullion was carried from Mexico City to Vera Cruz by mule-train or on the backs of Indian-carriers. It was usually accompanied to the shipping point by an armed escort and by one or more of the higher officials of real hacienda. In Vera Cruz it was weighed and boxed before load-

[24] Under Mendoza the offices of fundidor and ensayador were held by one person, Estévan Gómez, a silversmith by trade.

[25] Haring, "Royal Treasurers," in *Hisp. Amer. Hist. Rev.*, II. 182.

[26] Mendoza received warning concerning piratical preparations in Europe on a number of occasions even before the raiders left their home ports. An instance of the effective intelligence work of these early Spaniards is contained in a notice of six French corsairs off the coast of Tierra Firme, which news was immediately sent to Miguel Ruiz, captain of the armada in Havana, while at the same time Vera Cruz was prepared to meet an attack as a rich fleet was loading there.—A. G. I., 2-2-1/22, Mendoza, Carta, Mexico, March 3, 1544.

ing and the officials of the fleet attested to the amounts their vessels received.[27] Each ship was required by law to carry ten thousand pesos worth of gold[28] and shipments might be omitted every year or so to permit a large amount to accumulate or to avoid risk when the danger of the voyage was too great in any one year. These fleets carried not only the king's gold and silver but also that of merchants and other citizens. No direct shipment to Spain was permitted, however, as all vessels had to proceed to Santo Domingo first to join the fleet for convoy to Sevilla.[29]

Even after the ships had left New Spain with a carefully weighed and stowed cargo of yellow metal and white metal and had arrived in Spain unmolested, it was not always certain that all the gold and silver would reach the rightful parties. For instance, the money raised for the payment of the crews of the galleys commanded by the viceroy's brother, a sum of sixty thousand ducados, arrived in Spain short in weight on the consignment of metal.[30] To fix responsibility in such cases it was thereafter required that a sworn statement of the exact amounts loaded at Vera Cruz be forwarded to the oficiales reales in Spain to enable them to check the accounts of the receipt of gold and silver made by the House of Trade in Seville.[31]

[27] Gonzálo de Aranda was present in Vera Cruz when ten vessels were being freighted with gold and silver, and described the process in his report to the king. This fleet, which he observed, carried over 14,000 marcos of fine silver and 100,000 castellanos of gold.—A. G. I., 58-6-9, Carta al rey, Mexico, May 30, 1544.

[28] By a cédula of February 7, 1549, the king ordered Mendoza to increase the amount to 15,000 pesos as his expenses were very heavy and his need for more money imperative.—A. G. I., 87-6-2, Oficio y parte, Valladolid, February 7, 1549, XLVI.

[29] A. G. I., 145-1-10, Memorial, received in Sevilla, March 22, 1538. In this communication the merchants of New Spain protested against the necessity of going via Santo Domingo and complained of the delays it involved.

[30] A. G. I., 87-6-2, Oficio y parte, Valladolid, June 1, 1549, LXXVI.

[31] A. G. I., 58-6-9, Carta al rey, Mexico, May 30, 1544.

The viceroy was supervising director of this entire movement of the treasure of New Spain from the mines to the ships at Vera Cruz, and, although technically his responsibility ceased when the fleet set sail, his position as the highest imperial agent in North America gave him an interest in the defense of all America against possible foreign aggression and he followed the movement of the fleet with anxiety. Communication with the home government, supplies, and colonists from Spain, everything depended on the safe going and coming of the fleet. Mendoza's interest is seen in his early championship of Havana rather than Santo Domingo as a fleet-base.[32] It lay, as he pointed out, on the natural commercial highway to Spain and all the treasure from New Spain proper and its outlying provinces and even from Peru could be brought there in safety and convoyed to Europe.[33] Subsequent history bore out the wisdom of his choice.

[32] Mendoza, *Carta,* Mexico, December 10, 1537, in *Coleccion de Documentos Inéditos, relativos al Descubrimiento, Conquista y Organizacion de las Antiguas Posesiones Españolas de América y Oceania,* Madrid, 1864-1889, II. 186.

[33] The best discussion of the European end of trade regulation is contained in C. H. Haring, *Trade and Navigation Between Spain and the Indies,* Cambridge, 1918.

CHAPTER IV

SOCIAL AND ECONOMIC PROGRESS UNDER THE
FIRST VICEROY

The study of the wars, intrigues, expeditions, and brilliant deeds of the men who effected and maintained the conquest of Mexico is only of value in so far as it assists in
bringing about a better understanding of the institutions of
the new society which was in the process of formation. The
contact of two widely divergent races and of a higher and
a lower type of civilization in the relationship of conqueror
to conquered meant that an adjustment of those relations
would ensue, involving grave problems of race, religion, and
social and economic justice, and, eventually, the emergence of
a new society. This process had its inception under Cortés
and Mendoza and is still far from settlement in the Mexico
of today.[1]

It is very necessary, therefore, to give some attention to
the social and economic factors in the history of New Spain
under Mendoza. These were a break-up of the old social
organization of the sedentary Indians which had existed
prior to the conquest, the introduction of Spanish customs
and life, and the adoption of certain policies which, in one
guise or another, have persisted into the present. Society
was in a condition of flux and change when the viceroy
arrived, but when he left, the fundamental questions of
classes and their relations to one another had been settled, and
the policies he discovered to be most expedient and which
his successors adopted, had been formulated. There was
change, growth, the destruction of old ways, and the intro-

---

[1] For a masterly discussion of these problems in Mexico of the
twentieth century, see André Molina Enríquez, *Las grandes problemas
nacionales*, Mexico, 1909.

duction of new, but as to whether the new social organism involved progress towards something better was a question for the future to decide. Mendoza, acting with the king's interests paramount in his mind, did not do in all things what was just and most fair for the natives, but rather what he could do after his majesty's patrimony had been safeguarded. A strong, well-organized government resulted, but the new society was essentially undemocratic, and, despite much praiseworthy, humane legislation, unfair to the conquered race. When the needs of the royal revenue and humanitarian principles clashed, the latter were inevitably the loser and for that reason much of the legislation favoring the natives was never carried out.[2] This is a result one would expect in the sixteenth century and the Spaniards are to be commended for their moderation, since they did not exterminate the aborigines as other peoples did. From another point of view, they deserve little credit for this, but rather for the fact that they were acute enough to realize the exploitation value of the Indian and to conserve him as an indispensable source of cheap labor.

The two main elements in New Spain were the Spaniards and the Indians, but there were also Negroes, moriscos, and a growing number of mestizos. The class lines drawn were racial, with the Spaniards at the top as a privileged, dominant group, holding the offices of government, the best lands and concessions, and having first call on the Indian labor supply under the encomienda system. The highest government

[2] Mendoza, *Relacion sobre los servycios personales que facian los Yndios en aquellas provyncias,* Mexico, 1537, in Pacheco y Cárdenas, XLI. 149 ff. In this document the viceroy confesses that the two policies of the Spanish government—1, to increase the royal revenues, and 2, to convert and protect the Indians—cannot be successfully carried out at the same time. The economic wealth of the country was based on Indian labor and if extreme laws against their serving Spaniards were enforced, the ruin of the royal rents would follow. Faced by this dilemma, he sought to find a middle course and permit services with proper restrictions and supervision.

positions, viceroy and oidores, were occupied by appointees of the king who had not been concerned in the conquest, but aside from them, the most favored and most powerful class of Spaniards were the conquistadores, veterans of the wars that overthrew the Nahua Confederation. They were the mainstay of Spanish rule against any possible Indian uprising and had to be humored with grants of land, office, and encomiendas.[3] The late comers were not so well treated unless they happened to have influence in Spain and came provided with royal cédulas ordering the viceroy to give grants to them.[4] Next to being a conquistador, a good Christian of pure blood (de sangre limpia), and having influential friends, the possession of a wife and children was the best argument for gaining preferment in office, lands, or Indians.[5] The Spanish government wished to build up a strong Spanish population in the Indies and issued many orders designed to foster marriages and large families. To drive all unmarried Spaniards into matrimony, a number of decrees were published,[6] threatening loss of lands and office to anyone found unwed after a certain lapse of time, and the viceroy made it a rule to appoint only married men as corregidores. This policy seems to have been very effective.[7]

[3] On one occasion the viceroy called Alonso de Baçan, assistant to the treasurer Juan Alonso de Sosa, into his presence and asked him to provide for some blind conquistadores and said that he would give them the silver inkstand, bell, and salver on his table if the treasurer could not provide for them.—A. G. I., 48-1-9/31, Testigo de Franco de Coronado, Mexico, January 18, 1547.

[4] The viceroy found it difficult to provide offices and Indians for everyone equipped with a royal cédula and examined each case upon its merits, refusing to provide for those already sufficiently well off.—A. G. I., 48-1-5/27, Interrogatorio del señor vissorey, preguntas 36-52.

[5] The viceroy gave grants to Luís de Castilla, Antonio de Turcios, Antonio de la Cadena, and Francisco Maldonado to enable them to marry poor girls, and to Martín de Peralta because he had a wife and many sons and daughters in Mexico. Ibid., preguntas 81-84.

[6] Ibid., pregunta 39.

[7] "Es publico y noto en esta nueva españa que a cabsa de los corregimientos que da e a dado se an casado muchos españoles con donzellas e otras mugeres."—A. G. I., 48-1-6/28, Testigo de Ju Oliveras cura de Colima, Colima, February 21, pregunta 292.

Mendoza found the Spaniards of New Spain easy to govern and more obedient, if properly handled, than any he had come into contact with during the course of his career, but he warned his successor, Velasco, that these same Spaniards had respect for neither wea.th nor persons if not treated as caballeros.[8] The principal revenues of the king were derived from them, as they worked the silver mines, cultivated the mulberry tree and the silkworm, and pastured sheep in the fields, which, as he saw it, were the promise of a continued and greater royal income from New Spain.[9] On the other hand, the products made by the Indians were considered as of little value in comparison, unless they should happen to rise in price.[10]

The moriscos were few in number in New Spain and always slaves, but were regarded as very dangerous, since their conversion to Christianity was so recent that they might teach the Indians their Moslem religion and undermine the Christian faith. Every one brought to the New World required a special license and the fiscal was instructed to proceed against those owners who failed to comply with the law.[11] It was quite legal to own them as slaves in Spain, but special laws operated in the Indies, which were the king's own possession.

The Negro element was inconsiderable when compared with the total population in New Spain, but, as the Spaniards were also a minority, the fear of an Indian revolt engineered by the less docile Negro was always present. The Negroes had been introduced into New Spain from the West Indies, where they supplied a laboring class after the natives had been ex-

[8] Mendoza, in *Instrucciones que los Virreys dejaron á sus Sucesores,* p. 299.

[9] *Ibid.,* p. 234.

[10] *Ibid.,* p. 233.

[11] A. G. I., 48-2-20/2, El fiscal contra Rodrigo Alonso Maestro sobre haber llevado a la nueba España dos esclavas moriscas sin licencia, Mexico, May 21, 1544.

terminated. But even there they had shown themselves to be dangerous and, in 1523, their numbers had been fixed at one to every three Spaniards and severe restrictions were framed to keep them in check as their numbers increased.[12] To keep them contented, it was considered well to encourage them to marry, but under no circumstances to grant them freedom.

In New Spain the inhabitants were soon awakened to a realization that their fears of the Negro were well-founded when a wide-spread plot to revolt was discovered among them on September 24, 1536. The Negroes had elected a king and had planned to drive the Spaniards out with the aid of the natives. The plot was revealed to the viceroy by a faithful Negro, and, when the truth had been ascertained, he took prompt measures and seized the ringleaders before they could act, and, after wringing a confession from them, had them publicly drawn and quartered in Mexico City as an example to the subject population. In the mines where they were working ample warning was received and the revolt was suppressed. The Indians failed to respond to the incitement of the Negroes and were among the most active in hunting them down when the viceroy offered a reward to anyone bringing them in dead or alive. In one instance the Indians brought in four Negroes and a Negress whom they had killed and salted to make sure of their reward.[13] Mendoza found the causes of the attempted revolt in the knowledge the Negroes had of the military weakness of the Spaniards, the too infrequent arrival of boats from Spain, the injudicious publication of news of Spanish reverses in Europe, and the fierce nature of the Negro. He informed the Emperor "that if so small a number of Negroes in this country have dreamed of such an enterprise, for the present the

[12] Bancroft, *History of Mexico,* II. 384.

[13] Mendoza, *Carta,* Mexico, December 10, 1537, in Pacheco y Cárdenas, II. 209.

number of Negroes sent here should be curtailed, for a quantity of them under similar circumstances could place the country in grave danger of being lost."[14]   For a time their importation was stopped, but we find a similar attempt thwarted in 1542 and the influx continued so that the new Viceroy, Luis de Velasco, was granted a license to bring one hundred Negro slaves to the New World with him when he was appointed viceroy in 1549,[15] and a partial enforcement of the New Laws against service of the Indians in the mines led to their arrival in considerable quantities after 1544.   To control them Mendoza issued laws patterned after the black codes in use in the West Indies, forbidding them to carry arms, to assemble, or to be out at night.[16]

This abortive uprising caused the Spaniards to turn their attention to internal defense, and a muster of troops in Mexico City brought out six hundred and twenty horsemen, of whom four hundred and fifty were in condition to take the field, and the same number of foot soldiers.   Mendoza asked for more arms from Spain and for a supply of saltpeter for the manufacture of gunpowder.   The project for a citadel on the Tacuba Causeway leading into Mexico City was agitated; in it would be contained the residence of the viceroy, the oidores, the alcaldes, and a supply of wheat and maize besides munitions and artillery.[17]   The project was never realized as the shrinkage of the water in the lake made it impractical for use in conjunction with brigantines.[18]   In-

---

[14] *Ibid.,* II. 199.

[15] A. G. I., 87-6-2, Oficio y parte, Valladolid, September 4, 1549, XCIV.

[16] Mendoza, in *Instrucciones que los Vireyes dejaron á sus Sucesores,* p. 231.

[17] Mendoza, *Carta,* Mexico, December 10, 1577, in Pacheco y Cárdenas, II. 201.

[18] Numerous letters as to the advisability of constructing such a fortress passed between the officials in New Spain and the home government.   Mendoza wrote letters in December 1535, January 1536, and December 1536, concerning the project.—A. G. I., 48-1-5/27, Interrogatorio del señor vissorey, pregunta 25.

stead a munitions depot was established in Mexico City and
the viceroy was forced to store his palace with arms for his
guard and an additional emergency force of three hundred,
at his own expense, his brothers in Spain sending him munitions, arms, and armor.

The great mass of the subject population in New Spain
was Indian, but even here there were differences of treatment, privileges, and rank to be noted. The Spaniards considered certain Indians like the Tlascaltecans as friends and allies, owing to the aid received from them during the conquest,
and accorded them rights and privileges which were denied
the other natives. Spain's grip on New Spain was not secure
enough yet to permit them to alienate the friendship of this
powerful tribe which could be relied on for assistance in the
future, as in the case of the Mixton War. The Spaniards also
recognized, to a certain extent, the Indian aristocracy which
had ruled the country before they came and they acted as
local governors under Spanish supervision. Some of these Indians were very intelligent and were treated almost as well as
if they were Spaniards. A certain Hernando de Tapia, for
example, who spoke Spanish fluently and wore Spanish
clothes, served the audiencia as an interpreter and was allowed to wear a sword and marry the daughter of a Spaniard.[19] In like fashion a large number of Spaniards married
Indian women or lived with them out of wedlock.[20] Under-
neath was the great class of Indian laborers (maceguales),

[19] This daughter was probably a *mestiza*, half Indian and half white,
and indeed this period saw the beginning of Mexico's race problem, with
castes and privileges according to color. Mendoza granted the right to
wear swords to a considerable number of other Indians who were known
to be favorably disposed towards the Spaniards. *Ibid.*, preguntas, 68-78;
48-1-9/31, Testigo de Franco de Coronado, pregunta 74.

[20] Gines de Mercado was married to the daughter of Bernal Vásquez
de Tapia. She was "bastarda hija de Yndia" and so was not able to re-
nounce Indians owned by her father in Mercado's favor.—A. G. I.,
48-1-5/27, Interrogatorio del señor vissorey, pregunta 29. Indeed by
royal order of July 10, 1540, only legitimate sons could inherit Indians in
encomienda.

who served as carriers (tamemes), worked in the mines, toiled in the fields, and did the bulk of the manual labor. The Mexican peons of today are their lineal descendants.

When the viceroy arrived in New Spain he attempted to enforce better treatment of the natives than they had been accorded up to that time. He was forced to recognize the encomienda system, but he tried to check its abuses and to stop the extension of slavery over the natives. Whenever he could, he secured their transfer to Crown lands where they would be sure of better treatment than they received from the encomenderos,[21] and, seeing the evils of the unrestrained rule of the native chieftains over their subjects, he established Spanish town government in their pueblos by which the natives elected, subject to his personal confirmation, alcaldes, alguaciles, and regidores to the local cabildos, thus removing some of the power from these local chieftains and placing it in the hands of the natives and himself.[22] He was particularly desirous of correcting the abuses connected with the personal services of the Indians and passed laws fixing the amounts which could be carried by an Indian carrier at two arrobas and less on any given journey.[23] For the hot lands of Vera Cruz, Soconusco, Tehuantepeque, Oaxaca, Colima, and Zacatula special provisions were made, as the climate made overwork fatal, and it was forbidden to send the Indians from the hot lands to the cooler regions or vice versa,[24] and the limit of a day's march was fixed at six leagues. Horses and mules were introduced to do away with the need of Indian carriers, but the mines absorbed most of the available

[21] Bancroft, *History of Mexico,* II. 382.

[22] A. G. I., 48-1-5/27, Interrogatorio del señor vissorey, pregunta 298.

[23] *Relacion del virrey de Nueva España, Don Antonio de Mendoza, sobre las servycios personales que facian los Yndios en aquellas provincias.* (dated 1537 but must have been written after 1548 as references to the mines of Zacatecas occur in the document) in Pacheco y Cárdenas, XLI. 150. An arroba was equal to fifty pounds.

[24] Except when they carried fruit and fish for the monasteries and wine and oil for the celebration of the mass.

supply and forced the continuance of the system.[25] Mendoza argued that its abolition would be a hardship to the poor, who could not own carts in which to haul their goods to market, and they would be forced to sell them to Indian merchants, who would have them transported by Indian carriers anyway.[26] The nature of the country would not allow the use of carts very extensively and artillery had to be dragged by hand; the viceroy thus saw no way out of it but to use the Indians in such service when they were willing, paying what he considered a fair wage for their labor. As the chief reliance of the state in the case of war was on the Spaniards, and as they could not go to war without the services of Indian carriers, the state would be forced to recognize their legality.[27]

To safeguard Indian free labor the viceroy hedged its employment with regulations designed to prevent fraud. Employers were obligated to secure the viceroy's consent, and the Indians employed had to indicate to him that the work was undertaken of their free will and that their wages were satisfactory. In addition, pay-rolls had to be made up when the Indians were paid and certified as correct by an authorized escribano. These pay-rolls (cartas de pago), with the labor contracts with the Indians, could then be produced at any time in the future if the employers' treatment of the In-

[25] *Relacion del virrey* in Pacheco y Cárdenas XLI. 152. In the majority of the mines machinery run by water-power (yngenios de aqua) was utilized, but in the Zacatecas mines the machinery had to be turned by horses, as no river existed in the vicinity.

[26] "Asi mismo se me ofrese, que orden se dara para los hombres pobres que no tienen posybilidad para tener requas e carretas e tienen estancias donde tresquilan sus ganados e fazen quezos o tacinos e siembran trigos e otras legumbres, para que estos tales traigan a vender lo que tienen de sus granxarias, porque le sera forzoso de pardella o vendello a mercadores yndios para quellos lo traigan con tamenes; e asi esta ley es fecha contra los pobres e en favor de los ricos." *Ibid.*, pp. 153, 154.

[27] *Ibid.*, 154. Coronado testifies that the majority of the Spaniards "no bibieron en esta tierra syno tuberon yndios."—A. G. I., 48-1-9/31. Testigo de Franco de Coronado, Mexico, January 18, 1547.

dians were brought into question.[28] The only difficulty was that the native chieftains would rent out their subjects and pocket the proceeds themselves and actual workers got little chance to indicate their wishes in the matter.

Although unable to abolish the harsh service of the Indians in the mines, Mendoza did much to alleviate the attendant conditions. He brought order out of the confusion prevailing as to the numbers of Indians who were to serve in the mines and the kind of service they were to perform; he regulated their working hours, the food they were to receive, and how they were to be lodged.[29] The absolutely inhuman and shocking living conditions of the Indians before such regulations became effective are revealed by the report of Tejada of the visita he conducted in Nueva Galicia in 1544. He found free Indians, men, women, and children, forced to labor long hours in the mines without shelter, proper food, or compensation, dying in large numbers from exposure, undernourishment, and the hardships of the work. Coronado was directly responsible for this, and his loss of both his governorship and the viceroy's warm friendship was due to these and other acts of maladministration in Nueva Galicia, rather than to the failure of his expedition in search of the Seven Cities of Cíbola.[30] The matter of Indian villages and their lands also claimed Mendoza's attention. He discovered that there were endless legal disputes concerning lands, the status

[28] The oidor Lorenzo de Tejada employed Indians extensively on various projects. He introduced into his reply to charges made against him by the visitor Tello de Sandoval cartas de pago and his contracts with the natives, approved by the viceroy, covering the period from July 1543, to December 1547. In one case, when he was erecting flour mills near Mexico City, he paid the Indians of Otumba three tomines (about sixty cents) for every braza of stone they hauled.—A. G. I., 48-1-4/26, Memorial del Lic^do Tejada, Mexico, 1547.

[29] A. G. I., 48-1-5/27, Interrogatorio del señor vissorey, pregunta 288.

[30] A. G. I., 48-3-3/30, Residencia que el Lic^do Lorenzo de Tejada oydor de la Audiencia Rl. de Nueva España, tomo a Franco Vasquez de Coronado, Guadalajara, August-September, 1544. Cf. A. S. Aiton, "The Later Career of Coronado," in Am. Hist. Rev., XXX. 298-301.

of the Indians, and their right to move about freely. To end this, he had an account of the lands taken, indicating boundaries and the status of the Indians resident on them, and then gathered the Indians living scattered about the country into villages where the Church and the government could handle them with greater ease.[31] This was, in a measure, an anticipation of the later mission system.

We gain an insight into Mendoza's real opinion of the natives and the proper attitude of the viceroy toward them in his instructions to Velasco, where we find him to be somewhat divided in counsel. He first told his successor that the natives should be treated as sons and loved and punished in that spirit, that services and carrying should be done away with slowly so as not to offend the Spaniards, and that the conversion and hospitalization of the Indians should be carefully watched over.[32] Then he expressed distrust of their cunning and warned Velasco that they lied most shrewdly and were not to be trusted without a thorough investigation and that they had a habit, when a legal case was decided against them, of waiting until the decision was forgotten or until a new judge arrived, to bring it up anew. To circumvent them Mendoza had had his secretary keep a record of such cases,[33] and had forbidden them to have suits at law among themselves. He said that it was his custom always to hear the Indians and that although they lied to him often, it did not annoy him, since he never acted until he had verified their statements, nor had he punished them for their misstatements, lest they cease coming to him with their troubles and childish stories. He had kept regular hours for them

---

[31] A. G. I., 49-1-3/30, Interrogatorio del señor vissorey, preguntas 286, 287.

[32] Mendoza, in *Instrucciones que los vireyes dejaron à sus sucessores,* pp. 230-233.

[33] The viceroy was judge in the first instance of all cases involving Indians.

on Monday and Thursday mornings, sending them from his audience chamber to the oidores, alcaldes, or churchmen according to the nature of their business and its importance; but he had been ready to listen to them at any other time or place, "notwithstanding the smell of perspiration and other evil odors."[34] Some, he told Velasco, would paint the Indians to him as humble, abused, and misunderstood, others, on the contrary, as rich, idle vagabonds who would not sow or work. Neither viewpoint was correct, and the safest course was to treat with them as with the men of any other nation, openly and without prejudice.[35]

In 1539 Las Casas, the famous defender of the natives, had returned to Spain to lay their case before the royal court. He had almost given up hope of securing definite action and was on the point of departure for Guatemala, in 1541, when he was ordered, by Cardinal Loasia, then at the head of Indian affairs, to remain and lend his advice to the Council of the Indies. It was during this sojourn that he prepared and presented his "Brevissima relacion de la destruycion de las Indias" to the court in 1542, a work which was destined to color the writing of histories about the Spanish conquest in America for generations. This vehement advocate of the Indian cause succeeded in having his views embodied in a code of laws known as the New Laws, in the face of strong opposition by the representatives of the encomenderos in court and a memorial from Cortés, who was in Spain, urging that a modified encomienda system was necessary in New Spain.[36] The main provisions of these

---

[34] *Ibid.*, p. 229.

[35] *Ibid.*, p. 233. " . . . Aunque algunos les parezca que estos yndios naturales son bestiales y les quadra que no ai diferencia de unos a otros porque no les entienden pero yo que los he tratado y conversado hallo mucho dellos de buenjuizio y conrrespeto de hombres de bien y de servir a su magestad. . . ." A. G. I., 48-1-2/24, Descargos del Señor Vissorey, descargo 18.

[36] The text of the New Laws as passed November 20, 1542, and June 4, 1543, is contained in Icazbalceta, *Colección,* II. 204-227.

laws were: 1. Enslaved Indians were to be set free and enslavement should cease altogether; 2. those holding too many natives in encomienda were to give up a number of them and on their deaths their heirs should not inherit the Indians but should receive from the royal treasury compensation for their loss; 3. all church and governmental officials were to give up their Indians immediately; 4. no relative or servant of a member of the Council of the Indies was to act as solicitor or attorney in any case concerning the Indies; 5. the residencias of oidores and governors were to be sent to Spain thereafter; 6. the audiencia was empowered to take a residencia at any time; 7. henceforth persons asking for royal favors must be recommended by the audiencia; 8. further discovery was restricted in order that the Spaniards should have no further control over the Indians, their personal services, or tributes; 9. the natives were to be converted to the Catholic faith. There were thirty-nine points in the complete text of these laws, which, if properly enforced, would have freed the Indian.

The New Laws were first announced in Seville and a force of visitors was appointed to carry them to America and make them effective there. Alonso López Cerrato was sent to the West Indies and later to Venezuela and the Gulf of Paria; Miguel Díaz to the provinces of Santa Marta, Nuevo Reino, Cartagena, Popayan, and Río de San Juan; Blasco Nuñez Vela to Peru; and Francisco Tello de Sandoval to New Spain. New tribunals were to be established, one in Peru, and the other, termed the Audiencia de los Confines, in Central America.[37] Francisco Tello de Sandoval, the visitor-general for New Spain, was a member of the Council of the Indies, a canon of the Cathedral in Seville, and an inquisitor of the Holy Office. In addition to the duty of publishing

[37] These audiencias were to rule instead of the governors, and the new code was ordered translated into the various native languages and published throughout the Indies.—Bancroft, *History of Mexico*, II. 521.

and enforcing the New Laws he was empowered to take the residencia of all royal officials, to exercise the functions of an oidor, with both seat and vote in the meetings of the audiencia, and, as a church official, was entrusted with a papal bull conferring the power to extend or restrict bishoprics and was instructed to call a special meeting of the bishops to consider the welfare of the church.

Sandoval arrived in Vera Cruz February 12, 1544, and reached Mexico City, March 8th, where the evil tidings of his mission had preceded him. Before his entry into the city the conquerors, merchants, and citizens wished to sally forth to greet him dressed in deepest mourning, but were restrained by the viceroy. Mendoza and the oidores urged him to put off the publication of the New Laws as the attitude of the country was very hostile. Finally, on March 24th, in the presence of the viceroy, the visitador, and oidores, and the assembled citizens, Antonio de Turcios read the laws publicly.[38] They were received with great sadness and discontent and, heeding the viceroy's plea to proceed cautiously, Sandoval was prevailed on by the regidor Alonso de Villanueva, representing the cabildo of Mexico, to stay the execution of four or five of the provisions, which struck the encomienda system hardest, until representatives of the encomenderos could appeal to the king.[39] The country was thoroughly aroused and not only did the citizens protest but the three orders, Franciscans, Dominicans, and Augustinians, and the bishops reported in favor of the continuance of encomiendas. Six proctors, Alonzo de Villanueva, Gerónimo López, and Peralmendez Chirinos of the city council, and the provincials of the three orders, Francisco de la Cruz, Dominican, Francisco de Soto, Franciscan, and Francisco de San Román,

[38] March 23, 1544, according to the report of Gonzalo de Aranda to the king.—A. G. I., 58-6-9, Mexico, May 30, 1544.

[39] Herrera, *Historia General,* dec. VII, lib. VII, cap. XIV, p. 142.

Augustinian, went to Spain to plead against the laws and show their danger to the country.[40]

The danger was very real, as the Spaniards were absolutely dependent on Indian labor for subsistence, and a veritable panic ensued which might easily have led to revolt, as it did in Peru, but for the moderation which the viceroy succeeded in getting both on the part of the visitor and the citizens.[41] On the publication of the laws all business came to a standstill, wheat rose to eleven reales a fanega, maize to five reales, the merchants and citizens went about like men bereft of reason "saying that they would be forced to kill their wives and daughters lest they go to a life of shame," and the first fleet returning to Spain took 600 settlers with it, including thirty-five or forty families.[42] The viceroy, the visitor, and the oidores did their utmost to hold the conquistadores and their sons by distributing charity, as with their departure the vast Indian population would have driven out the rest of the Spaniards very quickly.[43] When news of the situation reached Spain, the threat of a great loss of revenue and the possible depopulation of New Spain soon overcame the religious ardor and humane intentions of the government and the obnoxious provisions of the New Laws, as they con-

[40] Beaumont, *Crónica,* IV. 502.

[41] The clamor caused by the New Laws is described in the letters of Gerónimo López to the king, of February 25, March 1, September 10, 1545, and March 1, 1547 (A. G. I., 58-6-10). But, as he was a representative of the encomenderos, his letters are not good evidence by themselves.

[42] A. G. I., 58-6-9, Carta de Gonzalo de Aranda, Mexico, May 30, 1544. Aranda came with Sandoval to New Spain to audit the accounts of the royal officials and wrote strictly from the point of view of the effect of the laws on royal revenues; his account is therefore to be trusted more than that of an interested party.

[43] In addition to supporting the religious orders the citizens, with the aid of the viceroy, had been feeding the three hundred survivors of the DeSoto expedition for ten months and, with their means of getting food gone, had no alternative but to leave New Spain, which, Aranda says, "would lose New Spain to the great loss of the faith and the Crown." His solution was that the king settle a specified number of Indians on the Spaniards and their children as encomenderos in perpetuity.

cerned encomenderos, were suspended, October 20, 1545. With this revocation of Spain's greatest program of humane legislation the social lot of the Indians was definitely decided and, despite subsequent attempts at enforcement of the laws, the principle of compulsory labor became fixed in the social system of New Spain.

In the struggle over the New Laws the viceroy and the oidores identified themselves with the interests of the colonists. Mendoza, writing later in defense of personal services with proper regulation, pointed out that the visitor himself had been compelled to use Indian carriers, and informed the Council of the Indies that personal services were not invented by the Spaniards but were an ancient practice of the natives without which the country could not be kept in normal order. He accused them of heeding the complaints of one or two friars who had noticed isolated cases of cruelty and, while granting the holiness and justice of the laws, remarked that "All the provisions made or which could be made would not be a sufficient remedy; even if his majesty deprived them of their offices and cut off their heads, he could not make them enforce the laws which destroyed his rents and his vassals and depopulated the country, which needed inhabitants."[44] The Audiencia wrote in a similar vein and asked what they were to do in case of rebellion, as the Spaniards certainly would not place their lives in jeopardy without the hope of some pecuniary rewards; and since the captured rebels were, like the Indians put down in the Mixton War, who were only possessed of a mantle and a stone in which to grind their corn, entirely without wealth, the only reward the Spaniards could expect was the persons of the rebels as slaves.[45]

[44] Mendoza, *Relacion,* in Pacheco y Cárdenas, XLI. 157, 158.
[45] A. G. I., 58-5-8, Carta del Audiencia de Mexico, Mexico, March 17, 1545.

It is difficult to reconstruct the manners and customs of the strangely composite society over which Mendoza ruled.[46] The subject population lived with the barest necessities of life and engaged in the hardest kinds of work in the mines and fields,[47] while the Spaniards lived in considerable luxury.[48] The church exercised a very salutary influence in restraining wild excesses, but its feast days were very often the occasion of celebrations not entirely of a religious character. On such days bull-fights would be held in the main plaza and considerable drinking was indulged in by the Spaniards.[49] Mendoza and the Bishop, Zumárraga, who were often together in the Monastery of Zeptharztec "where the discourse was of God and of what was best for His service in the country,"[50] worked earnestly to raise the moral and religious life of the country to higher levels, but it cannot be said that they were successful. Severe laws against gambling were passed which, the viceroy claimed, put a stop to it and its attendant disorders.[51] The sale of wine or pulque to natives, Negroes, or

[46] The earliest census figures, those of February 25, 1560, show New Spain in its widest extent to have had a population, at that date, of 13,180 Spaniards, 15,609 negroes, 2,425 mestizos, and 1,465 mulattoes, besides 3,000 Spaniards of unfixed habitation and 3,000 in Guatemala, Costa Rica, and Honduras. The number of the masses of natives is uncertain, but there were probably two or three million, despite the devastating effects of such epidemics as occurred in 1545.—"Relaciones geográficas de Nueva España," *Boletín del Centro de Estudios Americanistas,* Sevilla, VII. nos. 36, 37, 45, 46.

[47] Aranda thought that the Indians of Mexico City, who were more numerous than the Moors in Granada, could do much more than they were doing, as he saw them loafing in the streets when they might have been planting wheat and maize.—A. G. I., 58-6-9, Carta de Gonzalo de Aranda, Mexico, May 30, 1544.

[48] Numerous laws, forbidding the wearing of brocades, gold cloth, or other expensive stuffs, were passed. In 1537 the viceroy said that the sum wasted on these luxuries was great.—Mendoza, *Carta,* in Pacheco y Cárdenas, II. 182.

[49] As, for instance, when news was received of the safe arrival of the Emperor in Castile, Aug. 1, 1533, the Cabildo voted such a festival, the expenses of which were to be paid out of the fines collected by the city. —*Actas de Cabildo,* Libro 3, pp. 46.

[50] Sir Arthur Helps, *Spanish Conquest in America,* New York, 1900-1904, III. 282.

[51] A. G. I., 48-1-5/27, Interrogatorio del señor vissorey, pregunta 215.

Spanish miners was prohibited in a number of cédulas and ordinances, their repetition showing that the traffic was not
ended,[52] and after a sharp controversy between the cabildo
and the bishop, all shops and places of business were ordered
closed on Sundays and feast days, and even the small vendors
in the plaza mayor were forbidden to ply their trade on such
days.[53]

The puritanical cast of the thought of the times is perhaps
best illustrated by the charges brought against Alonzo Maldonado, President of the Audiencia de los Confines, concerning his conduct while serving as an oidor in Mexico, of having raced horses and played the game of ball known as pelota.
He admitted the first charge, but excused himself for the sin
on the ground that it had taken place on St. John's day, the
anniversary of the capture of Mexico City. The second accusation was also true, but in defense he alleged that he had
played ball for the sake of his health, on the advice of a
physician, quite privately in his own residence with all the
doors closed.[54]

The City of Mexico was a busy place, with its shops and
stores, where food, clothing, and luxuries from Spain were
sold, and its narrow streets thronged with Indians, Negroes,
and Spaniards.[55]   Horses, mules, clumsy carts, and Indian

[52] Bancroft, *History of Mexico,* II. 536; *Actas de Cabildo,* Libro 3,
p. 134.

[53] On August 25, 1542, the bishop's alguacil was ordered not to interfere with the immemorial custom of selling fruits and foodstuffs
in the plaza mayor before the cathedral on feast days. If he did interrupt such legitimate commerce, he was to be jailed by the alguacil mayor
of the city.—*Actas de Cabildo,* Libro 4, August 25, 1542. The controversy ended in a victory for the bishop.—*Ibid.,* Libro 5, August 31, 1545.

[54] A. G. I., 48-1-4/26, Carta del Lic^do Maldonado, Gracias a Dios,
October 23, 1546. An old love affair dug up by the visitor brought from
him the indignant reply: "haze Vra Mrd cargo q fuy enamorado pues
a tantos años y despues desto a my se me tomo ressidencia y ya soy
cassado de cosa tan olvidada poca nescesydad abia de hazerse mi publico
cargo."

[55] The viceroy had caused streets and bridges to be built and
repaired, but the overflow of water from canals and the heavy carts

carriers mingled there with friars, as did the gentry from the viceroy's palace, and the citizenry, proud of their right to wear arms. In it were apothecary shops, tailor-shops, pastry-shops, and taverns,[56] while outside the city numerous flour mills ground the wheat necessary for its provisioning, and the aqueduct from Chapultepec brought water.

The viceroy was greatly interested in the opening of high-ways from the City of Mexico in every direction, with all the roads centering on the capital. These were roads over which mule-trains and pack-horses could travel and, in some cases, carts.[57] The viceroy opened new roads (caminos de nuevo) from Mexico to Acapulco to Oaxaca, and from there to the ports of Zacatula and Tehuantepec, to Michoacán, to Jalisco, to Pánuco, and to the mines of Tasco, Zultepec, and Zumpango. In addition he had those repaired leading from Mexico City to Vera Cruz.[58] He issued a total of fifty orders concerning roads, their construction and repair, by 1546.[59] Despite all this, conditions of travel were far from ideal. A man travelling in New Spain had to take his bed and all necessities with him wherever he went, and in most cases Indians had to do the carrying, as horses were hard to obtain and very expensive.[60] To spare these Indians as much as

did great damage to them.—A. G. I., 48-1-5/27, Interrogatorio del señor vissorey, preguntas 22, 23; 48-1-9/31, Testigo de Franco Coronado, pregunta 23.

[56] The shops of Cortés brought him a rental of over three thousand pesos.—Bancroft, *History of Mexico,* II, p. 326, note 21.

[57] Francisco Presciado, writer of the diary of the Ulloa Voyage, claimed that he had travelled over the viceroy's roads from Colima to Mexico, to the port of Acapulco, to the mines of Zultepec, Tasco, and Zumpango, and had seen loaded carts on them.—A. G. I., 48-1-6/28, Testigo de Francisco Presciado, Cura de Colima, Colima, February 21, 1547.

[58] A. G. I., 48-1-5/27, Interrogatorio del señor vissorey, preguntas, 20, 21, 22, 297.

[59] A. G. I., 49-1-2/24, Resumen de los mandamientos del Sr Vissorey Dn Anto de Mendoza sobre los caminos de la Nueva España, Mexico, October 31, 1546.

[60] Mendoza, in *Instrucciones que los Vireyes dejaron á sus Sucesores,* p. 230.

possible, the viceroy had regular resting places established, numbered the halts, and left their upkeep in the hands of the alcaldes mayores.[61]

Out over these roads went not only the trade and the exploiting agencies of the Spanish government, but also the emissaries of the Church, to convert and civilize the native population. From the time of the arrival of the famous twelve, in 1523, the Church grew in the number of clergy, secular and regular, in membership, and in extent of territory under control. The natives were drawn from their bloody religion, their idols were overturned, and their children gathered into schools, where they were taught to read and write. They also displayed great capabilities in the arts and crafts and were quick to imitate their masters. Learned and zealous fathers like Benavente (Motolinia) and Pedro de Gante acquired the native languages and baptized thousands. The great orders established custodias and provinces, and appointed provincials over them, to push the great task of conversion. From very humble beginnings, when the first services were held in a room in the house of Cortés, to numerous churches with magnificent ceremonials, was but the work of a decade, and soon the country became dotted with monasteries.[62]

The Church was organized for administrative purposes into four bishoprics, Mexico, Michoacán, Tlascala, and Oaxaca, to which were added Guatemala and Nueva Galicia, with boundaries indefinitely fixed at fifteen leagues from the cathedral town and the intervening space equally divided between the bishoprics. It was supported by the tithes[63] and by grants of Indians in encomienda. Special costs like that of

---

[61] *Ibid.*

[62] When Mendoza made up his probanza of the religious in 1547, 167 friars and priests testified in answer to his interrogatorio in the vicinity of Mexico City alone.—A. G. I., 48-1-8/30, Probanza del Sr Vissorey, religiosos, February 6, 1547, to March 14, 1547.

[63] This tithe was paid by the faithful; the natives were exempted from it.

the erection of a cathedral in Mexico City were shared by the royal treasury.[64]   The outstanding figures of the Church were Bishops Zumárraga of Mexico, Quiroga of Michoacán, Zárate of Oaxaca, Castro of Tlascala, Maraver of Nueva Galicia, and Marroquin of Guatemala.   On the death of Zumárraga, 1548, as archbishop-elect, he was succeeded by Archbishop Montúfar and Mexico became an Archiepiscopal See.

The establishment of bishoprics, the organization of provincias of the regular orders—Franciscans, Dominicans, and Augustinians,—the founding of monasteries, and the constant erection of churches gradually established the Church as a powerful force in New Spain.   Hard on the trail of the missionary, and often preceding him, came the encomendero and the tribute collector, and the Indian soon found himself caught and held both in the spiritual and temporal.   Miracles, like the appearance of Nuestra Señora de Guadalupe to a poor Indian in 1531, were of tremendous help in impressing the natives, and the Church was not slow to realize this, as the good use it made of such occurrences proves.   To commemorate these marvels shrines were built, which acquired great fame and exist today.   The great work of the Church was to convert and civilize the natives, and these early friars and priests toiled in the Indian villages, built hospitals for the care of the sick, like the one in Santa Fé near Mexico, organized fraternal orders of a religious character (cofradías) and schools (colegios) for the teaching of grammar, reading, and writing.[65]

The Spanish government found the Church to be a very useful adjunct in its labors, especially in maintaining control

[64] Fonseca y Urrutia, *Historia General de la real hacienda,* Mexico, 1845-1853, I. 519.

[65] Like the Cofradía del Benditísimo nombre de Jesus founded by the Augustinians in 1537, and the colegio established in connection with it through funds willed by a certain Bartolomé de Morales.—A. G. I., 60-2-16, Carta a Su Mag*, Mexico, December 15, 1537.

over the natives. The clergy came closer to the daily life
of their charges than the Spanish officials could hope to come,
and were very useful as gatherers of information. Every
care was taken to keep up their prestige in the eyes of the
Indians and crimes committed by any churchman were punished secretly to prevent a loss of reputation. The viceroy, in
his capacity as vice-patron, exercised general supervision over
the affairs of the Church and strove to weed out unworthy
clergy,[66] reporting annually to the King on the churches'
progress.[67] Such matters as concubinage, as widely practiced
by the natives, and marriage within the forbidden degrees
of relationship were left to the Church for settlement, but its
use of the right of sanctuary to give shelter to refugees from
justice was challenged by the state.[68]

In its educational efforts the Church was ably seconded by
Mendoza, who received orders to have the Indians taught
the Spanish language by competent members of the clergy.[69]
In Mexico, in the quarter of Tlatelalco, he founded the college of Santa Cruz for the instruction of the children of
Indian nobles, who soon knew more Latin than their instruct-
ors and were badly treated for it.[70] Some of the best stu-
dents died in the pestilence of 1548, but the school was

[66] He found it necessary to make a careful check on what the Indians
gave the clergy, as many of the latter were ruined individuals who came
to New Spain to recoup their fortunes. In general, if it were not for
the need of baptism he thought the Indians would have been better off
without them.—Mendoza, in *Instrucciones que los Virreyes dejaron a sus
Sucesores,* 228. A summary of the laws concerning real patronato is
given in Solarzano, *Politica Indiana,* tom. II, liv. IV, caps. II *et seq.*

[67] Herrera, *Historia General,* dec. IV, lib. V, cap. IX, 122.

[68] As in the case of Francisco Flores, who sought to escape the consequences of the murder of a certain Francisco Manrique in Mexico
City.—A. G. I., 48-1-5/27, Interrogatorio del señor vissorey, pregunta 11.

[69] A. G. I., 87-6-2, Oficio y parte, Valladolid, June 7, 1550.

[70] A. G. I., 87-6-2, Oficio y parte, July 7, 1550, 253. "L'intelligence et la
capacité des Indiens sont très grandes, et leur font surmontés les dif-
ficultés de l'étude. Leur professeur me l'assure et je les ai interrogé sur
le latin et la grammaire et j'ai vu qu'ils étaient fort avancés pour le peu
de temps qu'ils y sont."—Mendoza, Lettre, in Ternaux-Campans, *Voyages,
Relations et Mémoires,* Serie 2, tom. V, p. 266.

maintained and did excellent work. Its program included reading, writing, Latin grammar, rhetoric, philosophy, music, and Mexican medicine. The college of San Juan de Letran was established for foundling mestizo boys and girls and lasted over three centuries, as a school where trades and letters were taught. The supervision of the girls was a part of the duty of oidor Tejada, and Dr. Quesada looked after the boys. In Michoacán a college for the instruction of the sons of Spaniards and of some Indian chiefs was instituted, while the famous convent school of fathers Juan de Tecto and Pedro de Gante in Tezcuco continued to teach great numbers of natives. The cabildo of Mexico fostered a foundling school for girls and many teachers taught private schools.[71] This interest in education, according to Antonio de Herrera, led the viceroy to petition the king to establish a university in Mexico as early as 1539,[72] but the royal order for such a center of higher learning was not promulgated until September 21, 1551, and the formal inauguration of America's first university took place January 21, 1553. Mendoza's record with respect to education is exceptionally good, and he is to be particularly praised for his advanced views on education for the priesthood. He was one of the first to advocate a trained native priesthood, and believed that proper conversion of the natives to more than nominal Christianity would never result from anything less uncompromising.[73]

Another important manifestation of civilization and culture was the introduction of the printing press. During the

[71] For example Baltasar de Salto, a notary, taught a school for children where they learned to read and write.—A. G. I., 48-1-5/27, Interrogatorio del señor vissorey, pregunta 44. For an interesting account of early education in Mexico, see H. I. Priestley, "The Old University of Mexico," *University of California Chronicle*, XXI. 369-385.

[72] Hererra, *Historia General*, dec. VI, lib. VII, cap. VI, 153. Icazbalceta and other scholars challenge the accuracy of this statement.

[73] Mendoza, in *Instrucciones que los Vireyes dejaron à sus Sucesores*, p. 229.

frequent conferences in Spain of Mendoza and the bishop-elect Zumárraga, during the winter of 1533-1534, the establishment of a press in Mexico City was, in all probability, decided upon.[74] The flourishing German printing house of Jácome Cromberger and his son Juan Cromberger in Sevilla was persuaded to undertake the enterprise and agreed to establish a branch shop in Mexico City.[75] The press and type were probably shipped to Vera Cruz on the spring voyage of 1536. For a time nothing but government printing was done, and the religious books for the use of the Church continued to be printed in Spain. These *Doctrinas,* little religious manuals, were printed in both Spanish and the native dialects, but unfortunately none have survived hard usage and time. In 1539 the printing of books in the New World was begun. On June 12, 1539, Juan Cromberger entered into a contract with Juan Pablos, a native of Brescia, in Lombardy, to print books in Mexico City bearing the legend, "printed in the house of Juan Cromberger."[76] Pablos brought a com-

[74] Medina, *La Imprenta en México,* I, xxxv, quotes memorials of Zumárraga to the king from November of 1532 to June, 1534; that of March, 1533, from Sevilla, being most pertinent as the following quotation shows. "Iten porque parece seria cosa muy util y conveniente haber alla imprenta y molina de papel, y pues se hallaran personas que holgaran de ir conque Su Magestad les haga alguna merced con que puedan sustentar el arte, V.S. y mercedes los mandan prover."

[75] Jácome Cromberger had opened his printing shop in Seville in 1500, and had been so brilliantly successful that branch shops had been opened in Portugal at Lisbon and Evora. In 1525 he secured the right to contract printing for the New World and began operations in Mexico with one Diego de Mendieta as his representative. The death of this factor and subsequent legal complications led him to send his son-in-law, Lázaro Norimberger, to handle this business. Juan Cromberger, the son, was associated with his father in Sevilla from 1525 to 1527, and succeeded him in the enterprise on the latter's death in 1535. On his own death in 1542, the printing rights passed to his wife and sons. *Ibid.,* I, lvii.

[76] Juan Pablos is preceded in the records of Mexico City by another printer, Estéban Gómez, who probably came to New Spain in 1533-1534, and was granted citizenship by the Town Council September 5, 1539. He could print books of large or small letter print, music, and illuminated texts. He may have printed books before the arrival of Pablos, but no example of the earlier works, for which claims to printing have been advanced, has come down to us. Evidence of a lack of paper seems to preclude crediting Estéban Gómez as the printer of the first book published in America. *Cartas de Indias,* p. 762.

plete supply of materials with him, and indeed, may have escorted the press overseas.[77] The press was set up in the bishop's house and there, in 1539, the first American book issued from a press, a *Doctrina Christiana* in gothic type of twelve quarto sheets. This work was last seen and described in Spain in 1870,[78] but diligent search since that time has failed to bring it to light. Despite this fact, the weight of evidence in its favor points to this book as the first product of American typography rather than the *Manual de los Adultos* of the following year.[79] The fact that a fragment of this last named work escaped destruction and is in existence today, does not impair the conclusion that the first American imprint appeared in 1539.[80]

Following the death of Juan Cromberger in 1542, Juan Pablos continued to print books in Mexico City in the name of the firm until January 17, 1548, when the first book of "the house of Juan Pablos" appeared. Juan Pablos continued to be the official printer of New Spain until his death in 1560, and then the office was taken over by Pedro Ocharte. Under the direction of Pablos were printed the first mathematical work published in America, the *Sumario compendioso* of Juan Diez Freyle, 1556, the first physics text, the *Physica Speculativo* of F. Alphonsus of the faculty of the University of Mexico, 1557; and before Jamestown was

[77] The value of the press, ink, paper, and other supplies amounted to 165,000 maravedís. On the ship Miguel de Juarregui, which brought him to the New World in 1539, he brought his wife, Jerónima Gutierrez, an Andalusian woman, and a Negro slave apprentice, Gil Barbero. The writer believes that the confusion of the evidence on this point, the date of the arrival of the press, may be accounted for by the presence of two presses, one of inferior value brought over by the viceroy on the spring voyage of 1536, and a second and better one by Pablos when he came to New Spain in 1539. Cf. Medina, *La Imprenta en México*, I. lvii.

[78] *Cartas de Indias*, p. 787.

[79] Medina, *La Imprenta en Mexico*, I. v.

[80] The great array of evidence marshalled by Medina in his introduction to his *La Imprenta en México*, makes the older view of Icazbalceta, as contained in his *Bibliografía Méxicana del Siglo XVI*, pp. 1 ff., no longer tenable.

founded a law code for New Spain, Vasco de Puga's *Cédu-laras*, of 1563, and a work on navigation, the *Instruccion Nautica*, 1587, besides numerous works of a religious character, had been published.[81]

Impressive beginnings in the development of industry and agriculture were made in New Spain under the first viceroy and before the stifling effect of the oppressive monopoly of Seville was felt. This unhampered growth suggests what might have been accomplished in the Spanish colonies if free competition with the mother country had been permitted.[82] The viceroy made every endeavor to encourage the natives in their indigenous cultivation of cotton, maize, cacao, the maguey plant, and numerous species of edible fruit, and orders were issued that all ships sailing from Spain to Vera Cruz bring European plants, seeds, and selected stock for breeding purposes.[83] Wheat, sugar, horses, and mules were introduced in large quantities and, as the population grew and new areas were settled, great ranches and plantations came into existence. New Spain in 1535 was economically an exporting region able to furnish the West Indies and Tierra

[81] The best and most comprehensive work on this subject of the introduction of printing into the New World is Medina, *La Impren-ta en México*. Icazbalceta's older work, *Bibliografía Méxicana del Siglo XVI*, is still useful, and important documents are to be found in the *Cartas de Indias*. For the Spanish side of the story those interested should consult the important work of Konrad Burger, *Die Drucker und Verleger in Spanien und Portugal von 1501 bis 1536*; also the monumental work of Konrad Haebler, *Bibliografía Ibér-ica del Siglo XV*, with segunda parte, and the local works on the history of printing in Sevilla, Francisco Escudero y Perosso's *Tipo-grafía hispalense*, and Joaquin Hazañas y la Rua's *La Imprenta en Sevilla*. To the list of books known to have been printed by the Crombergers in Seville the writer feels that these works should add the titles of works printed for America by them for which the copyright is extant. Such a work is the *Doctrina Christiana es-cripto en lengua de yndios de Michoacan* by Bishop Quiroga, for which a license to print in Sevilla was issued on October 25, 1538.

[82] Bancroft, *History of Mexico*, II. 135 ff., tells the story of the pioneer work of Cortés in agriculture and industry in New Spain.

[83] A. G. I., 87-6-1, Oficio y parte, libro 3, Medina del Campo, March 20, 1532, XXVII.

Firme with wheat.[84] The sugar crop was by 1546 of sufficient size to keep many domestic refineries at work, and the
remarkable multiplication of sheep gave rise to a prosperous
cloth industry. The silkworm proved so adaptable to the
climate that the same date saw a considerable silk industry
flourishing, with silk officials so numerous as to be noted
by visitors from Spain, and the product of sufficient quantity
and value for the Church to insist on its tithe of the product
as was customary in Granada in old Spain. The Spaniards
brought improved methods of agriculture along with their
new plants and animals, of greatest importance being the skill
in irrigation they had acquired from the Moors and the dex-
terity with which they dug ditches (acequias) to convey water
to dry waste lands.[85] To spare human lives by relieving the
Indians from severe labor, machinery was built in the refineries and in the mines, motivated by water or horse power,
and the wheat and maize were ground by windmills, as was
the practice in Spain.

Certain of the industries soon outdistanced all others.
This was noticeably the case with the cattle and sheep
industries, where the viceroy set an example by introducing
fine breeds like the merino on his own ranches and by aiding
wool cloth factories. So rapid was the multiplication of
sheep and cattle that, beginning in 1538, two judges-of-the-
sheepwalk were appointed annually by the Town Council
of Mexico City, and semi-annual meetings of the sheep and
cattle proprietors were held to restore stray animals to their
rightful owners.[86] All ranches had their distinctive marks

[84] Cédula, in *Documentos de Ultramar*, X. 309. After 1540 Indian
troubles and mysterious epidemics caused a sharp diminution in the
quantity of wheat produced.

[85] For instance, Lorenzo de Tejada, oidor of the audiencia constructed
an acequia, to bring water from the Tacuba river near Mexico City to his
fields, which was crossed by thirty bridges of wood and stone.—A. G. I.,
48-1-4/26, Memorial de Tejada, Mexico, December 20, 1546.

[86] The first election of alcaldes de mesta took place in Mexico City
January 1, 1538, and ordinances for the government of the sheep-owners'

or brands which were registered by the various cabildos to prevent rustling and to keep the flocks and herds separate.[87] The opening of the wild country of the Chichimecas to the northwest, by the Mixton War, was fortunate, for the flocks and herds about Mexico City had become a nuisance and hindered agriculture, as the crops tilled by the natives were consumed by unfenced animals. The new lands afforded fine pasturage on open ranges far removed from cultivated soil. This little known Indian war, like King Philip's War and the Yamassee War, furnishes another example of the breaking of an Indian barrier into the back country for economic reasons.[88]

The viceroy's pet interest was the sheep industry, which he fostered and encouraged. The woolen cloth industry of New Spain was the direct result of his orders that the raw product be woven into cloth. Its chief center was Tezcuco, the lake town near Mexico City, where he personally kept thirty-three slaves and their families engaged in weaving the wool into cloth.[89] One of the most prominent of the wool cloth merchants of the period, Gonzálo Gómez, likewise had his factories located in Tezcuco, where Indian labor— slave and free—was used, and the cloth produced was sold in stores which he owned in the Capital City and the province of Michoacán. The sheep were merinos, famous for their fine quality of wool, and the cloth found a ready market.

association (the Mesta) were drawn up November 14, 1542. The text is to be found in the *Actas de Cabildo*, IV. 313-315. For the background of this institution in Spain, see Klein, *The Mesta, a Study in Spanish Economic History,* Cambridge, 1921.

[87] The brands of the owners in the vicinity of Mexico City are reproduced in the *Actas de Cabildo* II. 196-210.

[88] Mendoza sent his own flocks to these new ranges. A. G. I., 48-1-5/27, Interrogatorio, preguntas 306, 307.

[89] *Ibid.,* preguntas 56-65. Klein, in *The Mesta,* p. 6, states that he found less than a dozen references to merino wool previous to 1600 in all his research, and on that basis concludes that its use was not general until the later seventeenth century. Mendoza, however, very clearly states that his sheep were "ganado merino muy buen de Castilla."

Mendoza consequently was not only able to sell his cloth but dressed his servants in the product of his own ranches and factory.

The silk industry was also favored and grew to such proportions that special inspectors (veedores) and notaries (escribanos) had to be appointed to supervise its manufacture. In fact, Francisco Preciado, the first man to apply the name California to the geographical region which bears it today, commented, in 1547, on the number of silk officials he saw when he visited Mexico City.[90] Ordinances for the regulation of this nascent industry were framed by the cabildo of that city, March 15, 1542, to stop the abuse of slave spinners in the factories, and the satisfactory remedy stipulated was complete prohibition of the employment of slave labor.[91] Mulberry trees were planted in many parts of the country and the silk manufacture of New Spain soon enjoyed a reputation that reached Spain.[92] Free native labor, under the encomienda system, worked in the mulberry groves and spun in the factories under Spanish overseers. The center of manufacture was Mexico City and the amounts which could be spun in each town were arbitrarily fixed by the viceroy.[93] So prosperous did the silkgrowers become that the Church demanded the tithe already alluded to and the jealousy of Spanish growers, which in the end would cause the suppression of this colonial industry, was aroused.[94]

Old towns grew, and new ones were established on the basis of these industries, the discovery of new mines, and the exploring activities of the viceroy. The entry port of San Juan de Ulloa was improved by the building of a mole and

[90] A. G. I., 48-1-6/28, Testigo de Franco Presciado, cura de Colima, Colima, February 21, 1547.

[91] *Actas de Cabildo,* Libro 4, p. 273.

[92] Martín Cortés was given a grant to plant some thousands of mulberry trees on his estate.—Pacheco y Cárdenas, XII. 563.

[93] A. G. I., 48-1-5/27, Interrogatorio del señor vissorey, pregunta 283.

[94] A. G. I., 140-3-9, Cédula, Valladolid, 1543.

a tower, in addition to which a lighthouse and a fort were projected.[95] The new town, Puebla de los Ángeles, increased in number of inhabitants and was favored with a license to found silk factories without being subject to control or interference. Two cities, which are state capitals in Mexico today, Valladolid in Michoacán and Guadalajara, were founded, the second in 1541, as the result of the removal of the old city to a better location, and the shipbuilding activities of the viceroy brought numerous Indians and officials to Navidad in Colima. In Nueva Galicia, Zacatecas was established and there was a great movement of population into the surrounding region.

This development of agriculture and industry was also attended by great eagerness to acquire more lands than were conferred by the act of becoming a citizen in a town or city. The oidor Tejada was particularly active, improving lands, purchasing, trading, building, so that he probably earned for himself the title of the first great real estate promoter in the New World. On one occasion he traded sterile land in Chalco two to one with natives for lands they possessed near Chapultepec and they discovered the poorness of their bargain to their great chagrin when it was too late.[96] Even the Church was interested, and the bishop of Oaxaca had to be warned to cease troubling the natives with his ranches and flocks.[97]

Since in New Spain no money save that brought from Spain was in use until 1535, the merchants were forced to use gold and silver by weight for the payment of larger amounts, and bits of gold for retail trade. The Indians bartered or used cacao as a medium of exchange. On May 11, 1535,

[95] A. G.· I., 48 1-7/29, Testigo de Alvaro Fernandez Piloto del galeon La Concepcion, testigo 194, pregunta 228.

[96] A. G. I., 48-1-4/26, Memorial de Tejada, Mexico, December 20, 1546.

[97] A. G. I., 87-6-2, Oficio y parte, Valladolid, October 9, 1549.

the establishment of a mint was authorized for the coinage of silver and copper.[98] The silver coins were to be reales, two reales, three reales, and quartillos.[99] In charge of the mint, under the viceroy and oidores, were two alcaldes, a balançaro (weighing and measuring), a treasurer, an escribano, a tallador, coiners (acuñadores), and a guard, besides Negroes and Indians for the manual labor involved.[100] The money was legal tender both for New Spain and the mother country, but the right to coin gold was reserved. The fact that the mint was not able to satisfy the needs of the country during these first years is evidenced in a number of requests for permission to increase the coinage and undoubtedly points to a considerable growth of trade.

The period also afforded interesting attempts to fix prices. The City Council of Mexico drew up lists of legal prices, with the approval of the viceroy, covering bread, wine, olive oil, and the other necessities of life, which were changed as conditions seemed to warrant.[101] When Tejada arrived in New Spain, in 1536, he found prices to be excessively high, much higher in fact than in Spain. He cites the fact that a pound (libra) of grapes cost him a peso of gold and a quince two

[98] Puga, Cédulas, I. 360; Documentas de Ultramar, X. 264-271.

[99] The monetary units of uncoined gold were:

Peso de Oro	
De Tepuzque	271 maravedís
Comun	300 maravedís
Comun con tres quilates añadidos	360 maravedís
De ley perfecta	450 maravedís
De minas	450 maravedís

—Haring, op. cit., in Hisp. Amer. Hist. Rev., II. 177.

[100] A. G. I., 48-2-20/2, Visita a la casa de Moneda, May 28, 1545. At this time one, two, and four maravedí pieces of copper were being coined. The coins of the period, with an account of the founding of the first mint, are pictured in Riva Palacio, Mexico à través de los Siglos, II. 242-249.

[101] Bread was to be sold 11 loaves (de a libra) for a tomín (575 milligrams) of gold. White sugar was to be sold for an arroba for three pesos or one and one-half silver reales a libra. Olive oil was to be sold for an arroba for four pesos of oro comun. Milk, that was good and not watered, an azumbic for a medio real of silver.—Actas de Cabildo, Libro 4, passim.

tomines, but that, owing to the great development of agriculture, he was soon able to sell for prices equal to those current in Spain, that is, a libra of grapes for a half tomín and one quartillo and one hundred quinces for a tomín.[102] If a conclusion can be drawn from this, it is that a considerable lowering of prices took place in New Spain following the increased production of the ranches operated by the Spaniards. Prices for hauling and carrying, and the wages of the Indians were also fixed by law.   Thus every twelve fanegas of wheat paid a cartage of six silver reales,[103] and every arroba of goods brought from Vera Cruz paid freightage at a legal rate of five tomines.[104]   Those who overcharged could be prosecuted, and the records of the Town Council in Mexico City are filled with complaints against profiteers. These attempts at government control of prices and wages are significant and merit more attention than has been paid them up to the present.[105]

[102] A. G. I., 48-1-3/25, Descargos del Lic^do Lorenzo de Tejada, Mexico, 1546.

[103] *Actas de Cabildo*, III. 12.

[104] *Ibid.*, II. 22.

[105] The reader will find a more elaborate discussion of this interesting subject in A. S. Aiton, "Early American Price-Fixing Legislation," in *Michigan Law Review*, XXV. 15-24.

CHAPTER V

EXPLORATION UNDER THE FIRST VICEROY

When Antonio de Mendoza assumed his duties as viceroy of New Spain, Cortés and Guzmán were still in the New World engaged in a bitter struggle for the right to explore the South Sea and the unknown northern interior. Guzmán, by virtue of his authority as governor of Nueva Galicia, was able to block the advance of his adversary by land and to place numerous vexatious hindrances in the path of his sea expeditions. Guzmán had acquired this position of advantage by his own efforts when it became apparent that his position as president of the first audiencia was in jeopardy. In December, 1529, he had set out from Mexico City to the west to look for new conquests which would rehabilitate his reputation, lured in that direction by tales of an Amazon island and rumors of seven opulent cities which had reached his ears. Within two years he conquered Jalisco and Sinaloa and founded the towns of Compostela and Guadalajara in the former, and San Miguel de Culiacán and Chiametla in the latter. He named his new conquest, Greater Spain (Mayor España), but the authorities in Spain felt this to be presumptuous and bestowed the less pretentious title of Nueva Galicia on the region.[1] In the meantime Cortés returned from Spain in 1530 with the title of Marqués del Valle de Oaxaca and armed with extensive privileges to continue his discoveries in the South Sea; while over against both of the rivals the second audiencia set up its claim to supremacy.

---

[1] Guzmán had first overrun Michoacán, but was merely repeating the earlier exploration of Francisco Cortés and Avalos until he crossed the Tololotlán River. When the new territory to the north failed to reveal the riches he was seeking, he then ignored the earlier claims of these agents of Cortés and devoted his attention to the south of the River along the coast as far as the borders of Michoacán and Zacatula.

Cortés, thwarted in his attempt to assume the military leadership of New Spain, turned immediately to his shipyards at Zacatula, Tehuantepec, and Acapulco, where he resumed work on a large scale, as failure to sail within two years would make his privilege void. With renewed hope he began the exploration of the coast northward, a task which had been abandoned after Saavedra's fleet had sailed as far north as Santiago in Colima in the year 1527.

In 1532, the first of his fleets was ready, and under the command of Diego Hurtado de Mendoza, his cousin, and Mazuela, its two vessels set forth up the coast. But ill fortune soon overtook them. Buffeted by storms, plagued by sickness, set upon by Indians, and refused permission to land for provisions and repairs within Guzmán's jurisdiction, both vessels and nearly all of the crews were lost. The discovery of the Tres Marías Islands was the barren result of this effort. Undaunted by reverses and opposition, Cortés despatched Bercerra and Grijalva the following year with two vessels and was rewarded by the discovery of the peninsula of Lower California. This voyage was not a complete triumph, however, as one of his vessels was lost and the other, after murder and mutiny, fell into the hands of Guzmán. Appeals to the second audiencia only brought orders to stop his exploring activities, as this body had been secretly instructed to undermine the conqueror's authority. In the teeth of this opposition, but with royal authority for his action, Cortés determined to follow up this discovery in person and, in midwinter of 1534-1535, he set out at the head of an expedition to plant a colony in the newly found land. The colony was established at Santa Cruz (La Paz) on the inner coast, but failed to be successful in that sterile region and he was forced to break it up in 1536.[2] The news of the arrival of

[2] For detailed accounts of these expeditions see Bancroft, *History of Mexico*, II. 419-425; Bancroft, *North Mexican States*, San Francisco.

the viceroy had been brought to him before this time by Francisco de Ulloa and hopes for better treatment at the hands of the new government had started him back to New Spain post haste. These hopes were transitory, however, as Mendoza could not recognize any personage as equal or greater than himself in governmental activity, including discovery. The exaggerated politeness which characterized the relations of the two at the outset inevitably gave way to open rivalry, emphasized by the enforced withdrawal of Guzmán from the field, which left Cortés and Mendoza alone as the two strong contenders for the right to discover.[3]

In 1536, a new glamour was thrown around the work of discovery which resulted in the definite exclusion of Cortés. Three strangely-clad Spanish wanderers, Alvar Núñez Cabeza de Vaca, Andrés de Dorantes, and Alonso del Castillo Maldonado, accompanied by a Moorish slave, Estevanico, came in from the mysterious north with new tales of marvels they had seen or heard of in the course of their journey. They were the only survivors, save one, of the three hundred men on the ill-starred Narváez expedition to Florida in 1528. After several years spent among the Indians in Texas they had managed to escape and had made their way westward across Texas, Chihuahua, and Sonora to Culiacán, the northernmost Spanish settlement on the Pacific coast. From there

1884-1889, I. 16-54; and Charles E. Chapman's *The Founding of Spanish California*, pp. 6-8, and *A History of California, the Spanish Period*, pp. 49 ff.

[3] Guzmán had failed to produce the wealth his reports had promised and fate in the person of his judge of residencia, Diego Pérez de la Torre, had overtaken him at the viceroy's palace in Mexico City when he was on the point of flight to Genoa in Italy. A period of arrest in the common jail in Mexico City ensued until his return to Spain in 1538, a disgraced and discredited man. The attempt of a servant of Cortés to place his master's chair on a line with that of the viceroy was the beginning of the open breach between the two men that was to bear fruit in the deliberate attempt of Cortés to get even with his rival at the time of the Sandoval visita.—Bancroft, *History of Mexico*, II. 425, note 49.

they were brought to Mexico City, where they lived for several months as the guests of the viceroy.[4]

Fired by their tales of Indian cities in the Northern interior, Mendoza determined to enter the field of discovery
and to appropriate to himself the fame of conquering new
and rich civilizations for the king. To profit by the experience of the wanderers, he tried to induce them to enter his
service, and one of their number, Andrés de Dorantes, was
tendered a commission to explore the northern country, but
for some unknown reason the project was never carried out.[5]
Mendoza purchased Estevanico, the Moorish slave, and made
his ambitions known by applying to the Council of the Indies
for permission to engage in discovery.[6] A large-scale ex-

[4] For a critical treatment of their route and wanderings, see Herbert
Davenport and J. K. Wells "The First Europeans in Texas," *The South-
western Historical Quarterly,* XXII. 111-143; 205-260. Translations of
the original narrative by Cabeza de Vaca are contained in Fanny and
Adolph Bandelier, "The Journey of Alva Nuñez Cabeza de Vaca," in
The Trail Maker Series and the *Narrative of Alvar Nuñez Cabeça de
Vaca* (F. W. Hodge Edition) in *Spanish Explorations in the Southern
United States, 1528-1542.*

[5] Mendoza, "Première lettre" in Ternaux-Campans, *Voyages,* IX.
287. The plan embraced the sending of a party of horsemen and friars
into the country Dorantes had heard about, under the latter's personal
command. Mendoza spent considerable money preparing the expedition
and in his letter is at a loss to explain the fact that nothing came from his
preparations. Perhaps the real reason was a decision to have one of his
own men, a personage of more consequence, or even himself, undertake
the enterprise. Cabeza de Vaca returned to Spain in 1537 and was rewarded for his services by an appointment to be adelantado of the Río
de la Plata country. In South America, he distinguished himself by
another remarkable overland journey and was finally sent back to Spain
to spend the balance of his days in comparative quiet as a resident of
Sevilla. Both Castillo Maldonado and Andrés de Dorantes remained in
New Spain. Dorantes was rewarded with the grant of a pueblo, married
the widow of Alonso de Benevides, Doña María de la Torre, and served
with some distinction under the viceroy's command in the Mixton War.

[6] Dorantes "experienced deep grief on being asked that Estebanico
serve the viceroy, Don Antonio, and would not give him up for five
hundred pesos in a plate of silver which the viceroy sent as payment
by a third person, but was willing that Estebanico serve the viceroy in the
name of His Majesty without payment because of the good which might
accrue to the souls of those provinces and to the interests
of real hacienda." Obregón, *Crónica,* April 16 and 18, 1584. This
testimony seems to indicate that Estevanico was lent to the viceroy, not
sold as usually stated in the histories which treat of this period.

pedition was not justified by the mere stories of Cabeza de
Vaca and his companions concerning the marvels which, they
had heard, existed in the north. To verify these stories and to
secure something definite enough to justify an expedition of
conquest, Mendoza sent out a small reconnoitering party
under Fray Marcos de Niza, vice-commissioner-general of
the Franciscan Order in New Spain. Simultaneously he began the preparation of the more formidable expedition that
was to depart on the receipt of a favorable report, by sending
a new governor to Nueva Galicia, Francisco Vásquez de
Coronado, a gentleman of his personal following.[7] Fray
Marcos was accompanied by Coronado to the limits of Spanish settlement at Culiacán, and was instructed to proceed with
Estevanico, a lay brother, Oronato, and a few friendly Indians, into the unexplored country to see if a large expedition
would be worthwhile. His instructions were precise, and their
minute directions admirably illustrate the training and administrative ability of the viceroy.[8] Fray Marcos left Culiacán, March 7, 1537, with his little band. Oronato soon fell
sick and had to be left behind while the rest pushed on.
Eventually, Estevanico, sent on in advance, while his com-

[7] There are unsubstantiated accounts of other expeditions into the
north. In 1538, Fray Antonio de Ciudad Rodrigo, provincial of the
Franciscan Order, is reported to have sent Fray Juan de la Asunción
and a companion friar to the lower Gila on the lower course of the
Colorado.—W. Lowery, *Spanish Settlements,* New York, 1901, pp.
258, 259; A. F. Bandelier, *Contributions,* Cambridge, 1890, pp. 79-103.
It is also supposed that the viceroy may have led an expedition into the
Topia region in northwestern Durango the same year, but lack of food
and the difficulties encountered in the mountains forced a return.—Ternaux-Campans, *Voyages,* IX. 285.

[8] They are to be found in Pacheco y Cárdenas, III. 325-328. Lowery
analyzes their contents in his *Spanish Settlements,* pp. 262-264, and points
out that they are "remarkable and unique" in that "the viceroy had
shrewdly disguised the arm of the flesh under the Franciscan gown,
and the expedition, ostensibly undertaken for the glory of God, and
prosecuted at the expense of the Church, received direct authority from
him to take possession of any discovery in the name of his imperial
master." The instructions are also noteworthy for their insistence on a
careful survey of the country traversed and by a wise admonition to
preserve the peaceful character of the expedition with the utmost scruple.

mander gathered information concerning the coast, sent back by Indian messenger, in accordance with a prearranged signal, "a great cross as high as a man," indicating that he had discovered a greater and wealthier land than New Spain. A second cross as large as the first and the messenger, who verified and amplified the first reports, confirmed Fray Marcos in his belief that great things were at hand. In reality, Estevanico had arrived at the Zuñi pueblo Hawaikuh in western New Mexico. On being informed that it was the first of seven, his imagination had connected it with the mysterious Seven Cities, long the object of search, and he miscalled it Cíbola. Inordinate vanity and mistreatment of the natives brought Estevanico death as a punishment, but Fray Marcos, undaunted by this sinister news, pressed forward until he caught a distant view of the pueblo, before prudence turned him back. In his report he stated, "judging by what I could see from the height where I placed myself to observe it, the settlement is larger than the City of Mexico. . . . It appears to me that this land is the best and largest of all those that have been discovered."[9] With this exaggerated notion of the importance of his find Fray Marcos then hastened back to Culiacán, and not finding Coronado there, continued his journey as far as Compostela. Here he composed reports of his journey for the viceroy and the Provincial of his Order which, by reason of the false hopes they gave rise to, were responsible for the ensuing expedition and its ultimate failure. While they failed to give first-hand information of the presence of great wealth in the north, they at least encouraged such a belief, and spurred the rival claimants for the right to discover and possess these new lands to still greater efforts.[10] In the courts of Spain legal suits were

[9] Quoted in G. P. Winship, "The Coronado Expedition," in *The Fourteenth Annual Report of the Bureau of Ethnology,* p. 362.

[10] As soon as the report of the successful issue of the journey of Fray Marcos reached the viceroy he took precautions to withhold the news

brought to determine the justice of the opposing claims in which Mendoza found ranged against him, not only Cortés, Guzmán, and De Soto, but also Pedro de Alvarado and Lucas Vásquez de Ayllón.[11] De Soto and Ayllón were too distant for their pretentions to receive serious consideration and Guzmán's career was over as far as the home government was concerned. The real contenders were the viceroy, Cortés, and Pedro de Alvarado. Cortés claimed exclusive rights on the basis of his commission as captain-general of New Spain and his contract with the King, but his star was on the wane and Mendoza treated him with scant regard. After this, Cortés sent out Francisco de Ulloa, in the face of a viceregal prohibition, in 1539, and explored the Gulf of Lower California to its head, but this defiance made relations between the two so unpleasant that Cortés, realizing the impossibility of making any headway against such a powerful personage, withdrew to Spain, never to return, cherishing the deluded hope that his past services would win him a restoration of favor, power, and privilege.[12]

The only immediate rival of the viceroy left in the lists was Pedro de Alvarado, former lieutenant of Cortés and conqueror of Guatemala. He had recently returned from Spain with high honors and a contract, dated April 16, 1538, to discover and conquer islands in the Pacific. His opposition could not be formidable, however, as his contract stated

from his rivals. In the case of Hernando de Soto, who had recently secured the right to discover in Florida and for that reason would claim it to be within his grant, all vessels en route to Spain were ordered to avoid the Islands of the West Indies on the home voyage. *Ibid.*, p. 370.

[11] A. G. I., 1-1-2/21, Processo del Marques del Valle, nuño de Guzman y los adelantados Dⁿ Pedro Alvarado y Hernando de Soto y el lic^{do} Lucas Vasquez de Ayllón sobre el descubrimiento que hicieron de la Nueva Galicia y tierras del Mar del Sur.

[12] The nature of his defiance and the uncompromising attitude of Mendoza may be gathered from the fact that the conqueror's petition of September 4, 1539, to secure permission to send a vessel with thirty or forty men and supplies to rescue Ulloa was refused by the viceroy and audiencia.—A. G. I., 1-1-2/21, Peticion del Marqués del Valle, Mexico, September 4, 1539, in Processo del Marques del Valle.

definitely that his was to be an expedition by sea and, moreover, the viceroy was granted, by the contract, a third interest in it, for what aid he might extend.[13] Alvarado arrived
off the coast of Colima in August 1540, with a fleet of
twelve vessels and a force of six hundred men. His need of
supplies and assistance from Mendoza threw him into the
latter's hands as an ally rather than an opponent. Luís de
Castilla and Agostín Guerrero, the emissaries of the viceroy,
met Alvarado on the coast and soon secured his consent to
a meeting between the two to take place at the home of Alvarado's kinsman, Juan de Alvarado, at Tiripitío in Michoacán. At this place, November 29, 1540, the two met and
after a series of conferences entered into a contract in which
Alvarado was given a fourth share in the proceeds of the
viceroy's expeditions and the viceroy was to have his share
in the adelantado's ships increased from a third interest to
a half and future expenses were to be borne equally by the
two contracting parties from that time forth.[14] By this
agreement Mendoza effectively barred Cortés from further
discovery and, to this New World triumph, was added the

[13] A. G. I., 139-1-3, Libro de la provincia del Poniente que começa
en la Villa de Valladolid a diez e seis dias del mes de abril de 1538.

This contains the complete contract with appointments of officials in
the lands to be discovered, with salaries and all the usual liberality contained in contracts with prospective conquerors by the Spanish government.

[14] A. G. I., 1-1-2/21. *Asiento y capitulacion entre el virrey de la
Nueva España, D. Antonio de Mendoza y el adelantado, D. Pedro de Alvarado,* Tiripitio, November 29, 1540; printed in Pacheco y Cárdenas,
III. 351-362. Bancroft, who makes Cortés the hero of his narrative,
berates the viceroy for his action in thus forcing a friend and former
lieutenant of Cortés to betray his interests. He also accepts the view that
Mendoza, holding the whip hand, practically used the advantage Alvarado's need of supplies gave him to force the latter to give him a share
in his enterprise. He pictures the interviews as quite stormy with only
the diplomacy of Bishop Marroquin standing between the two and open
hostilities.—Bancroft, *History of Mexico,* II. 495. This is an acceptance
of the embittered report of Cortés and fails to take into account the
fourth share in the viceroy's expeditions received by Alvarado and his
very evident satisfaction with the entire arrangement.

news of the report of the fiscal of the Council of the Indies
of May 25, 1540, which turned aside the requests of all
claimants for the right to discover to the north save that of
the viceroy.[15]

The choice of Mendoza for the leadership of his exploring enterprise was Francisco Vásquez de Coronado, who
was appointed governor of New Galicia in 1538 in preparation for the northward march. He was a native of Salamanca in Spain and had come to the New World in the viceroy's
retinue. In Mexico he had won the viceroy's confidence and
favor and had married a wealthy wife, Beatrice de Estrada,
the daughter of the royal treasurer. With such high patronage and with such a dazzling opportunity the future of the
young governor seemed to be assured. With the gathering
of men and provisions for the entrada under way in Nueva
Galicia, he sent out a new reconnoitering expedition of fifteen
men under Melchoir Díaz and Juan de Zaldívar, November
17, 1539, and with their departure from Culiacán hastened
to Mexico City to help recruit the requisite force. The viceroy's call for volunteers met with an enthusiastic response,
as all the unemployed adventurers of New Spain flocked to
Compostela to join in the venture.[16] Men and supplies con-
verged on this rendezvous and, by February of 1540, three

[15] Winship, "The Coronado Expedition," p. 373.

[16] The jaundiced eye of Cortés saw a grave peril in this popularity
and in 1540 he complained that New Spain was being drained of its
citizens and would be left defenseless against an Indian revolt. From
evidence gathered by Mendoza to refute this charge it would seem that
the majority of the adventurers who went with Coronado were not
citizens of the towns or encomenderos but newcomers from Spain and
the floating population that a chance for adventure always attracts.
Indeed, a goodly number of the three hundred Spaniards had been living
in Mexico City on the Viceroy's bounty and could no longer loaf at his
expense with good excuse. Mendoza was undoubtedly pleased to be able
to put his guests to some use.—*Informacion del Virrey de Nueva España
Don Antonio de Mendoza, de la gente que va á poblar la Nueva Galicia
con Francisco Vásquez de Coronado, Gobernador de ella*, Compostela,
February 21, 1540, in Pacheco y Cárdenas, XIV. 373-384.

hundred Spaniards and eight hundred Indian allies[17] were gathered there, together with a great store of culverines, horses, mules, cattle, pigs, and sheep provided at the viceroy's expense.[18]

On Sunday, February 22, 1540, all was ready for the start and the little Spanish town of Compostela became the center of European interest in North America. The viceroy was present in person with his guard and attendant officials to pass the troops in final review and to impart his last instructions. A host of notable personages were in attendance to witness the departure and to bid friends and relatives "godspeed." It was a brilliant spectacle as the three hundred mailed horsemen, armed with lances and mounted on picked steeds from the viceroy's ranches, accompanied by two hundred foot-soldiers and over a thousand native allies paraded by the king's representative. The whites in corselet, casque, and silks, with lance, sword, harquebus, and crossbow, made a striking contrast to the swarm of Indians in vivid paint, festive attire, nodding plumes, and with spears, clubs, bows, and quilted armor, that crowded the background. The following day, after they had sworn an oath of fidelity to their commander, with pennons unfurled and in organized companies, the expedition set forth. Regretting that he could not go all the way, Mendoza accompanied them on the march for two days. In the wake came almost a thousand camp-followers, black and red, with the baggage and supply train of horses and mules, the latter laden with light mountain guns, and accompanied by a commissary "on the hoof" of cattle, sheep, and swine. Vásquez de Coronado, resplendent

[17] Ten thousand Indians wished to go, but the viceroy limited their number to the neighborhood of one thousand.—A. G. I., 48-1-9/31, Testigo de Coronado, Mexico, January 18, 1547, pregunta 200.

[18] In certain narrow passes they counted the horses and mules after the expedition got under way and the total was 1005 beasts. *Ibid.*, pregunta 199.

in gilded armor and gay trappings, but loath to part with his wife, rode none too gaily to the fate that would mar his career.[19]

At Chiametla the main body was rejoined by Díaz and Zaldívar, who brought in advance an unfavorable report of the country, where some of their Indians had been frozen to death on the coast and they had been turned back by the excessive cold which they had encountered. The ill-tidings leaked out and spread discontent amongst the fine gentlemen of the expedition, who were already dispirited by the unexpected hardships they had been forced to undergo. At Culiacán, Coronado resolved to leave the main body behind to follow in easy stages and pushed on in advance with a small party. On July 8th, Hawaikuh was captured and shortly thereafter side expeditions, led by Pedro de Tovar and García López de Cárdenas, overcame the Moqui villages and gazed for the first time into the Grand Canyon of the Colorado River. Soon the other pueblo Indians had been visited and Alvarado went far to the East to the Pecos. Hither the entire army marched to spend the winter in the valley of the Rio Grande in the country of Tigueux.

The following spring, after a winter of almost constant warfare, Coronado started northeastward across the great buffalo plains in search of great towns and precious metals, which a wily Indian guide, El Turco, so-called because the Spaniards thought he looked like a Turk, informed him lay just beyond in a land known as Quivira. Coronado probably penetrated as far as the wigwam towns of the Wichita Indians in modern Kansas before he turned back in September 1541.[20] Expeditions were also sent far up the Rio

[19]Winship, "The Coronado Expedition," pp. 378, 382, note 2, gives a vivid description of the review and collates the authorities for the dates of the departure from Compostela and the arrival at Culiacán.

[20] Coronado was in Quivira for twenty-five days, and the country must have been fairly thoroughly explored, for he says, in his letter to the king, that he sent "Captains and men in many directions." Cf. Coro-

Grande in search of treasure, but, in the spring of 1542, after the governor had been seriously injured in a tournament and the men had become almost mutinous, it was decided that the expedition should be abandoned. Some friars elected to remain and were killed soon after the departure of the soldiers on the return march, in April 1542. The journey was characterized by insubordination, and by the time Culiacán was reached, late in June 1542, the army had become almost disorganized. Owing to the painfulness of his injuries Coronado had to be carried in a litter and arrived in Mexico City with barely a hundred men, so numerous were the desertions.[21] Mendoza was keenly disappointed in the outcome of his venture and showed it when Coronado " . . . very sad and very weary, completely worn out, and shamefaced came to kiss the hand of the viceroy,"[22] as he had expended a great sum of money on the expedition as a whole and to help equip private individuals.[23] Coronado had not displayed the great qualities of leadership expected of him, but his journey had accomplished certain very important things. It had made known the vast interior of the continent, and for a time had dispelled the current illusion that new Mexicos and Perus existed in that direction. The sedentary pueblo tribes of the Southwest, the Grand Canyon of the Colorado, the tribes of

nado's letter to the king, in Winship, "The Coronado Expedition," p. 582; for further information concerning the sojourn in Kansas, see Richey, "Early Spanish Exploration and Indian Implements in Kansas," in *Kansas State Historical Society Collections,* VIII. 152-168.

[21] A convenient English translation of Pedro de Castañeda's narrative of the Coronado expedition with a critical introduction and notes exists in *Spanish Explorers in the Southern United States, 1528-1543. (Original Narratives of early American History,* F. W. Hodge, ed.)   George P. Winship's account of the expedition in the *Fourteenth Annual Report of the Bureau of Ethnology,* Washington, 1898, is standard.

[22] Castañeda in Winship, "The Coronado Expedition," p. 539.

[23] A. G. I., 48-1-9/31, Testigo de Franco de Coronado, Mexico, January 18, 1547.   Suarez de Peralta, who as a small boy witnessed the entry of the unsuccessful explorer into Mexico City, says that the viceroy received him with sadness, for he saw the loss of his labor and capital, but found forgetfulness of his losses in the government of New Spain *(Tratado del descubrimiento de las Yndias).*

the plains, and the teeming herds of bison had been discovered, but the treasure so eagerly pursued did not exist. Coronado's great advance into the north ranks with the contemporary expedition of Hernando de Soto as the last notable conquistador effort before the Spaniards settled down to the slower movement of the cattle and mining frontier.[24]

Coronado returned to his governorship over New Galicia in 1542, but his rule was cut short in 1544, when a residencia revealed the shortcomings of his administration. Held guilty on a number of charges, involving at least gross carelessness, he returned to Mexico City where he spent the remainder of his days serving the city as a regidor. In 1552 and 1553 he was in poor health, and sometime between January and November the following year his death occurred. Coronado fell from favor not primarily as the result of the great failure of his expedition in search of Cíbola but because he lacked the qualities of leadership high positions demand, and because his maladministration of Nueva Galicia exposed his incompetence as an administrator. The measure of success enjoyed by the great pioneering enterprise which will always bear his name was due not to his abilities, but to the organizing genius that stood sponsor for him and inspired the expedition, Antonio de Mendoza.[25]

Since the report of Fray Marcos de Niza had given the viceroy the impression that the route Coronado's expedition would follow lay along the western coast, he ordered his chamberlain, Hernando de Alarcón, to follow the shore by vessel, keeping in communication with it. Alarcón left Aca-

[24] Coronado was awarded the grant of an encomienda for his meritorious services in discovery and conquest in 1549, but his maladministration of Nueva Galicia marred his record so seriously that the audiencia wrote to the king, February 20, 1548, that "ni el ni Castillo Maldonado estar para que se les cometa governacion ni cargos de justicia."—A. G. I., 87-6-21, Oficio y parte, Nov. 9, 1549, 121; 58-5-8, Consulta del abidencia de la nueva españa de XX de Febrero de 1548.

[25] For details and references, see A. S. Aiton, "The Later Career of Coronado," in *American Historical Review*, XXX. 298-305.

pulco, May 9, 1540, with two ships, the *San Pedro* and the *Santa Catalina,* and was joined by the *San Gabriel* at the port of Santiago. He knew of the earlier expedition of Ulloa and proceeded up the coast to the head of the gulf, reaching the shoals at the mouth of the Colorado where that navigator had turned back. A passage was found by the pilots, Nicolas Zamorano and Domingo de Castillo, but the swift current and the bore caused by the tides decided Alarcón to leave his vessels and go up the river by boat. On August 26th he started with two small boats and twenty men. For two weeks he toiled up the river and made the acquaintance of numerous Indian tribes, from whom he heard news of bearded strangers like himself in Cíbola, armed with swords and firearms, and calling themselves Christians. This was probably the advance guard of Coronado's army, but Alarcón could get no messenger to brave the unknown desert intervening and was obliged to turn back without having achieved his objective.

After Alarcón had careened the *San Pedro* and built an oratory to Our Lady of Buen Guia, whose name he bestowed on the river in honor of the viceroy, he started up the Colorado again, determined to effect a junction with Coronado. He ascended the river beyond the mouth of the Gila to a place where it flowed between high mountains, probably in the vicinity of Yuma.[26] Here he erected a huge cross and left a map of the stream with letters which were subsequently found by Melchior Díaz.[27] After rejoining his

[26] Lowery, *Spanish Settlements,* p. 294. For further details see H. R. Wagner, *California Voyages, 1539-1542,* San Francisco, 1925, pp. 82-85.

[27] Díaz, left behind with the main party when Coronado pushed on in advance, went in search of Alarcón with a party of twenty men and some Indian guides. He marched 150 leagues to the region near the mouth of the Colorado, and found the Alarcón letters about fifteen leagues up stream by land. There is no evidence, however, that he went above the mouth of the Gila, as he travelled only five or six days more on the Colorado in search of a ford, finally crossing it on a raft, recrossed, and returned down stream to the coast. Díaz died on the way back to San

ships at the river's mouth, Alarcón started on the return journey, skirting the coast and landing frequently, still in hope of getting into touch with Coronado. He reached the port of Santiago[28] in November, gave a narrative of his voyage to Agostín Guerrero and Luís de Castilla, the representatives of the viceroy, and sailed away by night to avoid trouble with Pedro de Alvarado's fleet, which was anchored in the harbor. The viceroy planned another attempt to communicate with Coronado by sea and to explore more extensively the following year, and issued instructions to that effect May 31, 1541. These vessels were made ready but the Mixton Revolt intervened, and Alarcón was placed on duty at Autlán with thirty men to aid in holding the country for the Spaniards. It seems, however, that after Alarcón's return Mendoza sent out another expedition under Francisco de Bolaños, which sailed up the outer coast of Lower California probably beyond Magdalena Bay late in 1541 or early in 1542.[29] No official account of the voyage has been brought to light as yet; therefore we know little concerning the details.

Alarcón's voyage had retraced the gulf coast, first followed by Ulloa, had explored the lower course of the Colorado River, and had made the first contacts of white men with

Gerónimo, which place his party reached early in 1541.—Bancroft, *North Mexican States*, I. 88, 89.

[28] Lowery (*Spanish Settlements*, p. 295) says, "The port of Colima." Bancroft (*North Mexican States*, I. 93) thinks it was probably Navidad, but an eye-witness of the arrival, Joan de Jaso, who had come from Guatemala with Alvarado, says he had seen Alarcón return—"estando en la puerta de Santiago de Buena Esperança de la Costa de Coliman donde estubieron juntos los navios q el dho Hernando de Alarcon haya estando a la sazon en el dho puerto el Armada del Adelantado Dⁿ Pedro de Alvarado."—A. G. I., 48-1-1/23, Testigo de Joan de Jaso, Mexico, May 8, 1546.

[29] "Y asi mismo envio otra vez el dicho vissorey con ciertos navios a un fulano de Bolaños a descubrir por la misma costa del poniente." *Ibid.*, "a un bolaños a descubrir por la costa del sur."—A. G. I., 48-1-1/23, Testigo de alo de Baçan, Mexico, May 10, 1546; also the interesting material in H. R. Wagner, *California Voyages, 1539-1541*, pp. 85-96.

the natives who lived there (which makes the report of the expedition valuable to ethnologists), and had established the fact that California was not an island.[30] When later geographers forgot these early voyages, California was believed to be an island for years, and was so shown on the maps until Father Kino repeated the earlier demonstration of Ulloa and Alarcón.

The death of Pedro de Alvarado in the Mixton War left Mendoza in possession of the fleet with which they had planned to engage in northern discovery under the terms of their contract. In 1542 the viceroy sent part of this fleet up the outer coast of California and despatched the rest across the Pacific to the Philippines under Villalobos. The *Victoria* and the *San Salvador* were equipped for the northern voyage and placed in the command of Juan Rodríquez Cabrillo, a Portuguese by birth and skilled in navigation.[31] Under him were, as chief pilot Bartolomé Ferrelo, as pilot Bartolomé Fernández, and as masters Antonio Carrera and S. Remo. Ferrelo, who took over the command after the death of Cabrillo, was a native of the Levant.

This little fleet of poorly built, badly provisioned ships set sail from the port of Navidad June 27, 1542, on one of the most remarkable voyages in the history of navigation. On July 3 the point of Lower California was reached and by August 5 the vessels anchored off Cedros Island on the outer coast, which was the farthest limit of previous exploration. Continuing up the coast, Cabrillo heard of men with beards, dogs, and Spanish weapons five days inland, and in an effort to communicate with them he confided a letter to the care of the Indians. In all likelihood this was a report

---

[30] Alarcón's narrative is accessible in *Le Voyage de Cibola,* appendice IV. 299. See also Pacheco y Cárdenas, IV. 218, *Relacion del Armada.* For the map of the Colorado made by the pilot, Domingo de Castillo, see Winsor, *Narrative and Critical History of America,* Boston and New York, 1884, II. 444.

[31] Herrera, *Historia General,* dec. VII, lib. V, cap. III, 89.

of Coronado's party in the interior at the time. The end of
the month of September brought the two frail vessels into
the harbor of San Diego, which they named San Miguel.

After Cabrillo left San Miguel harbor his real troubles
began. Sailing through the Santa Barbara channel and
discovering its islands, his ships encountered stormy weather
and head-winds at Point Concepción and were forced to make
port at Cuyler's Harbor on San Miguel Island. While
there Cabrillo fell and broke an arm, but would not consider
turning back, and, finally, on November 6, the barrier of
Point Concepción was rounded. Under most trying weather
conditions, the ships becoming separated, land was sighted
November 14, near the site of Fort Ross north of San
Francisco Bay, which they missed along with Monterey Bay
and the intervening havens along the coast. Turning south
again, they discovered Drake's Bay; and, driven south by a
storm, the ships once more anchored in Cuyler's Harbor on
San Miguel Island. Here, on January 3, 1543, Cabrillo died
and in his honor the Island was named Isla de Juan Rodríquez.

Ferrelo, the second in command, determined to make one
more attempt northward before returning to New Spain and,
after some preparations, sailed on February 18. By a
most extraordinary display of endurance and skill he reached
a northern latitude of 42° in the neighborhood of the Rogue
River in Oregon.[32] Driven apart by a heavy storm the two

---

[32] The diary, which is really a summary or *précis*, gives 44° north
latitude, but this has been corrected by G. Davidson to 42° in "An Examination of some of the early Voyages of Discovery," in *Report of the
Superintendent of the U. S. Coast and Geodetic Survey*, App. 7, pp.
155-253, and Geographical Society of the Pacific, *Transactions and Pro-
ceedings*, second ser., IV. 16, cited by H. E. Bolton in *Spanish Exploration
in the Southwest 1542-1706* (Original Narratives of American History,
J. Franklin Jameson, ed.), p. 9. This volume contains a very useful English translation of the diary of the Cabrillo-Ferrelo voyage, with a critical
introduction and footnotes. The original is printed in Pacheco y Cárdenas, XIV. 165-191, under the title "Relacion del descubrimiento q hizo
Juan Rodriquez Navegando por la contra costa del sur al norte hecha por

vessels as they turned south were reunited at Cedros Island, March 24, 1543. They completed the return voyage on April 14, when they cast anchor in Navidad after an absence of nine and one half months. The mariners who returned from this voyage were engaged by Mendoza to undertake the rescue of the Villalobos expedition. While he was preparing the armada, in order to occupy their time, he dispatched them to Peru with three vessels loaded with mares and colts from his ranches. The three vessels were held in Peru and with them, not only the viceroy's ships, mares, colts, and supplies,[33] but the men who

Juan Paez." As there has been some doubt concerning the authorship of Juan Páez, the writer examined the original in the Archivo General de Indias (1-1-1/20 [70]) and verified the note in handwriting of the time, "De Ju⁰ Paez" and also noted the additional annotation, which is not included in the printed document, "no ymporta," a common secretarial notation on the backs of documents not considered important enough for the consideration of the Council of the Indies. This whole subject of the Juan Páez Diary is treated in H. R. Wagner, *The Spanish Southwest, 1542-1794*, pp. 91 ff. Since writing that work he has, through further investigation to be published soon, determined that Juan Páez is Juan Páez de Castro, who was appointed royal Cronista in 1555, and that the document, as we have it, is an abridged transcript of the original for his use.

[33] "Q aviendo el d'ho vissorey enbiado ciertos navios al descubrimiento delas yslas del poniente, y otros al descubrim⁰ de la costa de la Mar del Sur en cumplim⁰ del asiento q el d'ho vissorey y don Pedro de Alvarado avian tomado con S. M., bueltos los q avian ydo en descubrimiento de la d'ha costa y queriendose despedir los marineros della por entretenellos para el socorro q esperava hazer á los q avia ynbiado á los d'hos yslas, concerto conellos de darles tres navíos con el bastimiento necessario⁻ para q hiziesen viajes al Peru, en el entretanto q aderecava el d'ho socorro; y por q no se querian encargar de los d'hos tres navíos sin q les diese carga, el d'ho vissorey les ofreció carga de sus yeguas y potros, en caso q no hallasen fletes de otras partes y q les dava de flete de cada cabeça sesenta p⁰s de oro de minas . . . q en cumplimiento del d'ho asiento los d'hos marineros se encargaron de los d'hos navíos y los fletaron á su voluntad, y llevaron en los d'hos navíos solas diez y seis cabeças de yeguas y potros del d'ho vissorey, de q no llegaron vivas salvo doçe, los cuales tomo Machacao, y les repartio entre los soldados; y los navíos, por detenellos, como los detuvo, se perdieron y se echaron al traves, sin q ninguno volviese á esta nueva españa, por manera q del d'ho viaje el d'ho vissorey no solamente no yntereso cosa alguna, antes perdio todos sus navios yeguas y potros y bastimientos. . . ."—A. G. I., 48-1-5/27, Interrogatorio del señor vissorey, questions 226, 227; full text printed by Joaquin García Icazbalceta, in *Colección de documentos para la historia de México*, Mexico, 1866, II. 125, under the title "Fragmenta de la visita hecha á Don Antonio de Mendoza."

might have given us a more complete account of their previous experiences along the coast of Upper California.

The Cabrillo-Ferrelo voyage had explored the Pacific Coast from Cabo del Engaño north to 42° for the first time, and from its record some seventy places have been identified by modern scholars.[34] It represents a great achievement in navigation, when the means at the disposal of the mariners is taken into consideration, which has not been given due credit in comparison with similar voyages on the eastern coasts of the continent.

While the Cabrillo-Ferrelo voyage was in progress, Mendoza despatched Ruy Gómez de Villalobos[35] with two ships and three smaller craft, carrying three hundred and seventy men, from the port of Navidad to found a colony on the Island of Zebú in the Philippines. These vessels were also some of those that the viceroy inherited from Pedro de Alvarado. The expedition failed to obey the instructions not to settle within the limits of the territory claimed by Portugal in the East and soon became involved in difficulties with the nationals of that country. The King of Spain advised Mendoza that since Portugal claimed the lands Villalobos had attempted to settle, the project would have to be abandoned.[36] Efforts were made to send vessels back across the Pacific to New Spain, but contrary winds prevented, and at last the survivors found their way back to Europe by way of the Cape of Good Hope.[37]

[34] That the name Mendocino was applied to one of the northern capes by Ferrelo is doubted by Davidson and other modern scholars.

[35] Sometimes given as "Ruy López," sometimes as "Ruy Gómez."

[36] Mendoza was quite vexed by this set-back and in a letter to Juan de Aguilar hoped that he (or one of his sons) might be permitted to go in person to the East, where he would stand on the line of demarcation, and, with only a cape and sword, would show the Portuguese what rightfully belonged to them.—*Carta á Juan de Aguilar,* in Pacheco y Cárdenas, III. 510.

[37] Some returned to New Spain, circumnavigating the globe, as for instance, Pero Belbas, who testified during the Sandoval visita: A. G. I., 48-1-9/51, Testigo de Pero de Belbas, Mexico, 1547. Villalobos, whom

It is probable that during this voyage the Hawaiian Islands were first touched by white men, when two vessels under Alvaro de Saavedra were lost from the rest of the expedition in a storm one thousand leagues from port. At least, Hawaiian tradition tells of a foreign vessel wrecked on the coast of Keei Ca at about this same time, and relates that two of the crew lived and became the ancestors of the royal line.[38] There is strong evidence of the discovery of this group by Juan Gaetano, the pilot of the Villalobos expedition, when in 1555 he named them the Islas de Mesa. No account of the discovery has been unearthed save an anonymous chart, believed to be that of the Spanish galleon, preserved in Madrid, which records the discovery as made by Gaetano.[39]

In addition to these larger movements of discovery, just reviewed, Mendoza was interested in the conquest of Yucatán, which was being pushed to a conclusion throughout his period, and in lesser entradas, of which we only have vague mention, into the Chichimec country to the north, which will be discussed in connection with the Mixton War. Under his direction and with direct aid from him in money, ships, horses, cattle, sheep, munitions, and supplies of all kinds, one of Spain's most remarkable exhibitions of exploring activity had taken place. The "Northern Mystery" had been penetrated by land and by sea and Spanish curiosity about current "tales of the marvelous" had been thoroughly

Burney describes as a brother-in-law of the viceroy, died on the Island of Amboyna in 1543, more from vexation than any actual sickness.—Burney, *A Chronological History of the Discoveries in the South Sea,* London, 1803, I. 226, 236.

[38] *The Discovery of the Solomon Islands by Alvaro de Mendaña in 1568* (The Hukluyt Society; Lord Amherst of Hackney, Basil Thompson, eds.), I, Introd. p. ii.

[39] *Ibid.,* I, Introd. pp. iii, iv; *Boletin de la sociedad Geográfica de Madrid,* tom. II. 347, tom. XI. 7. An original account of the Villalobos expedition is the *Relacion del viaje que hizo desde la Nueva España a los islas del Poniente Ruy Gomez de Villalobos, Lisboa, 1 de Agosta de 1548,* in Pacheco y Cárdenas, V. 117-209.

gratified by a revelation of less exciting truth. In the East, Portuguese mastery had been disputed and the Philippines named. If new wonders had existed, Antonio de Mendoza would have gone down in history as a greater conqueror than Cortés or Pizarro. As it is, he will be remembered as the greatest organizer of exploring expeditions in the sixteenth century.

CHAPTER VI

THE TESTING OF THE VICEROYALTY

The government which Antonio de Mendoza had instituted with such vigor and prudence during the first years of his rule was destined to experience two severe challenges before he achieved a generally acknowledged success. The first of these was a serious revolt of the natives in Nueva Galicia, known as the Mixton War; the second was a determined endeavor to discredit his rule and to oust him from his high office, headed by the visitor-general, Francisco Tello de Sandoval. The military skill of the viceroy saved New Spain from a general uprising of the natives, in the first instance, and the genuine merit of his work as viceroy, plus the powerful influence he was able to wield at court, permitted him to vindicate his reputation and to save the benefits of the viceregal rule for New Spain in the second. The successful weathering of these two storms, one from within and one from without, enabled Mendoza to face the last years of his rule as an official of demonstrated success, the undisputed master of the situation and an indispensable servant of the king. Indeed, he was almost too successful, as the firm conviction of his excellent qualities meant that no relief from office could be accorded him and that he should eventually die in the harness.

Nuño de Guzmán, as governor of Nueva Galicia, by his enslavement and mistreatment of the natives, had left a legacy of discontent in that province which in 1538 had flared up in a revolt of the inhabitants of the northern region lying about Jocototlán. His successor in office, Diego Pérez de la Torre, suppressed the movement by force but lost his life in the decisive battle of the campaign. Coronado was appointed acting governor as soon as the news reached the capital, but the actual labor fell on Cristóbal de Oñate and the chief-justice, Luís de Galindo. When Coronado departed to search for Cíbola, Oñate carried on the government, but with a great handicap since his superior had merely used the province as a base for his expedition and because of his absorbed interest in the new conquest had so neglected its affairs that he left portions of it in open revolt—a condition which was to spread and to threaten New Spain when he departed with his fine body of troops.[1] No blame for what happened was lodged at the door of Cristóbal de Oñate, the active head of the government of the province, by his contemporaries or by later historians.[2]

Various definite opinions have been advanced as to what were the immediate causes of the outbreak of widespread rebellion in Nueva Galicia. The cruelty of the encomenderos is given as the principal cause[3] and the departure of such a large body of soldiers as the opportunity for revenge and perhaps complete liberation. Sandoval, in his charges against the viceroy at the conclusion of his visita, placed the blame on Mendoza and alleged that the ill-treatment accorded the

[1] The inhabitants were apprehensive that the Coronado expedition would strip the province of its defenders, but at the review of the troops, February 27, 1540, an inspection of the roster showed that only two were citizens of Mexico and two of Guadalajara. The great bulk of the force were newly arrived adventurers attracted by the fame of the entrada. While useful in the event of an uprising, which seemed to be a rather remote contingency, they were merely a burden on the viceroy and the community in time of peace. Their participation in the expedition seemed to be a wise utilization of otherwise wasted energy.—Bancroft, *History of Mexico*, II. 468.

[2] Cristóbal de Oñate is praised by all who knew him and was one of the few to escape censure in the sweeping investigation of conditions in Nueva Galicia conducted by the visitor Lorenzo de Tejada in 1544. Tejada even goes out of his way to state that during Coronado's absence, Oñate, he found, "aver usado del dho oficio bien e diligentemente segun q buen gobernador debia hazer e aber syrvido S. Mt. en el dho cargo especialmente en la pacificacion de los rebeliones e levantamientos desta gobernacion e provincia."—A. G. I., 48-3-3/30, Residencia secreta con Cristobal de Oñate, sentencia, Guadalajara, September 16, 1544.

[3] Bancroft, *History of Mexico*, II. 493.

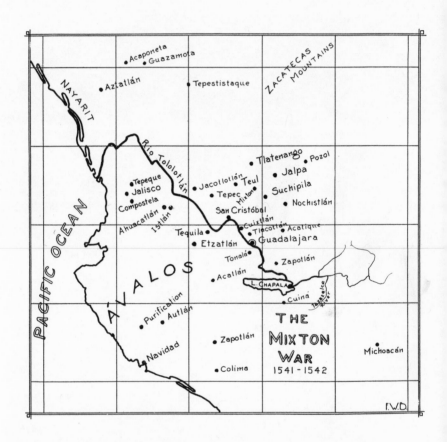

natives by the men on the viceroy's various exploring expeditions, particularly the Coronado party, provoked the revolt.[4] This accusation was indignantly denied by both Coronado and the viceroy, who pointed out that the route of the former's army lay through the pueblos of Ávalos fully forty leagues from Tlatenango and the fortified hill or peñol of Tepestistaque near by, the scene of the first revolt, and that the port of Navidad, the center of his sea explorations, was seventy leagues from that place, so that neither the land nor sea expeditions could have been responsible.[5] The administration claimed that the real cause was the incitement to revolt of the wild tribes in the north who came down from the mountains of Tepeque and Zacatecas and urged the peace-

[4] " . . . que ha entendido en enbiar gente de guerra por mar e por tierra a descubrir nuevas tierras e yslas y se ha ocupado en ello y por malos tratientos que Recibieron los yndios naturales de la provincia de Xalisco de la gente que enbiaua a las dichas armadas y descubrimientos especialmente de los que enbio a la tierra nueba de cibola los dichos yndios se Revelaron e alçaron contra el servicio de su magestad y mataron españoles legos y religiosos e quemaron yglesias e hezieron otros daños." —A. G. I., 48-1-2/24, Cargos que resultan de la visita secreta contra el muy illustre señor don Antonio de Mendoça, Mexico, June 21, 1546, Cargo 35. Sandoval based this charge on the similar complaint of Cortés voiced in Spain in 1543. Cortés had gone farther in his charge with an additional accusation that Mendoza had extorted men and provisions from the destitute Indians.—Cortés, "Peticion al Emperador," in Icazbalceta, *Colección de documentos para la historia de México*, II. 63.

[5] After demonstrating that the witnesses in the visitas who had testified against him were personal enemies and merely showing spite and that a host of worthy witnesses testified to the truth of his statement of the case, the viceroy said " . . . lo niego porque la gente de la armada passo y estuuo apartada sesenta leguas de los pueblos que primero rreuelaron y por estar tan lexos los dichos pueblos reueladas del camino por do la gente de la armada yva no pudieron rrecebir los malos tratamientos de que en el cargo se haze mencion. . . ."—A. G. I., 48-1-2/4, Descargos del Vírrey, Mexico, October 30, 1545, descargo 35. A similar statement is made by the viceroy in A. G. I., 48-1-5/27, Interrogatorio del señor vissorey, preguntas 130, 131. Coronado also claimed that Mendoza had purchased maize and other foodstuffs from the Indians in Ávalos in order to prevent any molestation of the natives of Jalisco. Miguel de Ibarra and a host of other witnesses concur and in addition point out that Alvarado's arrival could have nothing to do with the rebellion as he arrived after it was an accomplished fact.—A. G. I., 48-1-9/31, Testigo de Franco de Coronado, Mexico, January 18, 1547, preguntas 130, 131; A. G. I., 48-1-5/27, Testigo de Miguel de Ybarra, Compostela, January 26, 1547, preguntas 130, 131.

ful natives of the pueblos of Tlatenango and Suchipila to throw off the Spanish yoke. They pointed out the weakness of the Spaniards and their medicine men promised victory, telling them that they would no longer need to sow maize or any other grain, as food would be provided miraculously, and that the ancient gods and their resurrected ancestors with great riches in jewels of gold and turquoise, feathers, mirrors, magic bows and arrows, clothes for men and women, and many other wonders, would lead them to an assured triumph.[6] What the Spaniards were facing was a religious revolt from out of the north, with the superstition of the aborigine fighting against them, not with them, as had been the case in the conquest of Mexico. The new religion promised everything from sensual pleasure to immortality to those who would desert Christianity, and threatened unbelievers with dire penalites. Its political danger lay in its appeal to the native and in its declaration of unrelenting war against the Spaniards and all Christians in the New World.[7] The

[6] "Que estando los yndios de tlatenango de la dicha provincia que es mas de sesenta leguas de compostela muy qietos y sosegados y aviendo asentado monasterio de rreligiosos franciscos en suchipila vinieron vnos yndios de la serrania de Tepeque y çacatecas a ciertos pueblos que confinan con tlatenango que se llaman cuitlan y hueli y coltlan y tepeque con la habla del diablo que ellos llaman tlatol y llegaron a tlatenango donde juntaron los señores y principales y maçequales del a los quales hablaron diziendoles nosotros somos mensajeros del diablo el qual se llama tecocoli y venimos a hazeros saber como el viene y trae consigo rresucitados a todos vuestros antepasados con muchas rriquezas y joyas de oro y turquesas y plumas y espejos y arcos y flechas que nunca quiebran y mucha rropa para nuestro vestir y muchas quentas y otras cosas para las mugeres y hazeos saber que los que le creyerdes y siguierdes y dexardes la dotrina de los frailes nunca morireys ni tenays necesidad y los viejos y viejas se tornaran moços y concibiran por muy viejos que sean y las sementeras se os haran sin que nadie ponga las manos en ellas y sin que llueba y la leña del monte ella se os vendra a casa sin que la traiga nadie y el que fuere al monte despues del diablo venido comeran tigres y leones . . . y que a los yndios mandaria que tuuissen las mugeres que quisiesen y no uno como los frayles dezian . . . y que tuuiesen por cierto que el yndio, o yndia que creyase en dios y no en el diablo luego no veria mas luz y seria comido de los bestias. . . ."—A. G. I., 48-1-2/24, Descargos del Virrey, Mexico, October 30, 1546, descargo 35.

[7] " . . . rrobarian quanto tuuiesen y de alli [Guadalajara] a jalisco y mechoacan y a Mexico y a do quiera que huuviera Xrisptianos los

truth with respect to the cause of the Mixton War was probably a combination of both views. The Indians in encomienda in Jalisco were ripe for rebellion, owing to the harsh treatment they had received from their masters,[8] but no great revolt would have occurred without the incitement of the new religion introduced by the unconquered strangers of the north. A contributing cause was the slow realization by the Spaniards of the formidable character of the movement, so that much precious time was wasted in futile negotiation and small expeditions until the growth of Indian strength compelled them to jeopardize the entire military power of New Spain in a final desperate attempt to stem the rising tide of red.

The "messengers of the devil," as the Spaniards called those who preached the new religion, first appeared at Tlatenango and the chief men and their followers were soon persuaded to desert Christianity. At Suchipila, Xuitleque, chief of the Indians and respected by all, was likewise converted and the two peoples united in retirement to the rocky hill or peñol of Tepestistaque northward toward Zacatecas with the emissaries of the new god. While they fortified the peñol the messengers continued to impart their tidings to them and to delegations from other tribes. Petaçal, the chief of the pueblo of Jalpa, was won over with his people and came to Tepestistaque, as was Tenamastel or Tenemaxtli, brother of the Lord of Nochistlán (or Nuchistlán), who

matarian y rrobarian. . . ."—*Ibid.* " . . . Yria el diablo a Guadalajara y a jalisco y a mechoacan y a Mexico y a guatimalo y a do quiera que Xrispianos huiese. . . ."—*Ibid.*

[8] This harshness could not have been universal, for there are numerous examples of encomenderos rescued from death by their Indians during the course of the struggle and two Franciscan friars in Suchipila, Martín de Vera and Pedro de la Concepción, despite the branding they had suffered at the hands of the natives, expressed nothing but Christian forgiveness.—A. G. I., 48-1-5/27, Testigo de Miguel de Ybarra, Compostela, January 26, 1546, pregunta 125.

arrived with a contingent from that town.[9] This last defec-
tion was a good indication of the gravity of the situation, as
Tenemaxtli had been baptized and given the Christian name
Diego Zacatecas and was an alguacil of the church and the
king's justice in his district. On the peñol of Tepestistaque
the sorcerers or medicine men of the Zacatecas Indians continued to preach their faith, practiced the ancient bloody
rites, and predicted the defeat of the Spaniards as new re-
cruits came to join them.[10] To convince their growing following of the truth of their claims to supernatural powers
they conceived a clever stratagem. Toribio de Bolaños was
induced to come to Tlatenango in his capacity of alcalde of
Guadalajara to effect the arrest of a native chieftain, Teu-
quitate, under the belief that the natives had returned to their
homes, and then was followed and attacked two hours before
dawn while sleeping in the fields with his prisoner and one
Spanish companion, Alonso López. The latter was killed and
the prisoner lost, but Bolaños, though wounded, succeeded
in reaching Suchipila, where Miguel de Ibarra, visitor and
captain of Tlatenango, with Fray Antonio de Segovia, was
trying to pacify the inhabitants, following a fruitless visit to

[9] The movement was accompanied by deeds of violence. At Jalpa the
Cascanes drove out their encomendero, Diego de Proano, and his companion, Bartolomé de Mendoza, while at Tlatenango, Gonzalo Varelo was
set upon but managed to escape with some wounds, and one Gonzalo
Garijo narrowly escaped death by fleeing on horseback; while at Suchipila
two Spaniards and a Negro were killed and the encomendero was driven
out. Similar disturbances occurred everywhere in the area of the revolt.
—A. G. I., 48-1-2/24, Articulos para la provança sobre lo de jalisco,
Mexico, May 16, 1546.

[10] Bancroft (History of Mexico, II. 590-611), follows Mota Padilla,
Beaumont, and other writers in making the peñoles of Nochistlán and
Mixton the scene of early resistance and does not mention the more
northerly stronghold of Tepestistaque, although he does mention Tlatenango, Suchipila, and Jalpa in connection with the appearance of the
Zacatecan sorcerers. The writer in his account has followed the narratives of the actual participants, Miguel de Ibarra, Cristóbal de Oñate,
Antonio de Mendoza, and others, which are agreed that Tepestistaque was
the first armed camp organized by the natives.

Tepestistaque.[11] This bold attack had the effect anticipated by the Indians, who wished to lure Ibarra into an attack on their peñol, accompanied by a force of apparently friendly allies who would lead him into a preconcerted ambush.

Ibarra reacted as the medicine men had hoped. After a consultation with the Franciscans in charge of the area, Fray Martín de Vera and Fray Pedro de la Concepción, he sent out an emergency call to all Spaniards for reinforcements. The Spaniards in the vicinity responded, and the opportune arrival of others from Guadalajara swelled his little troop to seventeen Spanish horsemen, and fifteen hundred Tonalá allies were induced to accompany him.[12] In addition a number of Cascanes joined his little band from the towns of Suchipila, Jalpa, and others in the area of disaffection, with loud protestations of friendship, in order to carry out their treachery. Fortunately, Ibarra mistrusted them, as he was warned of their plot in advance. At his request Fray Martín

[11] Ibarra had set out to reconnoitre the situation with an escort of seven Spaniards, some friendly Indians, and a few Franciscan friars. He had penetrated to the peñol of Tepestistaque and had called on the revolted Cascanes in the fortress to lay down their arms and to return to their homes in the presence of the royal notary, Juan de Salinas. But their prompt answer had been an armed sally in such strength that Ibarra, in view of the weakness of his force, retreated to Suchipila.—A. G. I., 48-1-5/27, Testigo de Miguel de Ibarra, Compostela, January 26, 1547. Bancroft has no account of this first expedition in his history.

[12] Bancroft, *History of Mexico*, II. 493, says " some twenty-five Spaniards and a considerable force of friendly Tlajomulco and Tonalá Indians." Mendoza (A. G. I., 48-1-2/24, Descargos del Virrey, Mexico, October 30, 1546, descargo 35) sets the number of Spaniards at fourteen, but I have followed Ibarra's account cited above. Bancroft's story is based on the early chroniclers Fray Antonio Tello, Matias de Mota Padilla, and Fray Beaumont de la Purísima Concepción with some slight attention to the documents contained in Icazbalceta, *Colección de documentos*, II, namely, *Fragmenta de la visita hecha à don Antonio de Mendoza*, 72-140; *Peticion contra Mendoza*, 63-64; *Relacion de la jornada que hizo don Francisco de Sandoval Accazitli*, October 20, 1541, 141-154; and the standard secondary works at the time he wrote. As the sworn testimony of all the participants in the war, contained in the Sandoval visita, was not available when he wrote, Bancroft dismisses Mendoza's account as biased and, ever a staunch defender of Cortés, he accepts the conqueror's embittered criticisms as true. The writer has chosen to present the story of the revolt from the narratives of the military commanders, believing them to be better judges of what actually took place.

de la Coruña and his companions spoke to the Cascanes and admonished them to the effect that any traitorous act would be severely punished. Then he set forth once more for the peñol of Tepestistaque, bringing the friars along as witnesses to the sincerity of his offers of peace. On the line of march the Cascanes became unruly and threatened to kill the Tonalá Indians, who promptly deserted, with the exception of about one hundred chief men. The following day these Tonalá Indians divulged the full details of the plot and told him of the ambush that awaited in a gully wooded with cedars, where the Spaniards would be unable to use their horses. He seized the ringleaders and executed ten or twelve of them as a warning and sent the rest of them to their homes. This took place two leagues from the peñol, and two days later he arrived within sight of the strongplace and the Indians swarmed out to the appointed place of treachery.[13] Ibarra called upon them to lay down their arms and to return to their homes and promised them amnesty, but was answered by a fierce attack. The battle raged for over four hours before the onslaught was repulsed just at sunset.[14] Ibarra and several of the Spaniards were severely wounded and a number of the horses injured, but they camped on the field of the encounter that night.[15] When morning came Ibarra

[13] "Dos leguas antes del dicho peñol nuestro señor fue servido de descubrir la trama y traicion que los dichos Yndios tenian ordenada y el dicho Miguel de Ybarra prendio ciertos principales que eran en la traicion y sabida la verdad por su confision y informaciones hizo justicia dellos y a los Yndios cuyos caciques heran justiciados los despidio y ynbio a sus casas llevar las espaldas seguras y dos dias despues desto llegados los españoles, a uista del peñol los yndios salieron a ellos con mano armada al lugar senalada que era arroyo de los cedros donde estaua concertado."—A. G. I., 48-1-2/24, Descargo del virrey, Mexico, October 30, 1546, pregunta 36.

[14] Bancroft makes the peñol of Mixton the scene of this smart skirmish, which is an error, since Ibarra and the other veterans of the war describe it as being fought before the peñol of Tepestistaque.

[15] But not comfortably, for they were "harto heridos trabajados y maltrechos."—A. G. I., 48-1-5/27, Testigo de Miguel de Ibarra, Compostela, January 26, 1547, pregunta 125.

took counsel with the friars and resolved to retire, as his force was insufficient.[16] After a further ineffectual attempt to negotiate a peace with the natives, he retreated to Suchipila.[17] At this place new disorders had broken out which he quieted temporarily and proceeded to Teul, where he rescued one Bobadilla and his family from the revolted Indians. Ibarra then made his way as rapidly as possible to Guadalajara by way of Nochistlán, effecting the rescues of unfortunate Spaniards and Negroes as he went.[18] By this time peaceful measures had become useless. The movement had gathered such momentum that new posts on the peñoles of Mixton, Acactic, Nochistlán, and Cuinao had been established, and all the Cascane tribes were flocking to the conclaves of the "devil worshippers," and the Tonalá Indians were secretly represented at these gatherings. The spread of the revolt was everywhere accompanied by deeds of violence against encomenderos and Negroes. The only ray of comfort in the situation was the fact that the actual area in active rebellion was limited to the region north of the Tololotlán River and east of the mountains just west of Tlatenango, the focus of the disturbance. Conditions, while grave, were not desperate as yet, and prompt action could remedy matters. Failure to take these active measures would, on the other hand, give rise to most serious complications, as all the native warriors of Nueva Galicia from Culiacán in the ex-

[16] "Porque el dicho capitan Miguel de Ybarra no lleuaua mas de catorze españoles y un arcabuz y una ballesta y el peñol hera muy fuerte y de mucha gente y pertrechado de albarradas."—A. G. I., 48-1-2/24, Descargo del virrey, Mexico, October 30, 1546, pregunta 35.

[17] His encounter with Toribio de Bolaños, alcalde of Tlatenango, at this place occurred before this expedition, not after his return, as some writers state.—A. G. I., 48-1-5/27, Testigo de Toribio de Bolaños, Mexico, pregunta 7.

[18] A. G. I., 48-1-5/27, Interrogatorio del señor vissorey, pregunta 143. Bancroft and the writers he follows at this juncture indicate that Cristóbal de Oñate sent Diego de Vásquez posthaste to the viceroy in Mexico for help. As the viceroy was already present in Nueva Galicia this does not seem plausible.

treme north to the borders of Michoacán in the south only waited for the success of their kinsmen to make common cause with them.

When the movement of revolt began, Mendoza was just returning to Navidad from a cruise with his fleet, probably from Santiago, and dropped anchor on Christmas day, 1540, not quite a year after the departure of Coronado.[19] The revolt was apparently only local in character and could be handled by the local authorities, so he went about his regular business undisturbed. When Ibarra returned with the ill-tidings of the spread and magnitude of the rebellion at the time that the peñol of Mixton was converted into an armed Indian camp, he was in the Villa de Purificación, south of the river near the coast, conducting a visita.[20] When he was apprised of the new turn of events he hastened to Guadalajara to hear the details and to consult with the provincial officials. Before taking drastic measures, he sent to the Indians at Suchipila one more peace embassy, consisting of Fray Martín de Jesús, guardian of the monastery at Suchipila, and the notary Juan Leon, with a small armed escort under Miguel de Ibarra. When the Indians proved obdurate and attempted to kill his messengers of peace, it was decided that force must be used to bring them to their senses. A great junta was held in Guadalajara at which the viceroy, Pedro de Alvarado, Cristóbal de Oñate, Bishop Marroquin of Guatemala, Miguel de Ibarra, and most of the prominent personages of Nueva Galicia were present. Mendoza asked this body if they thought that he should go in person against

---

[19] ". . . Quando los Yndios de la dicha provincia se començaron a alçar fue quando los navios de mi armada y yo entramos en el puerto de la navidad que fue dia de navidad del año de quinientos y quarenta. . . ." —A. G. I., 48-1-2/24, Descargos del virrey, Mexico, October 30, 1546, descargo 36.

[20] " . . . Quando se encastillaron en el miston estaua en la villa de purificacion visitando aquella provincia y alli fue avisado de lo que pasaua. . . ." Ibid.; A. G. I., 48-1-5/27, Interrogatorio del señor vissorey, pregunta 143.

the rebels or send an agent. The unanimous decision was that the lieutenant-governor Oñate was the proper person to send and that he could bring the revolt to a successful conclusion. An armed force of over fifty Spanish horsemen from the province and the viceroy's ships, with footsoldiers, Indian allies, and a proper equipment of cannon and firearms was assembled under his command.[21]

When Oñate arrived at the peñol of Mixton his attempts to parley with the defenders were met with taunts and missiles; he then prepared to take the place by storm and pitched his camp before it. But Oñate had misgauged the strength of the natives, who had gathered in great numbers from the places near by and suddenly fell upon his rear simultaneously with a sally from the peñol. Over thirteen Spaniards, six Negroes, and three hundred Indian allies were killed. Defeat was saved from becoming utter rout by the bravery of Diego Vásquez, in command of the rearguard, and the survivors made their way to Guadalajara with great difficulty.[22] The

[21] Mendoza waited in Guadalajara until he received word from Oñate that he had surrounded the peñol of Mixton and, with the failure of peaceful measures, was about to apply force with every hope of success. He then returned to Mexico City where his presence was necessary, feeling certain that the problem of the revolt was in competent hands and would soon be settled. His own statement is " . . . y vista su rrebelion y determinacion el dicho Xrispoual de Oñate asento su rreal sobre ellos y me escriuio que el los tenia cercados y que no se podian yr y que el los castigaria y allanaria y yo le torne a escreuir que mirase si estaua poderoso para rresistillos y desbaratallos porque sino yria en persona a ellos y el dicho Xrispoual de Oñate me respondio que estaua bastante poderoso para deshazellos y castigallos que me decuidase de aquello y me viniese a proveer lo de esta governacion lo qual por tenello por muy bastantemente proveido me vine a esta ciudad porque avia necesidad de mi persona en ella . . ."—A. G. I., 48-1-2/24, Descargos del virrey, Mexico, October 30, 1546, descargo 36. Cortés and Sandoval both charged the viceroy with neglect of duty for returning to Mexico City and claimed that the revolt could have been easily suppressed at this time by the viceroy and that his departure meant defeat and the loss of many lives. To the writer Mendoza seems to be justified in his actions by the opinion of such expert Indian fighters as Alvarado and Oñate.—A. G. I., 48-1-2/24, Cargos que resultan de la visita secreta contra el muy illustre señor don Antonio de Mendoça, Mexico, June 21, 1546, Cargo 36.

[22] From the sequence of events April 10, 1541, is probably the correct date of this battle.

disaster was the signal for new revolts and the pueblos of Nochistlán, Tlacotlán, and many others which had been secretly in sympathy with the rebels went over to open espousal of the native cause. The garrisons of Culiacán, Compostela, and Purificación were hard pressed by besieging Indians and an advance on Guadalajara itself began. Oñate immediately sent news of his defeat to the viceroy, probably by Diego Vásquez, with an urgent appeal for aid.[23]

Mendoza, thoroughly aroused, now sent letters to Luís de Castilla and to Pedro de Alvarado, who were in Ávalos with the fleets ready to sail on a voyage of discovery, and asked them to abandon the ships if need be, until the revolt was crushed.[24] At the same time he sent one hundred men from Mexico City to Guadalajara under Captain Iñigo López de Anuncibay and ordered Juan de Alvarado to march from Michoacán with thirty horse and six thousand Indian foot soldiers.[25]

Alvaredo and Luís de Castilla answered the viceroy's request and an earnest personal plea for aid from Oñate with great promptitude. They sent fifty men to strengthen the garrisons in Autlán and Purificación, left fifty more in Zapotlán to hold the districts of Colima, and stationed twenty-

[23] Bancroft (History of Mexico, II. 493, 494, note 4) places Ibarra in command of this expedition in spite of contrary evidence in Herrera and in Mendoza's Interrogatorio as printed in Icazbalceta, Colección de documentos. He was also unaware of the junta which had preceded it and confused it with the earlier Ibarra entrada in many details.

[24] " . . . Estauan en los pueblos de aualos con la gente de mis armadas y del dicho adelantado que yuan a despachallos para el descubrimiento de la mar del sur si fuese necesario lo dexasen todo y fuesen a socorrer y poner rremedio en lo de la nueva galizia los quales lo hizieron asi por lo que yo les escreui como porque el dicho Xrispoual de Oñate les auiso . . ." —A. G. I., 48-1-2/24, Descargos del virrey, Mexico, October 30, 1546, descargo 36.

[25] At the same time Oñate sent all the information he possessed concerning the rebels to the audiencia of Mexico. As a punishment that body passed judgment on the revolted Indians and sentenced them to slavery for their misdeeds, and the royal brand for that purpose was sent to the lieutenant-governor Cristóbal de Oñate.—A. G. I., 48-1-5/27, Interrogatorio del señor vissorey, pregunta 157.

five soldiers at Atzatlán and Lake Chapala respectively, while they pushed on with all speed to Guadalajara with one hundred mounted troopers and as many foot. Within two days after receipt of the news, June 12, 1541, they were in the Capital City. Their timely arrival put a stop to the Indian advance on the city and enabled other points to be reinforced.[26] Oñate immediately called a new junta to formulate a plan of action, but its cautious deliberations caused Alvarado to grow impatient as he was anxious to depart on his voyage of discovery. He declared that the other members of the junta were like children in their timidity and that he would defeat the natives himself. Oñate and others tried to dissuade the adelantado, for they had experienced the mettle of the foe and feared the consequences of his rashness. He reminded them of his long experience in Indian warfare, scoffed at their fear of a few wretched Indians, and with characteristic impetuosity set forth on what was to be his last campaign, without waiting for aid from Mexico City and with a curt refusal of Oñate's offers of help.

Alvarado arrived before the peñol of Nochistlán, June 24, 1541, with an army composed of one hundred horsemen, an equal number of infantry, and five thousand Indian allies from Michoacán. After a brief attempt to treat with the defenders he contemptuously headed a direct charge on their

[26] " . . . A toda diligencia fueron dentro de dos dias en la ciudad de guadalajara con la gente de las armadas y con su llegada ceso la venida de los yndios sobre la dicha cuidad y rrepartieron parte de las dichas armadas en guarnicion para quel dicho leuantamiento no pasase adelante poniendo en yçatlan a diego lopez de çuniga con treinta de cavallo y en tonala a miguel de ybarra con quarenta de cavallo y en ameca a hernan nieto con doze cauallo y a la ciudad de compostela ynbiaron a francisco de godoi con treinta de cavallo y porque juan fernandez de ijar escriuio de la billa purificacion al puerto de la navidad que todos los yndios benian sobre la dicha villa se desamaron tres navios que estauan a la vela para yr con el capitan hernando de alarcon a poblar el Rio de buena guia y socorrer a francisco vazquez de Coronado . . . saco la gente de los dichos navios y la enbio a socorrer la dicha villa . . . con las armas y muncion de los dichos navios y porque la gente no queria yr la socorrio de nueva a mi costa. . . ."—A. G. I., 48-1-2/24, Descargos del virrey, Mexico, October 30, 1546, descargo 36.

entrenchments, only to find himself repulsed with heavy losses. He rallied his force for a new effort, but an ill-timed infantry charge in which the cavalry failed to coöperate, owing to a misunderstanding of orders, proved to be the decisive action of the battle. The rebels, worked up to a frenzy by the medicine men, took full advantage of the mistake and swarmed out of their defences in overpowering force. Alvarado's men were soon in panic-stricken flight with the Indians in hot pursuit; his frantic efforts to rally them were futile; and he was obliged to dismount and fight on foot in a vain endeavor to cover the headlong retreat. To make matters worse, it was a rainy day and the roads were veritable quagmires. In the mêlée of the pursuit, seeing that all was lost, Alvarado led his horse and tried to save himself by retreat on foot. His terror-stricken secretary, Montoya, madly spurring his jaded steed up a slope, slipped and fell and Alvarado, directly behind him, was thrown into a ravine with his horse on top of him. The cowardly secretary came off unscathed and lived to a ripe old age, but Alvarado received injuries which later proved to be fatal. Oñate, who had feared the worst, had followed Alvarado with a small force of twenty-five men and had witnessed the disaster from an eminence near by. He hastened to the scene and extricated the remnants of the expedition.[27] Alvarado was transported to Guadalajara in a litter, where he died July 4, 1541, at the home of his relative, Juan de Camino, a victim of his own rashness.[28] The immediate result of his fiasco was a great spread of the revolt and a siege of Guadalajara itself, which

[27] Herrera, *Historia General,* dec. VII, lib. II, cap. XI, pictures the attack and defeat as a combined attempt of the forces of Alvarado and Oñate, a version which cannot be accepted when confronted with the actual narrative of Oñate.

[28] For a discussion of Alvarado's will and the "seizure" of his fleet by Mendoza, see Bancroft, *History of Central America,* II. 208 ff. Bancroft once more allows his partizanship for Cortés to influence his good judgment and he speaks insinuatingly of the viceroy's "appropriation" of Alvarado's fleet.

PEDRO de ALVARADO'S LAST BATTLE　　De Bry: America, pt. V.

was invested, late in September, 1541, by fifty thousand jubilant Indians. The attack was beaten off with the greatest difficulty, despite the presence of the viceroy's soldiers. The defenders were able to hold only a few of the strong buildings about the plaza of the town by the aid of artillery fire. The heroine of the siege, Beatriz Hernández, wife of one of the captains, not only kept the women quiet, but fought like an Amazon alongside of the men. A series of successful sorties, during the course of which Santiago was reputed to have appeared on his white steed with an army of angels, finally caused the natives to retire and gave the city a breathing spell.[29]

Mendoza was greatly exercised by the tidings of continued disasters in Nueva Galicia and consulted the audiencia of Mexico as to the advisability of going in person to pacify the province. The audiencia felt that only the most serious conditions would warrant risking his person in the field and on their advice he sent the oidor Maldonado to Michoacán to gather first-hand information concerning the revolt. Maldonado moved from Michoacán to the towns of Ávalos and there soon realized the need of the viceregal presence and wrote to Mendoza that his intervention had become imperative. Similar communications from other officials decided the question for the viceroy, and he determined to put an end to Spanish defeats at the hands of Indians. He collected as large a force as possible, consisting of one hundred and eighty horsemen and a considerable body of friendly Indians,[30] and with cannons, the arm of greatest Spanish superiority in attacking a fortified place, and munitions in

[29] One of the consequences of this investment was the removal of the city to its present site south of the Tololotlán, where it was less exposed to such incursions from the north.

[30] The authorities vary as to the number of Spaniards from 180 to 500 and the native allies from 10,000 to 60,000.—Bancroft, *History of Mexico,* II. 505, note 16.

large quantities.[31] A dangerous concession to induce Indian
chieftains to enlist under him was permission to ride horses
and to use Spanish weapons, granted for the first time in
New Spain.[32] Late in September[33] the army led by the
viceroy in person, with Agostín de Guerrero as lieutenant
general, started for Jalisco. The question of white supremacy in New Spain was to be settled anew.

Mendoza led his army through Michoacán, receiving letters while there from Oñate, describing the attack on Guadalajara, which had been beaten off, and suggesting a juncture
of forces for an assault on the peñoles of Cuina (Coyna)
and Nochistlán. As the plan suited Mendoza's purposes,
he marched in that direction and at the Tazazalca river, a
day's march from Cuina, he was joined by Miguel de Ibarra
and Juan de Camino, to whom the Indians of the region were
granted in encomienda. The two had warned the natives of
the viceroy's approach, but their pleas for a peaceful rendi-
tion had been fruitless. Mendoza, after one last appeal to the
natives, proceeded to invest their fortress, which he captured
by use of the old stratagem of pretended flight. When he
found a temple and all the evidences of idolatry and sacri-
fice on the peñol, he condemned the Indians, as renegades, to
death or slavery, hoping that this example would make an

[31] Mendoza had his agents purchase powder and arms in Vera Cruz
and elsewhere in such quantities that sufficient weapons were left over
from the war to stock a munitions depot in Mexico City.—A. G. I., 48-
1-5/27, Interrogatorio del señor vissorey, preguntas 79, 239.

[32] There was some evidence of a plot to revolt among the Indians of
Michoacán and the tribes near Mexico City; therefore some thought it
unwise to acquaint them with the use of Spanish weapons.—Carta de
Gerónimo López al Emperador, Mexico, October 20, 1541, in Icazbalceta,
Colección de documentos, II. 141-154.

[33] Herrera, Historía General, dec. VII, lib. V, cap. 1, 87, says that
Mendoza left Mexico City, October 8, 1542, with an army of three hundred Spanish horsemen and some foot soldiers. Bancroft, ut supra,
places the number at "about four hundred and fifty Spaniards with some
thirty thousand Tlascaltec and Aztec warriors" and collates the various
authorities as to the date of the departure.

impression which would lighten his task at the other strong places. From Cuina, whose conquest had consumed two weeks, he pushed forward to Acatic, seven leagues distant. There for two days he treated with the natives, and with the terrible punishment of Cuina fresh in their minds, was able to persuade them to abandon their idols and to disperse to their homes. At the same time messengers to the inhabitants of Istlán and Cuyutlán, who had fortified a peñol on the ford of the river on the route to Guadalajara, secured a similar result.

Mendoza then headed for the strongest centers of resistance by way of Zapotlán, while the troops stationed at Guadalajara, which place was relieved of immediate danger, moved up to strengthen the number of effectives at his disposal. The army, so augmented, moved forward on the peñol of Nochistlán. The usual peace parleys were conducted by Miguel de Ibarra, Fray Antonio de Segovia, Fray Juan de San Román, and other priests, but without result. As long as he dared, in his desire to avoid bloodshed, Mendoza continued the negotiations,[34] but was finally forced to fight to avoid the contempt of his own Indians. The combat lasted from eight in the morning until four in the afternoon and only resulted in the capture of the outer lines of defense. Seeing that such procedure would be too costly, Mendoza settled down to regular siege methods, cut off the peñol's water supply and battered down the remaining obstacles with artillery fire. Before the final assault the Indians tried to stop it by offers of peace if the Spaniards would turn aside and march against Mixton. The viceroy rejected this proposal,

---

[34] "La dilacion que tuuo en el combate fue tanta que a mi me lo tenian la gente a poquedad y ellos cobrauan soberina y los yndios amigos que yuan conmigo se querian amontinar diziendo que pues no les dexaua pelear que se querian boluer a sus casas y visto esto hordene publicamente el combate. . . ."—A. G. I., 48-1-2/24, Descargos del virrey, Mexico, October 30, 1546, descargo 37.

and in the attack which followed the large force of defenders were either killed in combat or captured and enslaved.[35]

After the conquest of Nochistlán, the viceroy marched to Suchipila and while there discovered that the greater part of the Indians in rebellion were concentrated on the peñol of Mixton near by, an almost impregnable position.[36] The very name of the peñol, Mixton, which meant "subida de gatos" or "cat's ascent," indicated the nature of the task before the expeditionary force. The sides of the mountain were precipitous and the few practicable approaches had been fortified and were well defended. The earlier defeat of Oñate at this peñol had given the Indian leaders great confidence in their ability to defend the position, so the bulk of their forces had gathered here to try to conclude the war by a defeat of the viceroy. Miguel de Ibarra and Francisco Maldonado were sent in advance across the three leagues of territory lying between Suchipila, where the viceroy's camp was pitched, to make offers of peace, but they were obliged

[35] Ibarra, who had the official branding iron in his possession, was encomendero of the district and did not relish dividing his Indians among the victors, so he was conveniently absent in Guadalajara with the iron and connived at the escape of the majority of the prisoners.

[36] It was during a reorganization of the forces at Suchipila that Mendoza incurred the enmity of Iñigo López de Anuncibay, captain of one of the companies of cavalry. It had come to Mendoza's attention that a number of the so-called cavalry were incapable of so serving as they were not trained horsemen. He ordered all such persons to be placed in the foot companies so that the cavalry would not be hampered in critical moments by their lack of skill. The company of López de Anuncibay nearly melted away under the selective process and his mutinous attitude led to a stern reprimand from Mendoza. Smarting from the tongue lashing he received, López de Anuncibay was further guilty of leaving the artillery unguarded on the march from Suchipila to Mixton when some of the pieces were mired. As he was in command of the rearguard and responsible for their safety, this evidence of incapacity brought the viceregal wrath about his head once more and Mendoza "le rreprehendi con palabras asperas y afrentosas como el caso lo rrequeria." From that time forth he hated Mendoza and was the chief witness against him in the Sandoval visita. His abandonment of the artillery was due to a private trade in olive oil which he had pushed ahead to sell, to the complete neglect of his duty.—A. G. I., 48-1-2/24, Descargos del virrey, Mexico, October 30, 1546, pregunta 34.

to flee and leave their supplies in the hands of the enemy. The following noon a force of eight hundred Indians appeared on a hill above the Spanish camp at Suchipila and, chanting a hymn to the god Tlatl, sacrificed some chickens in full view of the viceroy. Mendoza sent Miguel de Ibarra to them to urge peace once more and to secure their leader Tenamaxtli, but was careful to secure Ibarra's retreat by placing a company of cavalry and a company armed with the arquebuse to hold the line of retirement. This was fortunate, as the Indians tried to entrap Ibarra's party and would have been successful if these reinforcements had not been posted.

With all chance of a peaceful conquest gone, Mendoza advanced upon Mixton with his entire army. In a steep pass leading toward the peñol he was attacked simultaneously in front and rear, but his dispositions were so well taken that the assault was beaten off by the vanguard and rearguard. Much of the day was taken by this skirmish. The main body spent the night in the pass, after carefully fortifying their camp, and the main position of the enemy on Mixton was not reached until the following day. For three weeks the fortress was closely invested with no visible sign of submission on the part of the Indians, despite daily offers of peace which were received with showers of arrows. Finally the continuous artillery fire and the persistence of the Spanish attack won out. A number of the Indians began to waver in their faith in Tlatl and the warriors of the neighboring town of Teul deserted to the Spanish side en masse in the hope of winning clemency. These deserters betrayed their erstwhile comrades by disclosing the existence of a secret pass to the top of the mountain, and the peñol fell before a combined frontal and rear attack. The viceroy restrained his horsemen and permitted the majority of the defenders to escape, feeling that the lesson had been severe enough and hoping to spare the local encomenderos the loss of all their

natives. With the capture of Mixton, where the bravest warriors had been assembled under Tenamaxtli to the number
of one hundred thousand,[37] the backbone of the revolt was
broken. After dividing the captives among his troops as
slaves, Mendoza extended his operations to the north and
then to the south of the Tololotlán to stamp out the remaining
embers of revolt. His line of march took him to Teul, Tlatenango, Jalpa, and Pozol and resistance ceased everywhere
at his approach. The itinerary of the expedition then led it
down the Suchipila river to San Cristóbal, where the Tololotlán was crossed, early in the year 1542. The region about
Tequilla and Etzatlan was soon pacified and the war was
terminated by the capture of Ahuacatlán, where the natives
of Compostela were assembled, by Juan de Villalba, just as
the viceroy prepared to march on the place. Mendoza had
completed his task in a manner worthy of the best traditions
of his training in the Moorish border wars in Granada; and
his military skill, by completing the second "Conquest of
Mexico," had demonstrated that New Spain could control
the Indians without the presence of Cortés. In the far
north Coronado's expedition, which returned at this time,
extinguished a few sparks of hostility near Culiacán, and the
inaccessible mountain districts of Nayarit and the north
were to resist conquest for nearly two centuries more, but the
danger of a general upheaval of the Indians of New Spain
against the Spaniard was over.[38]

[37] A large proportion of the force on Mixton were Chichimec tribes-
men and those that escaped death or slavery fled to the mountain districts of Zacatecas and Nayarit. The figures as to the numbers of
Indian participants vary greatly, but undoubtedly the number given above,
from the best obtainable authority, is an exaggeration. Fifty thousand
would be closer to the truth. The accounts of the siege likewise vary
considerably, and Herrera (*Historia General*) goes so far as to state
that the peñol was taken without any native resistance. Evidently Mendoza's account of the exploit was not available to this usually accurate
writer.

[38] During the course of the viceroy's military tour side expeditions
into the country of the "chichimecos blancos" were made and Franciscan
missionaries were sent there at his personal expense. These Indians were

Mendoza left some cavalry in Guadalajara and returned to Mexico City, where the lustre of his triumphs had preceded him and his entry was accompanied by "great solemnity, rejoicing and festivities."[39] The celebration was one of genuine thanksgiving, for they believed that a general uprising of the subject population had been averted and that their supremacy would henceforth be unquestioned.[40] In the land which had suffered from the scourge of war the lieutenant-governor Cristóbal de Oñate was able to report to the viceroy in 1542 that the Indians were back in their homes and that "the land, praise God, is fine, and I have never seen it better since I have been in it."[41]

While the celebration was at its height, news of the revolt of the younger Almagro in Peru and of the murder of Francisco Pizarro reached the viceroy. He was "scandalized" by the tidings and regarded the situation as nothing short of "diabolical." He wrote to the king and to Vaca de Castro, the special royal representative in Peru, offering ships, men, and artillery to aid in quelling the rebellion.[42] A body of troops for this service was organized in Mexico, but the prompt triumph of Vaca de Castro made a relief expedition unnecessary. When tidings of the events in Peru became

probably in the north between Zacatecas and Querétaro.—A. G. I., 48-1-6/28, Preguntas para la probanza de Mechoacan, 304. Bancroft, *North Mexican States*, I. 13, sums up the little that is known about early entradas into the region.

[39] Obregón, Crónica, cap. XLV.

[40] Miguel de Ibarra believed that the cordon of garrisons placed about the region in revolt prevented it from spreading to New Spain.—A. G. I., 48-1-5/27, Testigo de Miguel de Ibarra, Compostela, January 26, 1542, preguntas 162, 163.

[41] Mendoza, *Carta*, Mexico, May 10, 1542, *Cartas de Indias*, p. 255.

[42] *Ibid.*, p. 254. In this letter, Mendoza displayed great magnanimity or perhaps subtle irony toward his enemy Cortés by stating: "Parese me que el Marques del Valle seria muy bueno para remediar lo de ally, por la esperiencia que tiene de lo de aca y por el aparejo, y yo le ayudaria a ello lo possible." On the other hand, it may have been an attempt to placate the former ruler of New Spain in order to ward off such an attack as the Sandoval visita, which grew out of the conqueror's hostility toward him.

known, the celebration of the victory in Nueva Galicia was prolonged to recognize the complete vindication of royal authority.[43]

The second test of the Mendoza administration in New Spain came from without and was the answer of Cortés to the summary treatment of his pretensions to exploring rights which had been accorded by the viceroy. In 1540, when he found the way to further discovery blocked by the union of Mendoza and Alvarado, he had returned to Spain to seek redress at court. At the outset he met with little save rebuffs, but

---

[43] Mendoza had been accused by Cortés and the visitor Sandoval of great cruelty in the course of these triumphs in Nueva Galicia. Since that time historians have either justified or condemned him for his conduct. Bancroft (*History of Mexico*, II. 532) speaks with scorn of the viceroy's humanity and moderation, forgetful of his own rather singular blindness to the faults of his hero Cortés. In the matter of slavery it should be said that comparatively few slaves were taken and that, since slavery was a matter of justice, the viceroy was bound by the decision of his audiencia to give Indians captured in the field to his soldiers and, in addition, that the actual work of enslavement was in charge of the oidor Maldonado and that the branding iron was in Cristóbal de Oñate's possession. To this can be added the evidence of positive orders from the home government to place Indians in revolt in slavery as a better punishment than death, since the Indians were weak and prone to crime and the death penalty was no punishment in their eyes. A. G. I., 87-6-2, Oficio y parte, October 25, 1548, XVII, furnishes an even later expression of this attitude of the home government. The other charges, that he had had Indians blown from the mouth of cannon, mutilated by Negroes armed with knives, torn to pieces by savage dogs, and hanged, were brought originally by Sandoval and were refuted to the satisfaction of the viceroy's superiors. In the first place, all sentences were passed by the oidor Maldonado, not the viceroy, as the latter was not a letrado, and the sentences were carried out by Cristóbal de Oñate. In the second place, the stabbing was done by the Negroes and Indians in the heat of battle and was not a matter of justice at all but, as the viceroy puts it, "como se haze en españa con los erejes e ynfieles que la gente los acuchillan e matan en el camino sin que sea a cargo de la justicia." Finally, it was a matter of the sixteenth-century point of view admirably expressed by Mendoza in the following: "el apperrear algunos yndios de los mas culpados y ponellos a tiro convino hazerse para escarmiento y mas temor de los yndios . . . la muerte de la horca ellos se la dauan de su propia voluntad en estas partes . . . y en el rreyno de granada se acostumbra a cañauerear y apedrear muchos moros de los que an rrenegado nuestra santa fe"; and he closes by stating that as a viceroy and general in the field at war he cannot view the punishment meted out as doing more than fit the case, a necessary example, and for the good of God and His Majesty.—A. G. I., 48-1-2/24, Descargos del Virrey, Mexico, October 30, 1546, descargo 38.

the framing of the New Laws in 1542 and 1543, under the direction of Las Casas, gave him an opportunity to secure a hearing. In Valladolid, July 6, 1543, he presented a list of charges against the viceroy in which he set forth his complaint of unfair treatment at Mendoza's hands and charged that his administration was saturated with favoritism, gross inefficiency, and graft. In addition to introducing the New Laws overseas, he strongly urged that conditions in New Spain warranted the appointment of officials who would also be judges of residencia empowered to suspend the viceroy and his subordinates from office.[44] On July 11, he renewed his charges and petitioned that some action be taken to right the wrongs of New Spain. The members of the Royal Council were at last in a receptive mood and ordered an investigation by one of their own members, the licentiate Salmeron.[45] Cortés by this time had heard that only a visitor was to be sent, so was particularly solicitous that his powers be as great as those of a judge of residencia and include the right to suspend the viceroy from office, alleging that a simple visita[46] would be insufficient to free the inhabitants of their fear of Mendoza's revenge in cases of testimony against his rule. Cortés was given a hearing, July 19, and produced thirteen former residents of New Spain as witnesses to the truth of his charges, contained in thirty-five questions comprising a formal interrogatorio and

[44] "Suplico a vuestra alteza aya conpasion de aquella tierra y de sus subditas y naturales que en ella estan que tanto an servido a vuestra magestad y sea servido de proveher juez de residencia para el dicho vissorey y oficiales con suspension de oficios."—A. G. I., 48-1-1/23, El Marques del valle con el vissorey de la Nueva España Don Antonio de Mendoza sobre la residencia que pide se le mande tomar, Valladolid, July 6, 1543. On the reverse of the document are written these significant words: "dese traslado desto al señor licenciado Sandoval."

[45] A. G. I., 48-1-1/23, Peticion del Marques del Valle al real consejo, Valladolid, July 11, 1543.

[46] For a treatment of the origin of this institution and its history in New Spain, see Priestley, *José de Gálvez, Visitor-General of New Spain.*

designed to show specific instances of misrule by Mendoza.[47]
The former oidor of the audiencia of Mexico, Loaysa, who
happened to be at court, denied the truth of the charges in
his answer to the list of questions presented by the Marquis,[48]
despite the fact that his son, Diego de Loaysa, was married
to a niece of Cortés, and was joined in his negative testimony
by Juan de Najara, Andrés de Barrios, Diego de Zárate, and
Juan Cano.[49] Not satisfied with his showing at court Cortés
made certain that his accusations were given to the visitor
Tello de Sandoval and wrote to all his friends in New Spain
asking them to testify against the viceroy and the audiencia,
to permit the visitor to suspend them from office. He assured
his partizans that they would find every necessary aid[50]
in the visitor; and this coöperation between the visitor and
the Cortés party was not successfully concealed from the

[47] A. G. I., 48-1-1/23, Ynterrogatorio del Marques del Valle presentado en Valladolid a XIX de Jullio de 1543 con testigos.

[48] Loaysa and the veedor Peralmendez Cherino had been sent to Spain
with some laws concerning privileges which the inhabitants of New Spain
wished to see enacted in order to keep the Spanish element from leaving
the country.—A. G. I., 60-3-17, Carta del Cabildo de Mexico al rey,
Mexico, January 20, 1543. The list of witnesses who testified in the case
against the viceroy is as follows: Juan de Najara, resident of Mexico
and a conquistador; Francisco Tellez, resident of Mexico; Andrés de
Barrios, resident of New Spain; Diego de Zárate, resident of New Spain;
Andrés de Tapia, resident of Mexico; Juan Cano, resident of Mexico;
Martin Ruiz de Monaraz, resident of Mexico; Francisco de Lerma, resi-
dent of Mexico; Miguel Diez, resident of Mexico; Juan de la Peña, resi-
dent of Mexico; Francisco Rodríquez, canon of the church in Mexico
City; Francisco de Porras, and Francisco de Loaysa, former oidor of the
Audiencia of Mexico, now a resident of Cuidad Real.

[49] Juan de Najara said that some untoward things might have taken
place if the viceroy had not known ". . . lo castigaria muy bien por ser
el mas honesto honbre que puede ser . . . " Andrés de Barrios spoke of
Mendoza as " . . . buen governador que es muy temeroso de dios e que
disimule ni consienta hazer cosa mal hecha e que pluguiese a dios que
tal fuese el anima y conciencia deste testigo como es la del dicho vissorey
y tan buen Xrisptiano como el lo es." and Juan Cano put his finger on the
center of the trouble when he said "vio que entre el dicho virrey y el
Marques del Valle ovo manera de differencia en quel marques se quexava
porquel dicho virrey no le dexava yr al dicho descubrimiento."—Interrogatorio del Marques del Valle, ut supra.

[50] "Todo aparejo."—A. G. I., 48-1-5/27, Interrogatorio del señor vissorey, pregunta 225.

viceroy and his supporters.[51]   Indeed, a careful comparison of the thirty-three accusations of Cortés and the subsequent charges growing out of the visita, with respect to charges, even to specific cases, leaves only two possibilities open.   Either the accusations of Cortés were sufficiently correct to warrant the visitor's adverse judgment of Mendoza's administration, or Sandoval found it convenient to use the discontent of Cortés and his followers to further his own ends.[52]

Francisco Tello de Sandoval came to New Spain clothed in ample powers.   He brought with him a provision de visita which authorized him to investigate the conduct of the viceroy, the audiencia, treasury officials, and their subordinates down to most insignificant town officials in the most wretched town of New Spain.   He was empowered to bring charges against those found remiss in their duties and to pass sentence on such persons, subject to revision on appeal to the

[51] Speaking of the testimony of Anunciabay against him in the course of the visita the viceroy stated this knowledge clearly in the following and in a number of other places.   "Juro a dios que si supiera que le avian de tomar su dicho que huuiera huydo de la tierra por no lo dezir porque asi como asi se avia de yr de la tierra por aver dicho su dicho este fue ardid ynuentado por el y por otros apasionados conforme a lo que el Marques del Valle les tenia escripto por sus cartas que dixesen que por estar yo en el cargo no osauan dezir la verdad porque avisando por vuestra merced su magestad y su rreal consejo de yndias me suspenderian como en su tiempo y lugar parecera por sus cartas."—A. G. I., 48-1-1/23, Descargos del virrey, descargo 41.

[52] Cortés denounced the viceroy as being partial to his servants and friends.   Agostín de Guerrero is pictured by him as being able to secure advancement for anyone through his influence with Mendoza.   Francisco Vásquez de Coronado is singled out as a friend of the viceroy who had secured undeserved official positions and grants of land.   Juan Alonso de Sosa, the treasurer, declared that the explorer lived in wealth on money that rightfully should have been the king's, his virtual embezzlement of royal funds winked at by the king's representative.   Conquerors, married and possessed of family, went without Indians, while the friends of the administration were showered with corregimientos.   Mendoza's mole at Vera Cruz was a wasteful extravagance, his expeditions laid the country open to rebellion, the Mixton War was the result of shameful abuse of the natives and lack of leadership, the viceroy and his friends indulged in unlawful commercial enterprises and dodged the payment of customs duties, and so on the plaint goes.   A vindictive old man venting his disappointment is the answer.   Sandoval, the instrument of revenge, in his turn tried to make the situation into something advantageous to his own ambitions.

Council of the Indies. All royal officers were to render him every assistance in their power and his summons to them to appear before him was to be heeded on pain of condemnation as rebels. For the duties confided to his care he was granted full royal powers.[53]   In addition, he was granted the right to attend meetings of the audiencia with voice and vote, and was not obliged to act in accord with the viceroy, and, by a special commission from Cardinal Juan de Tavera, was made inquisitor of New Spain.[54]   The New Laws, already discussed in another connection, were also intrusted to him for publication and enforcement. Since his powers were really those of a super-viceroy, the presence of two men with such exalted authority might easily lead to a struggle for supremacy between the two. Only a man of exceptional devotion and character could safely avoid the temptation such a struggle involved.

After Sandoval received his instructions he went to Seville and embarked for the New World from the port of San Lúcar, November 3, 1543. After a successful voyage he arrived at San Juan de Ulloa, February 12 of the following year. The Contador Gonzalo de Aranda, who accompanied him, has left an account of the journey which fills out the meagre outline of times and places.[55]   They first landed on the small island in the harbor, inspected the mole which the viceroy had under construction, and slept there that night. The charges of Cortés concerning this work undoubtedly lay behind this visit. They found a tower there for the defence of the port with walls of cement as high as a man, and observed the progress of the work on the mole, which was in charge of a cleric and employed a large group of Negro laborers. Satisfied with what they had seen, they went

[53] A. G. I., 48-1-2/24, Probisyon e comision original del señor visitador.
[54] Puga, *Cédulas,* II. 452-453.
[55] A. G. I., 56-6-9, Carta de Gonzalo de Aranda al rey, Mexico, May 30, 1544.

next to Vera Cruz, five leagues distant, and waited there ten days while their baggage was being unloaded from the boats of the fleet, a wait which permitted an inspection of the customs and the town government. From Vera Cruz the party made its way overland to Mexico City, where they were greeted in sullen silence, as the ill-tidings of the New Laws had preceded them. With the unwelcome laws proclaimed and a stay of execution granted, Sandoval plunged into the more important duties of conducting a general visita.

The visitor instituted a vigorous investigation in all parts of New Spain, and every official of any importance within its confines soon felt the uncomfortable presence of the visita and had his official acts while in office subjected to an examination. The complete papers of the legal process involved in this extraordinary check-up on early New World administration fill nineteen bulky legajos and show conclusively that the visitor did accomplish a great deal and that the visita was no mere matter of form.[56] Evidence was collected on the basis of which charges were preferred, defenses were heard, and in numerous cases final sentence was passed. In the more important cases the list of witnesses called to testify ran into hundreds.[57] Statements with the sworn attestation of numerous citizens as to their truth or falsity (probanzas) were gathered in the mines, cities, and towns and even such a remote hamlet as San Estévan del Puerto (Pánuco) did not escape the sweeping inquiry.[58] The escribanos, abogados,

[56] A. G. I., 48-1-1/23 to 48-1-20/2, Visita hecha el ano de 1543-1547 al virrey de la Nueva España y Presidente de la Audiencia de Mexico Dn Antonio de Mendoza a los oidores de ella y demas oficiales por el licdo Dn Francisco de Sandoval, del consejo de S. M. en el consejo de Indias visitador general de la Nueva España. Bancroft dismisses the whole matter rather lightly, *History of Mexico,* II. 531-534.

[57] For example, 162 friars were called as witnesses for the viceroy's denial of the charges brought against him in the immediate vicinity of Mexico City, and in the city proper 108 citizens appeared as witnesses.

[58] A. G. I., 48-1-18/40, consists of an entire legajo given over to the trials of the individual regidores and alcaldes of that town, accompanied in each case by the final sentence of the visitor.

alcaldes mayores, alguaciles,[59] and all the other members of the officialdom of New Spain, in office at the time or out of office, were subjected to the prying scrutiny of the visitor. The mass of details thus collected by Sandoval is not only indispensable to a proper study of Mendoza's reign but also throws a flood of light on the organization and mechanism of visitas and on the institutional history of the sixteenth century in both Spain and New Spain.

In view of the extraordinary powers granted the visitor it is not strange that he was unwelcome to the viceroy and the oidores, who felt that they were temporarily deprived of the full powers of their offices while he remained in New Spain. ˙ The visitor's comportment aggravated rather than allayed this predisposition to dislike. Very shortly after his arrival he began to display certain unpleasant characteristics and rumors of his personal ambition to supplant the viceroy began to reach the latter's ears. Too much authority seemed to have turned his head. On the ship coming to New Spain he had boasted that he was going to bring order out of the chaos which existed there and at Vera Cruz he spoke slightingly of Mendoza as one he would ship home on a vessel whenever he saw fit.[60] In Mexico he let it be

[59] A. G. I., 48-1-15/37; 48-1-16/38; 38-1-17/39 contains the complete papers of the visitas of the escribanos. A. G. I., 48-1-14/36, is a bulky bundle containing the visita of the abogados, procuradores, and relatores. A. G. I. 48-1-12/34 and 48-1-13/35 contain the trials of the alcaldes mayores and ordinarios. A. G. I., 48-1-10/32, holds the visitas of the alguaçiles mayores and their assistants.

[60] ". . . Desde que el dicho licenciado partio de Sevilla mostro hodio y henemistad a mi parte y alla y por la mar yba deziendo y publica, do que a rredemir la tierra que estava perdida con mi parte y esto dixo muchos vezes como honbre que llevava proposito de le hazer mal. . . " Mendoza, A. G. I., 48-2-20/2, Resultas de la visita, le recusacion del virrey, Valladolid, May 7, 1548. As early as 1544 Mendoza wrote to Juan de Aguilar: "la primera cosa que en el puerto publico fue que traia todo el gobierno de la tierra, y preguntandole que sera del vissorey? respondio 'envialle en un navio cuando me pareciere'," and further complained that the visitor held the viceroy in such slight esteem as to publish his residencia throughout the land twice, "como si fuera el mas triste corregidor ó alcalde en ella."—Mendoza, Carta a Juan de Aguilar, in Pacheco y Cárdenas, III. 509.

known that he hoped to find the viceroy guilty and would welcome testimony against him. His overbearing attitude even evinced itself in the solemn sessions of the audiencia where, on one occasion, he placed one arm on the table about which they were seated with Mendoza presiding, and went through the pantomime of opening his eyes with his fingers when Lorenzo de Tejada ventured to vote with the opposition against him. With the completion of this extraordinary maneuver he shouted angrily at Tejada: "You had better open your eyes and remember that I am your visitor," together with other threatening remarks which ill became the character of his office, to the great amazement of the viceroy and the oidores, who considered his actions in the light of an open affront to the presiding officer.[61]

In the task of gathering information concerning the conduct of the viceroy in his office, Sandoval was accused of predetermining the former's guilt and of seeking only such evidence as would bolster his charges. He sought out the malcontents, who had run afoul of the viceroy's justice, and made their complaints the substantiating evidence of the formal accusations he brought against him; without waiting for the viceroy's side of the case he hastened to send these charges to Prince Philip and to the Council of the Indies. This was contrary to his instructions, as contained in his commission, which ordered him to gather full information, to formulate charges on the basis of this information, then to provide the viceroy with a copy of them and then, with that official's reply in hand, to notify the Crown of his findings. Vexed at every turn by Sandoval, who seemed to be attempting to badger him into an open act of defiance that would justify suspension from office, Mendoza wrote repeatedly to the home government complaining about his

<hr>

[61] A. G. I., 48-1-4/26, El lic^do Lorenzo de Tejada can Franco de Sandoval, visitador que fue de la Nueva España.

equivocal position.[62]   Sandoval openly consorted with the known enemies of Mendoza and entertained them in his dwelling, where he offered them government offices and boasted of the fact that he was going to be the ruler of New Spain.[63]   A fortunate turn in the wheel of affairs in Spain finally gave Mendoza a chance to present his side of the story to the home government.   In 1545 his brother, Bernaldino de Mendoza, captain-general of the galleys of Spain, was appointed president of the Council of the Indies and took up the cudgels in defence of the family honor.   At his instance, Philip ordered Sandoval to return to Spain so that the whole question might be sifted by the supreme governing body.   Sandoval was loath to return and only a repetition of the order in a series of increasingly stronger terms brought him to a realization of his true position as he clung tenaciously to his hope of succeeding Mendoza as viceroy of New Spain.[64]

It was not until June 21, 1546, that Sandoval made public a signed list of forty-four accusations against the conduct of Mendoza as viceroy, in the presence of the audiencia and the escribano mayor, Antonio de Turcios.   In these charges he accused Mendoza of favoring his personal friends, Luís de Castilla, Agostín de Guerrero, Antonio de Turcios,

[62] In a letter to the king dated from Mexico June 20, 1544, Mendoza took pains to point out the progress of New Spain under his rule, particularly stressing the increase of royal revenue.   In view of this evident success he protested against the power given Sandoval to pass sentence on him "sin embargo de qualquier apelacion" and protested vehemently that " . . . no estuviera mi honra puesta en manos de letrados a quien yo nunca servi ni conosci"; *Instrucciones que los Vireyes dejaron á sus Sucesores,* 240-241.   In 1548 he reported " . . . escrevio a vuestra alteza y a los de vuestro consejo muchos vezes contra el dicho licenciado Sandoval de lo que hazia y excedia en su officio. . . ."—A. G. I., 48-2-20/2, Resultas de la visita, la recusacion del virrey, Valladolid, May 7, 1548.

[63] " . . . Teniendo por cierto que abia ser governador abia dias que tenia ofrecidos officios y hecho Repartimiento dellos entre sus amigos y Alegados publicando ansi el como sus criados que benia por Governador . . . " *Ibid.*

[64] *Ibid.*

and others; of receiving gifts from individuals in return for his favor; of abusing the natives in the interests of his ranches and exploring expeditions; of not watching the collection of the royal revenues with sufficient care; of vacating corregimientos and applying the revenues derived from them to unlawful purposes, and so on through the long list. Two interesting items in the inventory of his crimes are first, an attempt to fix responsibility on Mendoza for the death of an unknown person at the hands of one Pedro Paco through an accident incidental to a fencing match in his palace,[65] and second, an allegation that he had forced his sister, Maria de Mendoza, to marry a rich mine-owner, Martin De Ircio, against her will.[66] Appearing against the viceroy were a number of his enemies, such as Bernardino de Albornoz, Alonso Ortiz de Zuñiga, and Tello de Medina. In general, the earlier complaints made by Cortés were repeated and amplified and, in particular, the conduct of the Mixton War came in for severe criticism.[67]

As soon as the viceroy was able to secure a copy of the charges which had been preferred against him by Sandoval he prepared a lengthy reply to them, which was completed

[65] Mendoza attacked this trivial charge with great vigor in his reply, stating that he might as well be held responsible for all those killed in bull and cane fights.—A. G. I., 48-1-2/24, Descargos del virrey, descargo 8.

[66] María de Mendoza was living with her husband and children at the mines of Zumpango during the year 1546-1547 and indignantly denied the truth of this charge against her brother in her sworn testimony.—A. G. I., 48-1-7/29, Probanza hecha en las minas de çumpango, testigo de María de Mendoza. The statements of many others, including no less a personage than Bishop de Zumárraga, corroborate her story. It seems that she had taken a certain vow before leaving Spain which prevented her from immediately entering into matrimony, but that after freely consulting letrados and churchmen, she had married De Ircio of her own volition.—A. G. I., 48-1-6/28, Testigo del Obispo Juº de Zumarraga, preguntas 26-27.

[67] A. G. I., 48-1-2/24, Cargos que resultan de la visita secreta contra el muy illustre señor Antonio de Mendoça, Mexico, June 21, 1546. Bancroft, *History of Mexico*, II. 532, states that no one dared appear against Mendoza.

October 30, 1546.[68]   In this rebuttal he assembled all his commissions and licenses from the government granting him power to do many of the things branded as illegal by the visitor and in general sought to show that the charges were false and placed against him by enemies who had been refused office by him or had been convicted of crime under his administration.   In order to make his case stronger and to prove his contentions, he petitioned for permission to call in witnesses on his own behalf, and drew up a list of three hundred and nine questions covering his entire administration to which they were to reply.   As soon as this permission was obtained his representatives took this list of questions (Interrogatorio) to all parts of the kingdom and nearly every Spaniard of any consequence, as well as a large number of Indians, gave answer to it in the course of the following year.[69]   Mendoza by this means secured an overwhelming mass of favorable evidence but Sandoval paid no attention to it and persisted in his attack.   Mendoza then transferred his case to the Council of the Indies and Sandoval was instructed to complete the visita within sixty days and was ordered home to explain his conduct.[70]

Sandoval departed in 1547, and the termination of his four-year sojourn lifted a great weight of uncertainty from the minds of those charged with the duty of governing New

[68] A. G. I., 48-1-2/24, Descargos del señor vissorey, Mexico, October 30, 1546.

[69] The first 303 questions have been printed under the title "Fragmenta de la visita hecha a don Antonio de Mendoza" by Icazbalceta, *Colección de documentos,* II. 72-140. This is the part drawn up by the notary Miguel López, which lacks the five additional questions framed by Juan de Salazar for the probanza in Michoacán.—A. G. I., 48-1-6/28, Probanza hecha en Mechuacan, 1546.

[70] Sandoval lingered in New Spain eleven months after his first order to return to Spain, to the great disadvantage and interruption of good government. It took "Carta sobre carta y tercera" to convince him that the home government was in earnest and he was furiously angry with the viceroy and his brother for the part they played in upsetting his plans to govern New Spain.—A. G. I., 48-1-2/24, Cargos que puesto contra el licenciado Tello de Sandoval, Valladolid, May 7, 1548.

Spain. He had been too long about his business and had become a hindrance to the proper conduct of affairs rather than the beneficial stimulant intended by the home government. Everyone had been so busy defending himself that little time was left for his real duties. Sandoval's effort to enforce the New Laws had failed and the rather meaningless vote of an ecclesiastical congress to the effect that slavery was unlawful had only afforded Las Casas an opportunity to show that his hands at least were clean of the offense. The visitor had done nothing of a constructive character and his numerous inspections and threats against the administration had brought progress to a standstill.

In the case of the viceroy, no stone was left unturned until the stigma of Sandoval's accusations had been removed. Mendoza sent Agostín de Guerrero and Juan de Aguilar to Spain to push the case to a conclusion before the Council of the Indies, and retained Sebastian Rodríquez as his legal adviser in Spain. The first gun of the legal battle was fired in Valladolid, May 7, 1548, when Mendoza's representative presented a petition to the Council of the Indies asking that Sandoval, a member of that body, be barred from consideration of the visita findings against the viceroy as an acknowledged enemy incapable of an unprejudiced decision.[71] The Council of the Indies granted the petition as one based on good grounds and, after viewing the credentials of the viceroy's agents, accepted a bond of 30,000 maravedís as a guarantee of their good faith. Sandoval was then summoned to appear before the Council for a formal hearing.[72] At the

[71] A. G. I., 48-2-20/2, Recusacion del señor vissorey, peticion, Valladolid, May 7, 1548: ". . . por ende pido y suplico a vuestra alteza mande aber al dicho licenciado sandoval por Recusado y que no haga Relacion de la dicha bisita ni de parecer en ella ni conosca de las causas que mi parte tiene y tubiere ni sea juez en ellas y se avstenga de conocer de todas ellas . . . "

[72] A. G. I., 48-2-20/2, Peticion al Consejo de Yndias, Valladolid, May 24, 1548. On the back of the petition, the consent "que esta bien provey do que se cumpla lo mandado," dated May 28.

same time a list of twenty-eight reasons why he should be so barred out of the case was presented in order that Sandoval could answer them before the Council.

The former visitor appeared before the Council, June 2, 1548, and replied briefly with negations, half admissions, and lack of memory concerning some details. In general he denied unfriendliness and that he had hoped to become governor of New Spain in the viceroy's stead, but two admissions damaged his case severely in the eyes of his fellow members of the Council. He admitted that he had wished to prolong his stay in New Spain for another year,[73] and that he had been asked by many to stay in New Spain as president of its audiencia, when it was rumored that Mendoza would go to Peru, but that he had replied that he lacked the necessary qualifications.[74] The decision of the Council of the Indies, September 14, 1548, was in favor of the viceroy, and Sandoval was ordered to abstain from taking any part in the examinations of the visita which concerned Mendoza. After two meetings which ended in disagreement, it was finally shown by an actual examination of the files of the archives of the Council that Sandoval had sent a letter and memorials to the king against the viceroy immediately after his arrival in New Spain and before he could possibly have made a judicial inquiry.[75] Not satisfied with this vindication

[73] "Por que si otro año mas estaviera pensabe de hacer mucho servicio a su magestad . . . pero que niega aver dicho las dichas palabras por tener pensamiento de quedar por governador."—A. G. I., 48-2-20/2, Testigo de Francisco Tello de Sandoval, Valladolid, June 2, 1548.

[74] *Ibid.*, pregunta XVIII.

[75] ". . . Cierta carta e capitulos quel dicho licenciado sandoval confeso que avia enbiado al dicho vuestro Real consejo de yndias luego que llego a la nueva españa. . . ."—A. G. I., 48-2-20/2, Resultas de la visita, Valladolid, August 24-September 14, 1548. The decision was signed by the licentiate, Hernan Martínez de Montalvo, Doctors Anaya and Castilla of the Royal Council, and by the licentiates Gutierrez Velázquez, Gregorio López and Doctor Hernan Pérez of the Council of the Indies and it reads that " . . . Sanctdoval se abstenga de la vista y determinacion del proceso de la visita que por mandado de su magestad tomo en la nueva españa en lo que tocare al dicho virrey don Antonio de Mendoça . . . " *Ibid.*, September 14, 1548.

of their master, the viceroy's representatives pressed the case further and on September 22, 1550, secured an extension of the prohibition so as to include any case which might involve Mendoza.[76] Even after the viceroy's death the case was continued by his son, Francisco, who obtained an injunction which excluded Sandoval from any case in which the children of Mendoza were parties, July 29, 1555.[77] Thus the attempt to oust the viceroy, which had its genesis in the charges brought by Cortés in 1543, ended in ignominious failure; and the viceregal system as represented by Mendoza was vindicated as a successful means of maintaining imperial control in the distant Spanish Indies.

[76] A. G. I., 48-1-20/2, Mandamiento de los señores del consejo Real de Indias, Valladolid, September 22, 1550.

[77] *Ibid.*, Valladolid, July 29, 1555.

CHAPTER VII

THE LAST YEARS OF ANTONIO DE MENDOZA'S RULE

The fifteen years of Mendoza's government in New Spain fall naturally into four periods; first, the era of beginnings, characterized by a struggle between the viceroy and Cortés for the right to engage in discovery (1535-1540); second, the years of the remarkable voyages and exploring expeditions under viceregal promotion and direction, during which time there also occurred the last great native rebellion, the Mixton War (1540-1544); third, the period of the visitor Sandoval's sojourn in New Spain (1544-1547) as a menace to Mendoza's continuance in office, and noteworthy for the failure of the New Laws; lastly, the days of recognition, when, despite failing health, the "good viceroy" could get no relief from the office he had fought the visitor so strenuously to retain. This final series of years, stretching from 1547 to the time of Mendoza's departure for Peru in 1551, brought many new problems to be solved as well as continued progress and increased prosperity. The viceroy had to devote much attention to the questions concerning the relations between the conquered race and the Spaniards, which arose as an aftermath of the Mixton War and from the great scarcity of labor caused by a destructive epidemic which broke out among the Indians in 1545 and ran its course the following year.[1] In addition to the great social unrest which these conditions produced, the period was characterized by continued expansion on the northern frontier, where the

[1] It has been estimated that as many as 800,000 natives perished from this disease, but the figures seem to be greatly exaggerated. The epidemic is believed to have been small-pox, first introduced into New Spain by a Negro with the Narváez expedition. The Indians apparently had no immunity and in most cases the results were fatal.—Bancroft, *History of Mexico*, II. 529.

breaking of the Chichimec and Otomí barriers prepared the way for the advance into Nueva Vizcaya under the succeeding viceroys. The development of mining and ranching, the founding of new towns, and the establishment of an audiencia in Nueva Galicia, were indeed the preliminaries to the great advance of the frontier of settlement in the second half of the sixteenth century when Francisco de Ibarra, Luís de Carabajal, the two Urdiñolas, Juan de Oñate, and others opened up vast new regions in the north of New Spain. From the standpoint of the viceroy, Mendoza's determined but unsuccessful effort to make his office hereditary in the person of his son, Francisco, was the outstanding feature of these last years.

The failure of the New Laws, and with them Spain's greatest program of humane legislation, coupled with the disorder occasioned by the Mixton War and the Sandoval visita, left a trail of discontent in New Spain of which traces were to be found in all classes—among the Spaniards, Negro slaves, and subject Indians alike. The victors in the Mixton War petitioned for rewards for their services and were highly discontented with their lot. War, pestilence, and conscription had killed off so many of the natives that the problem of securing enough laborers to gratify these demands became a most serious one; for the government could only pay its obligations to its servants by granting them the right to exploit the labor of the servile classes. Since the small number of slaves captured during the war were far from sufficient, Negroes were imported in increasing numbers, those in service were subjected to increased exactions, and, under the guise of chasing runaway Indians, an extensive illicit slave-trade grew up on the northern frontier. This was particularly true of Nueva Galicia, where such raids had been customary from the time that Cabeza de Vaca met such a party north of Culiacán.

The undercurrent of discontent engendered by the existence of these oppressive conditions found expression in sporadic revolts on the part of the servile classes and in attempts to overturn the government on the part of dissatisfied Spaniards who fancied that such violence would remedy the economic situation. These disgruntled Spaniards went so far, in one instance, as to plot the murder of all the magistrates in Mexico City, whom they felt were responsible for their grievances. Fortunately for the government, two of the conspirators weakened and betrayed their accomplices before anything had been accomplished. The government seized those concerned and executed them with utmost promptness as an example, for the very thought that such an act even could have been contemplated thoroughly alarmed the authorities.[2] During the same year, 1546, the Negroes were discovered in a conspiracy to throw off the yoke of slavery in the region about Tlatalulco and Tenocha and were dealt with in summary fashion. This was a repetition of the earlier attempt, in 1536, of the less docile African to substitute black for white rule in New Spain, and again the viceroy's quick action and effective measures quelled the insurrection before it got under way.

In like fashion the Indians manifested their restiveness under the harsh and often intolerable life of serfdom they were forced to live. These uprisings were scattered and ill-timed and there was no evidence of leadership or concerted action. Accordingly the viceroy was never hard pressed, as his full military strength was available in each instance. Among the more important of these social revolts was that of the Tequipans of Oaxaca in 1548 and that of the Zapotecans in 1550. The Tequipans, like the Cascanes in Nueva Galicia, retired to mountain fastnesses in their country in a vain attempt to shake off Spanish rule. Men-

[2] Bancroft, *History of Mexico*, II. 538.

doza struck hard at the very outset this time, having learned
a valuable lesson from the Mixton War, and nipped the
movement in the bud by sending Tristán de Arellano with an
overwhelming force against the insurgents. The Zapotecans
enjoyed a brief success in 1550, when they renounced their
allegiance to Spain under the leadership of a chieftain who
claimed to be Quetzalcoatl himself, returned to free them
from oppression. It was one thing to convince the natives
of his supernatural mission and quite another to display the
military skill which his rôle required. A few well-directed
blows delivered with great vigor by the viceroy caused the
movement to collapse and the chieftain to topple from his
exalted position.[3] While none of these outbreaks were serious they were symptomatic of underlying conditions of social
injustice and inequality existent in New Spain.

In 1544, Blasco Núñez de Vela had been sent to Peru
to create a second viceroyalty. His instructions ordered the
strict enforcement of the New Laws within his jurisdiction.
Unlike Mendoza, he was a man of little tact and refused to
listen to the pleas of the angry encomenderos, on the ground
that he had no power even to delay the execution of a royal
order. Peru, as a result, was plunged into a series of profit-
less wars culminating in the assassination of the viceroy.
Gonzalo Pizarro, the bastard son of the colonel of the same
name, profited by the disorder to make himself ruler over
Peru. Fearful of losing this rich area the Spanish government despatched a very able diplomat to right the situation,
the licentiate Pedro de la Gasca. Having been appointed
president of the royal audiencia of Peru, this agent of the
king reached Panamá early in 1547, and called on Mendoza
to furnish him with military aid in his task of wresting the
control of Peru from the hands of Gonzalo Pizarro. Men-

---

[3] Cavo, *Trés siglos de Méjico*, I. 155-156, cited by Bancroft, placed the
blame for this outbreak on the corregidores and the cruel treatment they
accorded their charges.

doza answered very quickly and a force of six hundred men was enlisted. This army was placed under the command of Francisco de Mendoza, son of the viceroy, and Cristóbal de Oñate, of Mixton War fame, was appointed maestro de campo.

In Mexico, before the troops departed, a review was held on March 1, 1547. In order to inspire the soldiers on this occasion Francisco de Mendoza and Hernando de Salazar, the king's factor, "spurred on their horses and attacked each other so furiously that they shivered their lances, and the two horses met head to head and breast to breast, so that from the force of the shock they fell down and were left dead, without, however, the knights being killed, although they were racked and wounded because of the great force of the horses and the encounter which took place." This was the first jousting that took place in New Spain of which an account has come to light.[4] On the eve of the departure of this expeditionary force, probably from Tehuantepec or Navidad,[5] when all was in readiness for the sailing of the armada for Peru, news that Gasca, by the prestige of his commission and the adroitness of his diplomacy, had gained a bloodless victory over the insurgents arrived, and the army was recalled and disbanded.[6] As Mexico City had furnished a large quota of the men who volunteered for the campaign,

[4] F. M. García Icazbalceta, "El primer torneo habido en la Nueva España," in *Hisp. Amer. Hist. Rev.*, V. 749, quotes this description from Torquemada and ventures the opinion that the tourney must have been held in the main square of the city about the middle of 1547.

[5] Diego de Ocampo, a knight and native of Cacares in Castile, is credited with the achievement of having opened the navigation route from New Spain to Peru at his own expense. Santiago in Colima was another possible port, as the viceroy used it for the despatch of most of his exploring expeditions by sea.

[6] One hundred and ninety-two thousand pesos were expended on munitions, provisions, and the accoutrement of the men who volunteered for the enterprize, a heavy expense when one considers that the outcome showed the needlessness of such extensive preparations.

after proper representations had been made, the king rewarded this display of loyalty and zeal for the royal service by conferring on the city the title of "muy noble, insigne y leal" and granted special immunities and privileges to it.[7]

In the region directly north of Mexico, around the modern city of Querétaro, even before the advent of the Spaniards, the Indians had never yielded to outside rule. From the time of the conquest a struggle was in progress against these roving native tribes, who were designated by the Spaniards by the general term Chichimecas.[8] The Spaniards adopted the policy of the former Nahua Confederation, entrusted the subjugation of this area to native caciques, and treated the region as a buffer state. The obscure wars which ensued were largely fought by christianized Mexicans and Otomí under Spanish direction against the Chichimecas and unconverted Otomí of the country about Querétaro. Two native chieftains were conspicuous in the pacification of this frontier, Nicolás de San Luís de Montáñez, created a knight of the order of Santiago and a captain-general in the army by Charles V, and Fernando de Tapía. In 1531 Querétaro was captured and by 1550 San Luís had made it safe for settlement. Mendoza at that time referred to this place as Taxco, the Mexican equivalent of Querétaro, and, in 1551 and 1552, grants of town-lots and orchards were made to incoming settlers. Warfare on this frontier continued under Indian leadership, the caciques being permitted to ride horses and use Spanish weapons, almost down to the close of the century. However, as need of ready communication with the Zacatecas mines made control of this border-

[7] June 20, 1530, Mexico had granted to it the special privileges enjoyed by the city of Burgos in Spain. The new title and privileges were received by the cabildo in the meeting of June 7, 1549.—Rivera Cambas, *Las Gobernantes de Mexico*, I. 32.

[8] A generic term which they applied to all the wild tribes of the north who, in contradistinction to the Aztecs, had no fixed abode.

land essential, no effort was spared by Mendoza and his successors to secure a safe passage through.[9]

On August 8, 1544, in Guadalajara, the oidor Lorenzo de Tejada inaugurated a searching visita, having assembled the leading citizens of Nueva Galicia in his residence on the main square of the town.[10] Francisco Vásquez de Coronado, the governor, Juan de Saldívar, Pedro de Placencia, alcaldes of the town, Diego de Proano, Juan de Ojeda, contadores, Miguel de Ibarra, Juan Sánchez, regidores, Alonso de la Vera, escribano, Cristóbal de Oñate, Juan Michel, Cristóbal Romero, Pedro Quadrago, Diego Hurtado, Juan de Cubia, Bartolomé García, citizens, Francisco de Godoy, Alvaro de Braçamonte, citizens of Compostela, and Juan Fernández, captain in the Villa de Purificación, were present when Tejada's royal provision was read and the alcaldes surrendered their wands of office into his keeping. Two days later he began to call in witnesses to testify concerning the conduct in office of the incumbent, and past officials of Guadalajara,[11] and of the governor and his lieutenant Cristóbal de Oñate.

[9] For a summary of this contest see H. E. Bolton and T. M. Marshall, *The Colonization of North America*, New York, 1921, 39, 58. A rather unsatisfactory account of this confused and relatively little-known series of wars is to be found in Bancroft, *History of Mexico*, II. 539-546.

[10] By a royal order dated in Valladolid, September 7, 1543, Tejada was allowed two ducats a day in addition to his salary as oidor for a period of eighty days, in order to defray the expenses he incurred during the visita.—A. G. I., 48-3-3/30, Residencia que el Lic^do Lorenzo de Tejada oydor de la Audiencia R^l de Nueva España tomo á Franco Vazquez de Coronado Governado que fue de la nueva Galicia y su teniente Xpoval de Oñate, 1544. The legajo contains the complete papers of the visita of all the officials not only in Guadalajara but elsewhere in Nueva Galicia and no further citations to it will be given except in the case of particularly important documents.

[11] Soon after the siege, during the Mixton Revolt, Guadalajara had been moved to a new site south of the Tololotlán. The old city had been abandoned, October 6, 1541, and, on February 11, 1542, town officers had been elected in the new settlement. It was located in the fertile valley of Atemajac, where it grew rapidly into one of the most important centers in New Spain. The visita included the officials who had served in the old Guadalajara.

Alldes q han sido (Miguel de Ybarra, Diego Vásquez, Juan de Villa Royal, Diego de Colis, Hernan Flores, Toribio de Bolaños, Alonso de Castañeda), A. G. I., 48-3-3/30.

Charges of a serious nature, with ample proofs, were brought against Coronado during the days which followed until the fifth of September, when Pedro de Placencia, the twenty-ninth and last witness, was heard. From the information collected under oath in the course of this secret inquiry Tejada drew up a list of thirty-four formal charges, of which a copy was presented to Coronado with a request that he file his answer within a week.[12] Chief among the charges were gross mistreatment of the natives and mishandling of the royal funds. He was accused of having sent heavily loaded Indians all the way to Mexico City and return, driving them so relentlessly that a considerable number died on the march and many more later in the hospital at Patzcuaro; and, moreover, of exacting this toll without remuneration. He was declared to have forced the natives to labor under inhuman conditions, to have taken them from their villages without permission or just cause, to have separated families, and to have taken whatever he wanted from them without compensation. In connection with the journey to Cíbola it was stated that he had left a considerable portion of the country in revolt behind him and had drawn his salary as governor all the time he was absent.[13] In matters of justice, religion, industry, and all the varied interests which should have been his, he was declared to have been remiss and negligent. In one specific instance he even was said to have gone so far as to have used his authority as governor to force Juan de Villa Real on the cabildo of Guadalajara in the place of Colis, the regularly elected regidor. A few days later Coronado returned his replies, admitting most of the charges but pleading extenuating circum-

[12] Cargos que resultan de la residencia secreta contra Francisco Vasquez de Coronado, Guadalajara, September 5, 1544, in Coronado residencia cited above.

[13] " . . . Q sin tener facultad a llebado el salario de gobernador tres años q tubo absente desta provincia q es en cada un año 1500 ducados de buena moneda." *Ibid.*

stances.[14] He was placed in his home under arrest for a time but allowed to go free on an appeal to the Council of the Indies.

Cristóbal de Oñate, who had served as lieutenant governor during the absence of Coronado, was cleared of all guilt by the visitor and, what is quite unusual in a residencia, praised most warmly for his splendid record as an official in the sentencia at the close of his case, September 16, 1544. Tejada fined, suspended from office, and otherwise punished eight of the lesser officials of the province for laxness in office before he closed the official business connected with his task on the following day. On his return to Mexico City he wrote a report of what he had accomplished and sent it, accompanied by a number of constructive suggestions for the betterment of the province, to the king.[15]

The most important remedy for the maladministration of Nueva Galicia advanced by Tejada was the establishment of an audiencia in one of the chief towns, Guadalajara, Compostela, or Purificación.[16] These were the only Spanish towns of any consequence and what is more to the point, were possessed of the only cabildos and jails.

Coronado was replaced in 1545 by Baltasar de Gallegos, who ruled over Nueva Galicia as alcalde mayor until the

[14] The reply bears the title "Descargos Confesantes."

[15] A. G. I., 58-5-8, Carta del Oidor Lorenzo de Tejada al Rey, Mexico, March 12, 1545.

[16] ". . . Parceme que para pacificar aquella probincia y reducirla a la obediencia de vuestra magestad y conserver los naturales e industriarlos en las cosas de Nuestra santa fee catolica que conbiene y es necessario que vuestra magestad probea aquella provincia de audiencia y perlado proprio y que este sea Religioso y se le apliquen pueblos dabalos y provincias de Colima y Cacatula que confinan con Galicia y estan muy lexos desta Real audiencia y con el mismo salario que se da a los oydores desta los quales se podran pagar con lo que se a quitado a gobernadores e oficiales y de algunos Residuos." Ibid. It would seem from this that no bishop had been appointed for New Galicia at this time, although 1544 is usually the date given for the establishment of a bishopric there. The first bishop, Maraver, is referred to in the Sandoval Visita as bishop-elect, so it may be that the generally accepted date is wrong.

recommendation of Tejada was carried into effect by a royal decree, February 13, 1548, ordering the installation of an audiencia at Compostela subordinate to that of Mexico.[17] The oidores Hernando Núñez de la Marcha, Lebrun de Quiñones, and Miguel de Contreras arrived in Mexico in July of 1549, after having been appointed to office in Spain during the month of May of the previous year.[18] They proceeded to Compostela together, where, after a brief survey of the situation, they reported to the king, November 28, 1549.[19]

Just before the arrival of the new administration for Nueva Galicia the town council of Compostela wrote a lengthy report on the actual state of the province and earnestly requested the appointment of Cristóbal de Oñate as governor and captain-general.[20] His earlier services had been so effective that they thought him to be the best man to handle the peculiar difficulties of the local situation. Conditions as described were indeed very grave. The Spaniards, originally attracted to the region by the gold mines within three leagues of the town, had left for Peru and other more prosperous settlements because a plague had carried off all but four thousand natives within a radius of fifteen leagues of Compostela and the mines could no longer be worked at a profit.

[17] Bancroft, *History of Mexico,* II. 547, note 26, collates the printed authorities on the date of founding, jurisdiction, and first oidores.

[18] A fourth, Sepúlveda, died on the voyage over from Spain. Lebrun de Quiñones had arrived in Mexico City in 1548, where he awaited the arrival of his colleagues, as it appears from a list of recommendations to the Emperor on the government of his future charge of November 2, 1548. He had served as an oidor in Española and as governor in Santa Marta, where his conduct had not been above approach. Complete freedom from supervision by Mexico and the fixing of the capital at Guadalajara were the principal points in his communication.—Pacheco y Cárdenas, X. 52-56.

[19] A. G. I., 67-1-18, Carta al Rey de los oydores y Alldes mayores de la Nueba Galicia, Compostela, November 28, 1549.

[20] A. G. I., 67-1-18, Carta á S. Mt de la justicia y rregimio de Compostela, November 1, 1549.

Only the poor and the married remained. It was requested that permission to import six thousand Indians from New Spain with their families be granted by the viceroy so that the land could be cultivated for the purpose of reducing the excessive price of food transported from New Spain and even from Castile. The citizens lamented that theirs was the poorest province in the Indies since the cultivation of the vine had been prohibited; they felt, however, that if Colima were added to it, if his majesty would grant them two thousand Negroes at a moderate price, and if the royal fifth be reduced to a twentieth, they would make it the richest by developing the mines. Even the mines of Zacatecas were declared to be in straitened circumstances owing to their distance from Guadalajara and to their being situated in an uninhabited region. This was a condition which was not rectified until the Otomí barrier was broken in 1550 and a direct road to Mexico City opened.

The new oidores reported to the king, November 28, 1549,[21] on what they thought would be the measures most conducive to the prosperity of the Audiencia. They particularly felt their subordination to Mexico and asked that they be given preëminence, as in the case of the Audiencia de los Confines, and pleaded for more oidores as it would be impossible to keep two out on visitas if one should become ill. They put off the matter of choosing between Guadalajara and Compostela as the seat of their government until the relative merits of the two places could better be ascertained, although a hint at the ultimate triumph of the former is contained in their description of the latter as a town where only about twenty people actually had houses and about one hundred and thirty-one claimed residence be-

[21] A. G. I., 67-1-18, Carta al rey de los oydores y alldes de la Nueba Galicia, Compostela, November 28, 1549.

cause of their encomiendas and offices.[25] To increase the population they requested a repartimiento to attract men capable of bearing arms and repeated the earlier plea for the incorporation of Colima into their jurisdiction. Indian troubles, the need of clergy, the danger of the Negro slaves who were joining the war-like tribes in the north, their action in placing alcaldes mayores in the mines of Zacatecas, the inconvenience of sending silver from there to Compostela to be stamped and a plea that a mint be established in the capital city made up the balance of this account.

The royal officials in Nueva Galicia throw additional light on the progress of affairs in Nueva Galicia in a report to the king at about the same time.[23] They felt that the province was showing distinct evidences of progress and that new mines were being discovered in every direction.[24] Their view was too narrowly restricted to revenue, however, to be given much weight. Like the oidores they felt the superiority of the audiencia of Mexico keenly and said that they had refused to appeal to it up to that time. They advised that the new oidores were inexperienced and that a president to keep them in check would be expedient. An interesting opinion of the viceroy is revealed in their request that if they are to be subjected to a visita, Mendoza be sent rather than some inexperienced and overzealous official.

Simultaneously with complaints against the oidores,[25] news of the unexampled richness of the mines of Zacatecas

---

[22] Bancroft, *History of Mexico,* II. 549, note 32, says the government was transferred to Guadalajara somewhere between 1550 and 1569, the seat of the bishopric being removed at about the same time. The year 1560 seems to be the most reliable date.

[23] A. G. I., 67-1-18, Carta de los oficiales de V. Mt de Nueva Galicia, Compostela, December 20, 1549.

[24] *Ibid.,* "Al presente como dios es servido q las cosas desta provincia vayan de bien en mejor con el describimo de las minas."

[25] A. G. I., 67-1-18, Carta de Juo de Cespedes, Guadalajara, August 25, 1550. He alleged that they were drawing their salaries while neglecting their duties and that the settlers received nothing but "molestias y aggravios" at their hands.

started a rush to that district which almost depopulated Nueva Galicia.[26] This movement of the population and the success of the mining operations almost coincided with the opening of a direct road through Querétaro to Mexico from Zacatecas, which probably means that the improved communication was responsible for the "boom" which resulted.

In the month of April of 1550 the licentiate Hernando Núñez de la Marcha,[27] in the course of a general visitation of New Galicia, lasting from December 9, 1549, to December 7, 1550, visited the Zacatecas country and made a valuable report on what he observed there.[28] He found a total of thirty-four companies owning and operating mines with smelters to extract the metal, with free Indian and slave laborers. The companies were headed by such men as Cristóbal de Oñate, who had thirteen stamp-mills and foundries (yngenios de moler y fundir), one hundred and one slaves, his residence, and a church for the workmen, Juan de Zaldívar, Baltasar de Bañuelos, the oidor Santillán,[29] and the factor Juan de Salazar. In addition there were numerous residences, merchant stores, churches, and an Indian quarter. To take care of the royal interests he appointed, to reside at the mines, Alonso de Roa, as veedor, with two lieutenants, one to serve as contador, the other as treasurer. On the journey, both going and coming, he visited the vari-

[26] A. G. I., 67-1-18, Carta al rey de los Justicias y Regimi⁰ desta Cibdad de Guadalajara. So great was the loss of population—as the encomenderos took their Indians with them—that the four oidores had little work to do and were almost unnecessary.

[27] Sometimes the name of this official is also given as Hernan Martínez de la Marcha.

[28] A. G. I., 66-5-14, Relacion sacada en suma de vesita general hecha por el señor licenciado hernan martinez de la marcha oydor allcalde mayor en la Real Abdiencia que Reside en la cibdad de Compostela.

[29] And this in spite of royal decrees against any member of the audiencias engaging in business. Santillán had a foundry, stamp-mill, a residence for himself, and five houses for his slaves. By a royal cédula, May 7, 1550, he was given a year in which to dispose of his holdings. —A. G. I., 87-6-2, Oficio y parte, Cédula, Valladolid, 227.

ous towns, held trials, inspected boundaries, settled disputes, and inspected the conduct of officials.

New Galicia then, at the close of the viceroy's reign, was a vast district as yet inadequately populated by Spaniards with probably only about five hundred settlers, exclusive of the mines in the neighborhood of Zacatecas. These Spaniards were largely dependent on mining and stock-raising, the actual labor involved falling on the Indians, slave and free, and imported Negro slaves.

Mendoza, from the time that he arrived in New Spain, had tried to secure a measure of social justice for the Indians. He had published on June 30, 1536, his first ordinances regulating their services in the mines.[30] The succeeding years of his rule were given over in large part to efforts to better the harsh lot of the subject population, by reiteration of the laws, by investigations, and by constant support of the Church. This was particularly true of the period immediately following the elimination of the effective provisions in the New Laws.

Before the visitor Sandoval arrived, Mendoza had ordered the inspection of the mint in Mexico City, but as the visitor conducted a regular visita there, the viceroy had postponed his own investigation. However, when Sandoval had returned to Spain he proceeded to examine the work there in person and found every official guilty of fraud of one kind or another even to the extent of debasing the coinage. The situation demanded heroic measures but, as the country needed money badly, he could not dismiss all the officers and close the doors of the establishment, no matter how damning the evidence in the case might be. He wrote to the king, summing up the problem and indicating the various remedies which might prevent a recurrence of the scandal he had

[30] A. G. I., 58-3-8, Hordenanças para la conservacion y buen tratamiento de los naturales libres y eslavos q sirven y andan en las minas de plata. Mexico, June 30, 1536.

uncovered.[31] The chief cause he found in the system whereby men were permitted to hold positions in the mint by merely
possessing a title of office from the king and subletting the
actual work to substitutes who paid for the privilege and,
naturally, would take advantage of any chance to take more
of the silver they coined than was their legal right. In addition to changing this method of appointment, he recommended the payment of the quinto in coin rather than silver,
which could be changed to a lower grade, and that weekly
accountings be made in the presence of all interested parties.

From the time of Mendoza's visit to Nueva Galicia in
1540, to participate in the final organization and start of the
Coronado expedition, he suffered from intermittent fevers
which left him weak in body for a brief period.[32] Soon after
the death of his good friend and fellow-servant of the
king, Archbishop-elect Zumárraga, May 4, 1548, these at-
tacks and other complications so reduced his physical strength
that he could not tend to the affairs of state. A year before
this he had expressed a desire to return to Spain to discuss
a repartimiento of the land which he had made and matters
of finance with the Prince, topics which it was inconvenient
to write about without being prolix and perhaps misunderstood. He also intimated that he had served loyally and
needed some time to look after his own business in Spain.[33]
Despite his declaration that New Spain was now so well
organized that it could do without him, no relief was ac-

[31] A. G. I., 58-3-8, Consulta del Virrey, Mexico, July, 1549.

[32] A. G. I., 2-2-1/1, no. 30, Carta del Virrey, Jacona, April 17, 1540.
At this time he contracted a fever in Colima and wrote to the king that
he was "muy flaco de una calentura continua q tuve en Colima que aun
no fue mas de seis dias me appretto muy rezio a nro S^r plazios q ya
estoy bueno y encamiendado."

[33] "Ya catorze anos que sali de Espana a servir en estas partes, y con-
viene á mis negocios y hazienda visitalla; y asi suplico á V. A. me mande
dar liçençia por el tpo que fuere servido, porque, á Dios gracias, lo de
estas partes está assentado de manera que no Ay de que tener cuydado
mas de los negoçios ordinarios." Carta de D. Ant° de Mendoza, in
Cartas de Indias, pp. 253-55, Mexico, October 30, 1548.

corded. The feeling of discontent which this rebuff produced may well have contributed to the seriousness of his illness.

In 1549, while about to leave Mexico to visit Oaxaca, Mendoza was stricken with an illness which forced him to go to the hot lands for his health. On June 10, 1549, he was still in bed but convalescent.[34] During the period of his indisposition his son Francisco de Mendoza was given charge of the ad interim administration of the affairs of the kingdom, instead of the audiencia as was customary. The home government at the same time was deluged with requests that Francisco be appointed as his father's coadjutor in office and, when the time came, viceroy.[35] The petitioners described Mendoza as being so sick that his ultimate recovery was doubtful and said that even if he did survive he would be left without his former vigor. He was reported to have one leg paralyzed and a pronounced tremor in his hands which would incapacitate him greatly. They asked that Francisco be given official recognition as his father's assistant and in case the viceroy died that he succeed to that office until someone else was appointed. This, they alleged, would insure continuous government by a capable man who had the confidence of the citizens and who had already shown great aptitude for the task.

The king, as soon as he saw the trend of Mendoza's ambitious project to make his office hereditary, hastened to check the movement, but was careful not to offend his faith-

---

[34] *Carta de D. Antonio de Mendoza,* Guastepeque, June 10, 1549, in *Cartas de Indias,* 258-259. He was alert enough at this time to protest against the royal project of abolishing personal service in the mines, which he pointed out was too drastic and would lead to a repetition of the former troubles and a let-down in the production of the silver mines. Such reforms must come slowly, he stated.

[35] The regular and secular clergy and numerous officials sent such letters. A. G. I., 60-4-8. *Carta del Obispo de Tlascala,* Los Angeles, May 24, 1549; *Carta de Fray Domingo de Santa Maria y otros Clerigos en nombre del Orden de los predicadores,* Mexico, June 13, 1549; *Carta de Fray Alonso de la Vera,* Mexico, October 1, 1549, in *Cartas de Indias,* pp. 86-88. The above are just a few of a long list which might be cited.

ful servant. In a communication dated at Peñafiel, May 8, 1550,[36] the government intimated that it had heard of the satisfaction derived from the rule of his son Francisco through letters received from oidores, prelates, and many others and that, while recognizing his loyalty and great services, could not approve this action "por ser cosa nueva y Contra la universal costumbre destos Reynos." In such emergencies the crown held that it was the business of the audiencia to govern and such was to be the practice from then on. His motives were recognized as being pure and he was addressed as "tan servidor nuestro," but a mild rebuke was intended. Thus ended the project to establish a line of Mendoza viceroys in the New World.

The Emperor Charles V at last became aware of the fact that even a good servant like Mendoza could not remain forever in the same place and replied to Mendoza's request for release and permission to return to Spain by appointing as his successor in office Luís de Velasco, a member of the noble house of the constable of Castile and a knight of the Order of Santiago with a long career as a military man and royal servitor behind him. On July 4, 1549, in the city of Brussels, the appointment was officially made[37] and the offices of viceroy and president of the audiencia of Mexico were conferred on Velasco. His salary was fixed at ten thousand ducados beginning the day he should set sail from San Lúcar[38] and an additional sum of 4,000 ducados was provided for his expenses in Seville.[39]

Mendoza was too useful in the New World despite his enfeebled health to be free from service; therefore he was

[36] A. G. I., 87-6-2, Oficio y parte, 231, El Rey á Don Antᵒ de Mendoza.

[37] A. G. I., 87-6-2, Oficio y parte, título de Presidente, título de Visorrey. Brussels, July 4, 1549, LXXXV, LXXXVI.

[38] A. G. I., 87-6-2, Oficio y parte, El Rey al oficiales reales de la Nueba España, Brussels, July 14, 1549.

[39] A. G. I., 87-6-2, Oficio y parte, El Rey a los oficiales reales en Sevilla, Valladolid, August 5, 1549.

promoted to the viceroyalty of Peru. In case he was too ill
to make the journey Velasco was to proceed to that charge
and Mendoza was to continue his rule in New Spain. The
salary of either in case he went to Peru was fixed at 20,000
ducados, with an allowance of 6,000 ducados for the costs of
the voyage.[40] This possible trip of Velasco to Peru from
New Spain was previsioned by the Spanish government and
orders were sent to oidores of New Spain that they were to
provide him with the necessary ships even if those of private
individuals had to be requisitioned, and a trustworthy person
was to be appointed to accompany him to Peru.[41] In case
either of the viceroys became sick so that he could not govern, the audiencia was ordered to govern until he recovered,
and in the event of the death of either, until the king appointed a new representative.[42] Soon after May 8, 1550,[43]
Velasco set sail for New Spain and arrived in Mexico during
the month of November of that year.

Mendoza sent representatives to receive Velasco when
he arrived at San Juan de Ulloa and agreed to meet him in
person at Cholula twenty leagues from Mexico.[44] This
meeting was held "so that they might agree upon what was
best to do and which one of the two was to go to Peru as
governor, considering that his majesty had left charge and
choice of the two in the hands of and subject to the desire

[40] A. G. I., 87-6-2, Oficio y parte, El Rey a los oficiales reales de la
Nueva España, Valladolid, March 11, 1550.

[41] A. G. I., 87-6-2, Oficio y parte, El Rey al Presidente y oydores de
la Nueva España, Valladolid, March 11, 1550.

[42] A. G. I., 87-6-2, Oficio y parte, El Rey al Presidente y oydores de
la Nueva España, Valladolid, March 19, 1550.

[43] Date of the last royal order to him before he left Spain. His
instructions are printed in Pacheco y Cárdenas, XXIII. 520-547 and were
dated in Valladolid, April 16, 1550.

[44] Before the arrival of Velasco an impostor landed who called himself the licentiate Vena and announced himself as a new visitor. He was
accompanied by a beautiful woman companion and for a time defied
detection while spreading consternation among the office-holders.—Bancroft, *History of Mexico*, II. 559, 560.

of the viceroy Don Antonio de Mendoza. It was because of his humbleness that he agreed to take upon himself the voyage to Peru and so that his choice should not be attributed to laziness and cowardice he chose the most dangerous and arduous journey, evidence that he was an obedient and loyal servant of his Majesty."[45]

The two viceroys were accorded splendid receptions on their way to Mexico City in passing through the close-by towns. "Great rejoicing and happiness prevailed, which involved considerable expense and novel entertainments on the part of the natives."[46] After the ceremonials of the transmission of power were over, Mendoza remained in Mexico for some time advising Velasco and preparing for his journey to Peru. During this period he compiled at the king's command a lengthy written instruction for Velasco concerning the government of New Spain and the proper course of action for the incoming viceroy to adopt.[47] This became the model of a long series of such instructions given by each viceroy to his successor.[48] Mendoza, in his instruction, laid particular stress on the conversion of the natives, on real hacienda, on the relations of the viceroy to the various elements in New Spain, and on the promotion of new discovery. It was extremely valuable to Velasco as it was the result of many years of hard-won experience and dealt very explicitly with the problems the new administration was forced to face.

Mendoza, before setting sail for Peru, sent his son, Francisco, on in advance, to determine the state of affairs there.

[45] Obregón, Crónica, cap. V.

[46] Ibid.

[47] Relacion, apuntamientos y avisos, que por mandado de S. M. dió D. Antonio de Mendoza, virey de Nueva-España á D. Luis de Velasco, nombrado para sucederle en este cargo in Pacheco y Cárdenas, VI. 484-515.

[48] These documents are printed in Instrucciones que los Vireyes de Nueva España dejaron à sus Sucesores.

Francisco, after a brief stay in that country returned to Spain to report to the Council of the Indies on behalf of his father.[49] With a small retinue he sailed from one of the ports on the South Sea about the middle of 1551 and, after an uneventful passage, arrived in Lima September 12, of the same year.[50] He was received with regal honors, as his reputation had preceded him, but he modestly refused to enter under a canopy as the city of Lima (Villa de los Reyes) desired.[51]

Mendoza fulfilled the good hopes of the inhabitants of Peru in the brief period of his rule, although greatly handicapped by his poor health. He forgot all the past mistakes of his subjects and endeavored to show no favoritism to any group. He interested himself in the Indians and their conversion to the faith, but felt that some relief from their forced labor in the mines must be afforded first. His son Francisco was sent to the mines of Potosí to see conditions at first hand for his father and every effort to ameliorate harshness in the services required of the natives was made.[52] It was this virtual enslavement which finally brought on the storm which contributed materially to Mendoza's death.

[49] The Marqués de Cañete, who followed Mendoza in Peru, reported that he brought out one Francisco de Mendoza with him in 1554 and there is a grant of a repartimiento of a cocoa plantation to such an individual, but we know that Mendoza's son died in Spain after holding the important positions of governor of the mines of Guadalcanal and captain-general of the galleys.—*Carta del Marques de Cañete al Emperador,* Pacheco y Cárdenas, IV. 96, 110.

[50] Velasco, when he accepted the office of viceroy, had been given to understand that at the end of two years Mendoza would return and he would go to Peru. He states that the journey to Peru had cost Mendoza 210,000 ducados, 6,000 of which were covered by the royal allowance. *Carta de Don Luys de Velasco,* Mexico, July 12, 1552, *Cartas de Indias,* 260-262.

[51] Herrera, *Historia General,* Dec. VIII, lib. VII, cap. 1, 146.

[52] In 1551 Baltasar de Zárate presented the viceroy with a royal cédula granting him the sole right to "traer camellos al Peru" for a period of ten years, in view of the fact that with no personal service they would be most desirable for the carrying of burdens ". . . q dicen algunos, que siendo grande el çelo de D. Antonio de Mendoza para sacar aquellos naturales de todo trabajo." *Ibid.,* dec. VIII., lib. VII. cap., III. 148.

Bartolomé de las Casas, when he heard of the non-enforcement of the royal orders against personal service in Peru, wrote a letter of protest to the head of the Dominican order there which precipitated a crisis. The oidores resolved to promulgate the original order even though it had been revoked. Mendoza was fearful of the results of such an injudicious act and counseled against it but gave the audiencia full liberty of action. With great rashness these officials defied the public sentiment of Peru and promulgated the obnoxious orders of June 23, 1552. Discontent was immediate and widespread and the cabildos met to find a remedy. Some petitioners of the cabildo in Lima secured permission to protest to the viceroy, but he was too ill to hold an audience, and the audiencia met their advances with rudeness.[53] When he heard of this ill-advised action Mendoza ordered his secretary Pedro de Avendaño to write the king a full account of the happenings. A month later, July 21, he died and the disorders he had predicted broke out shortly thereafter.[54] His body was buried with full honors in the cathedral next to the conqueror Pizarro. Thus the New World was deprived of the services of its first great administrator.

[53] They stated that they obeyed only the King and the Council of the Indies and would not "dar lugar á juntas, ni congregaciones de pueblos, que es adonde, por la Maior parte, se fraguan las rediciones." *Ibid.,* dec. VIII, lib. VII, cap. III. 189.

[54] *Relacion cierta y breve de los desasosiegos sucedidos en Perú despues de la muerte del Señor Visorey D. Antonio de Mendoza* in Pacheco y Cárdenas, III. 246-271. When Mendoza was sick and dying the decree of the audiencia was brought to him for his signature but he refused, saying it was inconvenient and that its execution should be suspended until he could go to Spain and consult the king.

CONCLUSION

When the career of Antonio de Mendoza is summed up, his imposing record as a pioneer administrator and the part he played in creating and sustaining the colonial empire of Charles V strike the attention most forcibly. One needs but to consider that the superstructure of Spain's three hundred years of rule in New Spain rested on the sure foundation which he laid to appreciate the importance of his achievement. That his immediate successors in office were likewise able men who continued his policies and that they conserved what he relinquished into their keeping no more detracts from the lustre of his performance than the fact that capable and courageous navigators followed Columbus deprives him of the credit for his first voyage. It is as an administrator, then, the first, and, from many points of view, the ablest, of a long line of imperial agents in the New World, that he should be remembered.

Mendoza's success was in the main due to three things: his prestige, his statesmanship, and the reasonable use he made of the wide powers of his office. He came to New Spain a great nobleman, possessed of ample wealth, from the immediate circle about the Emperor, to be his personal representative. No later word or act of his lessened the original respect this inspired. On the contrary, he bent every effort and made use of every means to enhance the prestige of his person and, by so doing, to establish a tradition of proper awe for authority. His bodyguard, his palace, and his open hospitality were all elements which contributed to this end. So well did he reflect the Imperial splendor in his entertainments that years afterward, when alluding to the celebration of the peace with France in 1538, the bluff veteran Bernal

Díaz was moved to remark: "They decided to hold great festivals and rejoicings, and they were such that it seems to me I have not seen others of the same quality [even] in Castile . . . "[1] The reputation he acquired in this manner served the viceroys well, although in the end it proved to be too costly for men who were without private fortune and therefore were forced to lavish state money on such functions in a later age when great achievement no longer existed to accompany the grand manner.

Mendoza's statesmanship is mirrored in his ordinances, his recommendations to the king, and his instructions to his successor Velasco. His mining regulations, his laws calculated to moderate the services of the Indians, his encouragement of the clergy, his schools, and his provisions for defense show him to have been a man of broad vision for his time and a prudent servant of the state. By nature firm and just, he knew when to yield to popular clamor in order to avoid destruction, not only of his own influence but of the new society. He never antagonized the Spanish settlers un-

---

[1] Bernal Diaz, *True History,* V. 188. His description of the happenings on this occasion is most vivid and what he writes concerning the viceroy's banquet is worthy of quotation. He relates "that supper was given by the viceroy, and this feast took place in the corridors of the Royal Palace, which were transformed into bowers and gardens . . . and for each seat of honor there were stewards and pages and a full and well-arranged service." Then, after mentioning all manner of pasties, salads, birds, and rather exotic dishes served, "together with much music of singers . . . and trumpetry and all sorts of instruments, harps, guitars, violas, flutes, dulcimers, and oboes, especially when the stewards served the cups . . . to the ladies," he speaks of the *pièce de resistance,* consisting of huge pasties filled with live quail and rabbits which were brought on and afforded much merriment when these animals escaped. There were jesters and versifiers at this remarkable dinner also and the redoubtable Diaz dwells on fountains of white wine, Indian sherry and red wine and other store of bottles. "Over three hundred men and more than two hundred women were present and the banquet lasted until two hours after midnight, when the ladies cried out that they could stay no longer at table, and others were indisposed." Everything was served on gold and silver and none of it was lost, for the major-domo, Agostín Guerrero, had placed an Indian on guard over each piece of plate. Silver salt cellars, many table cloths, napkins, and knives disappeared, but that was not regarded as serious. *Ibid.,* V. 188-197.

necessarily but rather chose to obtain his ends by diplomacy, management, and, if necessary, on occasion by intrigue. The one great failure of his administration, the failure of the laws emancipating the natives, was in reality an evidence of his common sense, for he saw that the alternative to Indian labor was revolt and the loss of New Spain, since his own countrymen were too few, too little acclimated, and, in general, regarded work as degrading. He chose to keep New Spain and to do his utmost to protect the Indian from want or inhumanity.

The powers he enjoyed were not abused but rather wielded in useful service. In his administration the encomenderos were brought under control, the royal authority established, and the ground laid for a period of peace. He gave a new impulse to industry and agriculture; cattle multiplied extraordinarily, new mines were opened, and exploration pushed far into the unknown north, while at the same time his vessels plied the Pacific Ocean. Under his direction the conquests of Nueva Galicia and Yucatán were extended and consolidated and the remnants of disorder which were the heritage of the conquest were almost completely eradicated. In brief, confusion gave way to the order and system of a regular state, and Mexico of the conquest became Mexico of the viceroys.

BIBLIOGRAPHY

MANUSCRIPT MATERIAL

I. Archivo General de Indias. (A. G. I., abbreviation used in the text.)
   A. Patronato Real section.
      1-1-1/20
         Carta escrita por fr. Gerónimo de Santistevan a Dn Anto de Mendoza en la q le relaciona la perdida de la armada q salio en 42 para las yslas de Poniente a el cargo de Ruy Lopez de Villalobos.
            No. 10. Relacion del descubrimiento q hizo Juo Rodriquez navigando por la contra costa del mar del Sur hecha por Juan Paez.
      1-1-2/21
            No. 72. Cartas de Nuño de Guzman sobre la Jornada q hizo en 1530 y 1531, sobre q restituyere ciertas armas y sobre descubrimiento del mar del Sur y Nueva Galicia.
         Ynformacion del virrey de Nueva España Dn Anto de Mendoza de la gente q va a poblar la Nueba Galicia con Francisco Vásquez de Coronado Gobernador della. Compostela, February 21, 1540.
         Asiento y capitulacion de compania que celebraron Dn Anto Mendoza Virrey de la Nueva España y el Adelantado Pedro de Alvarado sobre el descubrimiento q este ofrecio hazer en el mar del Sur. Tiripitío, November 29, 1540.
         Processo del Marques del Valle, Nuño de Guzman y los adelantados don Pedro de Alvarado y Don Hernando de Soto y el Licdo Lucas Vasquez de Ayllon sobre el descubrimiento que hicieron de la Nueva Galicia y tierras del mar del Sur. 1541.
            No. 297. Carta de la Nueva tierra de Santa Cruz descubierta por Hernan Cortes el dia 3 de Mayo de 1535 de promovieron Nuño de Guzman, Pedro de Alvarado y otros. Se acompaña el acta de posesion.
      1-1-1/23
         Relacion del viage que hizo Ruy Lopez de Villalovas desde la Nueba España a las Islas del Poniente el año de 1542 por orden del virrey Don Anto de Mendoza.

Cédula al virrey Don Ant⁰ de Mendoza, Brujas, November 9, 1545.

1-1-2/28

No. 72. Carta de Nuño de Guzman sobre descubrimiento del Mar del Sur y Nueva Galicia, diario que escribe de este viage y un plano siquiendo dicho descubrimiento. 1540.

2-2-1/1

No. 30. Carta del virrey, Jacona, April 17, 1540.

No. 63. Copia de todas las ordenes e instruciones que se han dado a D. Ant⁰ de Mendoça quando fue nombrado virrey de Nueva España, Barcelona, April 17, 1535.

No. 67. Ordenanzas hechas por el Virrey de la Nueva España Dⁿ. Ant⁰ de Mendoza sobre el buen trat⁰ de los Yndios. Mexico, June 30, 1536.

No. 68. Obligacion q hace Martin Cortes al virrey de Nᵃ España de plantar en las provincias de Guapocingo Cholula y Tlascala 100,000 pies de morales en 15 años para la Crianza de la seda y dice que fue el primero q la crio en aquel reyno. Mexico, October 6, 1537.

No. 70. Relacion del Virey de Nueva Espana D. Antonio de Mendoza sobre las servicios personales que hacian los Indios de aquellas provincias, 1537.

No. 73. Ordenanzas hechos en la ciudad de la Vera Cruz para el buen gobernacion desta ciudad se Aprovaron ciertos capitulos dellas por el Virrey D. Ant⁰ de Mendoça. Mexico, July 3, 1539.

No. 76. Ordenanzas hechas por el Virrey de Nueva Espana D. Ant⁰ de Mendoza sobre prohibicion de todo juego de Naypes. 1539.

No. 77. Real provision por la que se senala al virrey de Mexico Dⁿ. Ant⁰ de Mendoza 15 leguas de termino para entender en negocios civiles y criminales. Madrid, October 24, 1539.

No. 77. Carta de Joan de Alvear en no'be de cavildo Justicia y regimiento de la Ciudad de Mexico. (Mexico, 1592?)

Relacion de Bᵉ de Zarate. 1543.

2-2-2/2

No. 3. Ordenanzas hechas en la Ciudad de Megico por su Virrey D. Ant⁰ de Mendoza sobre el Modo de labrar generos de seda en aquella ciudad. 1542.

No. 15. Tetimonio informacion hecho en Mexico
contra Luis Roman y otros sobre haber tratado de robar
las minas de Tasco matiar al virrey y ministros de
aquella audia y levantase con el gobierno.   1550.
2-2-2

No. 5. Minuta de los despachos que el secretario
Samano enbia al Lic^{do} Fran^{co} Tello de Sandoval sobre
puntos de buen gobierno.   1543.

No. 10. Testimonio de la comision que se dio a Gonzalo de Aranda para las cuentas de Real Hacienda en
Nueva España y otros puntos de buen gobierno.
2-2-5

No. 12. Cartas del Lic^{do} Salmeron de Mexico; January 22, 1531; March 30, 1531.

No. 15. Carta al consejo del Lic^{do} Quiroga sobre la
venida del obispo de Santo Domingo.   Mexico, August
14, 1531.

No. 17. Cartas de Nuño de Guzman, Mexico, January 15, 1531, to the council; January 15, 1531, to the
king; June 7, 1531.

No. 21. Cartas del Obispo de Santo Domingo.
Mexico, April 30, 1532; July 10, 1532; September 8,
1532; September 20, 1532; November 3, 1532.

No. 22. Carta de Nuño de Guzman, Compostela,
July 12, 1532.

No. 24. Cartas originales de Nuño de Guzman.
Santiago de los Valles, March 10, 1534; Valle de Bande-
ras, March 9, 1535; June 8, 1535.

No. 25. Carta del Obpo de Guatemala, Santiago,
February 20, 1542.

No. 27. Cartas a la Emperatriz de Dⁿ Anto de Mendoza, sobre Cabeza de Vaca y puntos de buen gobierno.
Mexico, 1537.

No. 30. Cartas del Obispo de Guatemala. Mexico,
October 24, 1537; November 10, 1540; Mechoacán,
November 30, 1540.

No. 31. Carta a S.M^t. del virrey Don Anto de Mendoça. Jacona, April 17, 1540.

No. 35. Carta de obpo de Guatimala, Mexico, February 20, 1542.

No. 41. Cartas originales del obispo de Mexico al
Emperador y Principe. Mexico, March 31, 1547; December 4, 1547; February 18, 1548; May 15, 1548;
June 2, 1548 (advise of his death from officials, July
13, 1548.)

2-5-1/22

Traslado de una carta que el Virrey de Nueba España escribio a Miguel Ruiz Avisandole que Ju⁰ de Anasco iba a tierra firme en busca de unos Cosarios franceses a fin de ayudarle en la comision. 1544.

B. Justicia.

47-4-20/15

El licenciado Diego de la Torre juez de residencia en la Nueva España con Gonzalo Lopez, Cristoval Oñate vecinos de Mexico y salvador Martel vecino de compostela sobre derecho a cierta numero de esclavos cavallos yeguas y otras cosas. 1537.

47-4-28/23

No. 3. Franc⁰ Montejo con el adelantado Pedro de Alvarado sobre ciertas encomiendas. 1541.

47-4-34/29.

El obispo de Mechuacan Vasquez de Quiroga con el obispo dean y cavildo de Mexico sre demarcacion de estos obispados y diezmos que a ellos pertenece. 1542.

47-4-36/31

Gonzalo Zerezo Alguaçil Mayor de la Audiencia de Mexico con Juan de Samano Alguazil Mayor de Aquella ciudad sre las preheminencias de sus oficios. 1543.

47-6-8/3

El fiscal con Martin Ibañez y Hernani residente en Mexico sre que pagase de sus Mercaderias los derechos que estaban impuesto para la obra del muelle de San Juan de Ulua. 1539.

47-6-13/43

Residencia tomada el ano de 1535 y 1536 a los Lic⁴⁰ˢ Juan Salmeron Alonso Maldonado Francisco de Loaysa oidor de aquella audiencia juez nombrada para este efeto.

48-1-1/23-48-2-20/2 (inclusive)

Visita hecha el año de 1543-47 al virrey de la Nueva España y Presidente de la real Audiencia de Mexico Dⁿ Antonio de Mendoza, a los oidores de ella, al fiscal, a los alguaçiles mayores, a los relatores, a los escribanos de camara a los abogados, a los regidores e los alcaldes, a los ess ⁿ⁰ˢ del numero y demas oficiales de Real hacienda, contador, tesorero, fator, y a sus tenientes y oficiales sobre el cumplimiento de sus deveres por el Lic⁴⁰ Dⁿ Francisco Tello de Sandoval del consejo de S. M. visitador General de la Nueva España.

48-1-1/23

El Marques de Valle con el Visorrey de la Nueva España Don Antonio de Mendoza sobre la residencia que pide se le mande tomar. Nota: se unira a la Residencia del dicho visorrey. Valladolid, July 6, 1543.

Ynterrogatorio del Marques del Valle presentado en Valladolid a XIX de Jullio de 1543.

48-1-2/24

Fees de la guarda años 36 hasta 46.

Visita hecha a Juᵒ Alonzo de Sosa Tesorero, Mexico, May, 1547.

Cargos que resultan de la visita secreta contra el muy illustre señor Antonio de Mendoza, Mexico, June 21, 1546.

Visita hecha a Rodrigo Muñoz, teniente de Tesorero de la ciudad de Vera Cruz.

48-1-4/26

Testimonio de varios autos sacado por orden del Licᵈᵒ Tello de Sandoval.

Diego de Esquivel con Francᵒ Maldonado sobre ciertas casas. Mexico, December 12, 1542.

Descargos del oidor Tejada, Mexico, December 20, 1546.

Relacion de los cargos que se le podian hacer al fiscal. Mexico, 1547.

Testimonios y pleitos se unirar a la visita de la Audiencia, Mexico, 1547.

El fiscal de S. Mᵗ con Don Antonio de Mendoza sobre la visita que se le tomo.

Memorial de los cargos q hizo el muy Magᶜᵒ Senor Licenᵈᵒ tello de Sandoval del consejo de su magestad al Licᵈᵒ Tejada oydor del audiencia Real de Mexᶜᵒ.

La acusacion puesta contra el Licᵈᵒ Sandoval de consejo Rˡ de las Indias por el Licᵈᵒ Tejada.

Cargos que resultan de la visita secreta contra el Licenciado Alonzo Maldonado oydor que fue del audiᵃ Real de Mexico y los descargos q por su parte fueron dade a ellos.

48-1-5/27

Interrogatorio de los descargos del Señor Visorrey (con las preguntas de Johan de Salazar.)

Probança fha por parte del yllmo Señor Visorrey en las minas de Tasco. April 14, 1547.

Provança fha por parte del yllmo Señor Visorrey en la Nueva Galicia.

48-1-6/28

Probança de Don Antonio de Mendoza hecha en Mechuacan. 1546.

Probanças que dio el Virrey de la Nª Eª Dⁿ Antonio de Mendoza en la visita que hizo el lizdo Dⁿ Fr Tello de Sandoval del Consejo de Indias, 1546-1547.

Provança hecha en la provª de Zacatula. 1547.

Probanças que dio el Virrey de la Nª Eª Dⁿ Antonio de Mendoza en Colima (pa lo de los Navios de Navidad) 1547.

48-1-7/29

Probanza hecha en la Ciudad de la Vera Cruz por Franco Duarte en nombre del Virrey Dⁿ Antonio de Mendoza. 1546.

Probanza hecha en las minas de Çunpango y su jurisdicion por parte del yllmo Señor Don Antonio de Mendoza vissorey de nueba España.

Probanza hecha en las minas de plata de Zultepeque por el señor virrey Dⁿ Antonio de Mendoza.

Probanza hecha en la Ciudad de Antequera por el Sor Virrey Don Antonio de Mendoza. 1547.

Probanza por parte del virrey Dⁿ Antonio de Mendoza hecha en la ciudad de Santiago de Guatemala.

48-1-8/30

Probanza hecha en la Cibdad de los Angeles en nombre de yllmo Sor Visorrey desta Nueva España por los descargos de la visita.

Probanza del yllmo Senor Dⁿ Antonio de Mendoza Vissorey y gobernador en esta nueva España. En Mexico, religiosos.

Probanza hecha en la cibdad de los Angeles en nombre del yllmo Sr Vissorey. Los Angeles, January 8, 1547-February 9, 1547.

Probanza de descargos fecha con rreligiosos por parte del yllmo Senor Don Antonio de Mendoza, February 23, 1547-March 21, 1547.

48-1-9/31

Provanza del virrey de la Nueva España don Antonio de Mendoza, testigo de Francisco Vasquez de Coronado. (IX) Mexico, January 18, 1547.

Probanza del virrey de la Nueva España Don Antonio de Mendoza hecha en Mexico por Johan de Salazar. 1546-1547.

48-1-10/32

Visita a el fiscal de la R^l Audiencia de Mexico el lizdo
Cristoval de Benavente a los relatores y a los escribanos
de cámara y a sus oficiales a el Alguaçil Mayor y sus
tenientes por el Lic^{do} Dⁿ Franco Tello de Sandoval
visitador general (Processo de la visita secreta contra
los oficiales de Addia rreal de Mexico).

48-1-11/33

Gabriel de Castellanos de la Ciudad de Mexico con Juan
de Samano Alguaçil Mayor de la dha Ciudad sobre cierta
acusacion.

El fiscal de S. M. con Gonzalo Terezo Alguazil Mayor
de la cibdad de Mejico sobre el nombramiento de los
oficios de Alguaçiles.

Visita a Pedro Nuñez Alguacil Mayor de Mexico. 1544.

Visita a Alonzo Perez Tamayo teniente de Alguazil
Mayor de Mexico por el Lic^{do} Fr Tello de Sandoval.
1544.

Proceso de la residencia contra Franco Lopez de Archoleta teniente de Alguazil Mayor. August, 1544.

Los cargos que se hazen a Franco Lopez de Archoleta
por la residencia se puesta del tpo q fue teniente de
Alguazil mayor en esta cibdad de Mexico. 1544.

Proceso de la Residencia contra Diego de Piñeda teniente
q fue del Alguazil mayor, 1544.

Proceso de la Residencia contra Lope de Valdes teniente
q fue del Alguazil mayor. 1544.

Proceso de la Residencia contra diego de Puelles teniente
q fue del Alguazil mayor. 1544.

Proceso de la residencia contra Juan de Calahorra
teniente de Alguazil Mayor de Mexico. 1544.

Proceso de la residencia contra Franco Hernandez
teniente de Alguazil M^{or} de Mexico. 1544.

Proceso de la residencia contra Juan Sanchez teniente
de Alguaçil Mayor de Mexico. 1544.

Visita a Juan de Segovia teniente de Alguacil Mayor de
Mexico por el señor visitador. 1545.

Proceso de la visita contra Gonzalo Cerezo Alguazil
Mayor de la abdiencia de Mexico del tiempo que tuvo a
su cargo dicho oficio por el S^r visitador. 1546.

Cargos q resultaron de la visita contra Lope de Valdes
teniente de alguaçil mayor de Mexico. 1546.

Visita a Juan de Samano alguazil mayor y regidor de
Mexico. 1547.

Proceso de la residencia contra Ju⁰ de Samano alguazil mayor por el Lic^do Fr Tello de Sandoval.

Proceso criminal de Gabriel de Castellanos con Juan de Samano Alguazil mayor de Mexico sobre los prejucios q le havia originado.

48-1-12/34

Visita a Bernardino Vasquez de Tapia V⁰ y Regidor de Mexico del tiempo q fue allde ordinario en la dha Ciudad. 1544.

Libro de la Residencia secreta de las Justicias desta cibdad de Mexico. 1544.

Visita a los alcaldes mayores y ordinarios de Mexico a los Alguaçiles Mayores y sus tenientes y demas ministros del distrito. 1544.

Visita a Fran^co de Terrazas del tiempo q fue allde en la cibdad de Mexico. 1545.

Visita a Luis Marin del tpo q fue Alcalde Ordinario de Mexico. 1545.

Proceso de la Residencia contra Ju⁰ Xaramillo Alcalde q fue de la cibdad de Mexico. 1545.

Visita a Luis de la Torre allde de la Cibdad de Mexico por el Lic^do D^n Fran^co Tello de Sandoval. 1545.

Proceso de rresidencia con Juan Perez de boca negra del tpo q fue allde en esta Ciudad. 1545.

48-1-13/35

Visita a Alonzo de Bazan ald^e ordinario de la Ciudad de Mexico por el Lic^do Fran⁰ Tello de Sandoval. 1546.

Proceso de rresidencia con Ant⁰ de la Cadena del tpo q fue allde Hordinario en la cibdad de Mex^co. 1545.

Proceso de la residencia con Juan de Burgos del tpo que fue alld ordinario de Mexico. 1546.

Visita a los alcaldes de Mexico Geronimo de Medina y Gonzalez Lopez por al Lic^do Fran^co Tello de Sandoval. 1546.

Proceso de Residencia con Gonzalo Lopez del tpo q fue Ald^e en esta Cibdad de Mexico. 1546.

48-1-14/36

Visita a Agustin Guerrero Chanciller de la Real Abdia de Mexico y contra Ju⁰ de Salazar su oficial y teniente y los descargos por su parte dados. 1546.

Visita a Ant⁰ de Almoguer Registrador de la Real Abdia de Mexico. 1546.

Cargos que resultaron de la visita secreta contra Franco Ramirez Procurador de la Real Audiencia de Mexico. 1546.

Los cargos y descargos de Hernando de Herrera relator de la audiencia de Mexico. 1546-1547.

Visita a Anto de Turcios Escribano de camara de la Real Audiencia de Mexico. 1546.

Visita al commendador Juan de Baeza Herrera escribano de camara de la Real Abdiencia de Mexico, por el Lic Tello de Sandoval. 1546.

Visita a los abogados de la cibdad de Mexico el licdo Diego Tellez el licdo Bartolome Melgarejo el licdo luys Rodriguez el licdo Nicolas Aleman el licdo Hernando Caballero. 1544-1547.

Visita a los Relatores, Hernando de Herrera, Juan Alvarez de Castañeda. Mexico, December 30, 1546-March 21, 1547.

Visita a Franco Ramirez procurador de la Real Abdia. Mexico, November 19, 1546.

Visita a Anto Almoguer registrador de la Real Audiencia de Mexico. Mexico, November 20, 1546.

Visita a Agustin Guerrero, Chanciller de la Real Abdia de Mexico y a Juo de Salazar su teniente. Mexico, November 20, 1546.

Visita a el Doctor Juan Alvarez de Castañeda Relator de la Real Abdiencia de Mexico. 1547.

48-1-15/37

Visita a los Escribanos de la Ciudad de Mexico por el Licdo Dn Francisco Tello de Sandoval. 1545-1546. (Entire legajo.)

48-1-16/38

Visita a los escribanos de la Ciudad de Mexico por el Licdo Dn Francisco Tello de Sandoval. 1545-1546. (Continued.)

48-1-17/39

Visita a los escribanos de la Ciudad de Mexico por el Licdo Dn Francisco Tello de Sandoval. 1545-1546. (Concluded, the acts of forty-seven officials examined in the visitas included in the three legajos.)

48-1-18/40

Visita a Vicencio Corzo Alde de la Villa de Santistevan del Puerto de la Provincia de Panuco y a Andres de Valladolid Alguaçil por el Licdo Tello de Sandoval. 1544.

Visita a los Alcaldes y regidores de la villa de Santistevan del Puerto de la Provincia de Panuco por el Licdo Tello de Sandoval. 1544-1546.

Pedro Becos contra Martin de San Juan, Benito de Cuenca, Juan Acedo y otros Alcaldes y Regidores de la Villa de Panuco—salio el fiscal y entiendo en estra causa el juez visitador Dn Francisco Tello de Sandoval. 1545.

Juan de Becos = con el cabildo de Panuco = sobre agravios = Juez el Licdo Dn Francisco Tello de Sandoval. 1545.

48-2-19/41

Visita a Alonzo Perez Tamayo Alcayde de la carcel de Mexico por el Licdo D. Franco Tello de Sandoval. 1545.

Visita a Franco Hernandez Alcayde de la Carcel Rl de Mexico. 1546.

Visita a Bernaldino de Albornoz Alcayde de los atarazanas de la ciudad de Mexico y regidor por el Licdo Dn Franco Tello de Sandoval. 1546.

Visita a Juan Fernandez Berdejo Carcelero Alias alcayde en la de corte de Mexico. 1546.

Visita a Juan Xaurez Alde Mor de las minas de Ayoteco de la Provincia de Chiautla. 1545-1546.

48-2-20/2

El fiscal = sobre denuncia de dos esclavos = Juez de visita El Lic Tello de Sandoval. Mexico, 1544.

De oficio y el fiscal contra Rodrigo Alonso Maestre sobre haber llevado a la Nueva Espana dos esclavas Moriscas sin licencia. 1544.

Visita a el cabildo de Mexico por el Licenciado Dn Franco Tello de Sandoval. 1546.

Don Anto de Mendoça Virrey de la Nueba Espana sobre la recusacion q puso al señor Licdo Tello de Sandoval del Consejo de Indias. 1546.

Visitacion de la cassa de la Moneda de la Ciudad de Mexico hecha por el Señor Visitador Año de 1546.

Visita a Estevan Franco fundidor y ensayador de la Casa de Moneda de Mexico por el Licdo Dn Franco Tello de Sandoval del Consejo de Indias. 1546.

Proceso del fiscal con Sebastian de Moscoso sobre una morisca q vino sin Licencia de S. Mt. 1546.

Proceso de oficio de Rodrigo Cordero (sic) 1546.

Proceso de residencia de Ruy Gonzalez regidor. Mexico, 1546.

Mandamiento del Juez visitador a el Alcàde Ordinario
de Mexico Alo Garcia Bravo para q hiciese diligencia del
pasadero de Juan de Salamanca meztizo y se lo enviase.
1547.
Proceso de residencia de Anto de Carabajal rregidor.
Mexico, 1547.
Resultas de la Visita de don Antonio de Mendoza, Virrey de la Nueva Espana. 1545-1547.
(1) La recusacion del virrey. Valladolid, May 7.
1548.
(2) Poder e sostitucion a sebastian Rodriquez.
Valladolid, May 7, 1548.
(3) Peticion que pide que jure de calunia y la cedula
de deposito. Valladolid, May 17, 1548.
(4) Carta de Agustin Guerrero y Juan de Aguilar
al Consejo. Valladolid, May 23, 1548.
(5) Pusiciones que ha de responder el senor licenciado tello de sandoval. Valladolid, May 28,
1548.
(6) Juramento y depuso del licenciado Tello de
Sandoval Cerca de la Recusacion que le fue
puesta por parte de Antonio de Mendoça. Valladolid, June 2, 1548.
(7) Peticiones de Agustin de Guerrero y Juan de
Aguilar al consejo. Valladolid, June 13, 1548;
June 20, 1548; August 13, 1548.
(8) Mandamiento de los señores del consejo Real de
Yndias. Valladolid, September 14, 1548.
(9) Recusacion General puesta par parte del virrey
don Antonio de Mendoça con mandamiento de
los señores del consejo Real de yndias. Valladolid, September 22, 1550.
(10) Mandamiento de los señores del consejo Real
de Yndias. Valladolid, July 29, 1555.
El thesorero Juan Alonso de Sosa sobre la accusacion q
ha puesto en el señor Licdo Sandoval. Mexico, 1550.
La ciudad de Mexico con el señor Fiscal sobre excesos q
cometio en una visita q hizo Diego Ramirez en varios
pueblos de Yndios. Mexico, 1554.
48-3-1/17. (Guadalajara.)
El fiscal con Frano Vasquez de Coronado vecino de la
ciudad de Mexico sre malos tratamientos hechos a los
Indios de diferentes pueblos. 1553.

48-3-3/30

Residencia q el Liz^do Lorenzo de Tejada oydor de la Audiencia de Nueva España tomo a diego de colis alde ordinario que fue de la ciudad de Guadalajara en el Nuevo Reyno de Galicia. 1544.

Residencia que el Lic^do Lorenzo de Tejada Oydor de la Audiencia R^l de Nueva España tomo a Franco Vazquez de Coronado Gobernador q fue de la Nueva Galicia y a su teniente Xpoval de Oñate y demas oficiales. Nueva Galicia, 1544.

52-1-1/10

Informacion hecha en la ciudad de Mexico a instancia de los mineros de Zumpango Tasco y Zultepeque acerca de los crecidos gastos que importavan al labor y beneficiar las minas solicitando rebaja de derechos. 1540.

52-1-5/2

El fiscal con D^n Garcia Ramirez de Cardeñas Vecino de Madrid sobre los escesos que cometio cuando fue el maestro de campo a la jornada a Cibola desde la provincia de Cuyuacan en Nueba Espana. 1551.

El fiscal con D^n Bernardino de Mendoza Capitan General de las Galeras de España sobre paga de una libranza en las caxas de Nueva España. 1550.

51-6-5/22 (Mexico)

Pedro de Membrilla residente en Madrid con Fran^o Rincon vecino de Mexico sobre derecho a los oficios de fundidor y ensayador de la casa de moneda de Mexico. 1544.

C. Consejo

58-3-8

Hordenanças para la conservacion y buen tratamiento de los naturales libres y esclavos q sirven y andan en las minas de plata, Mexico, June 30, 1536.

Consulta del Virrey. Mexico, July, 1549.

58-5-8

Carta del Presidente y oidores. Mexico, May 11, 1544.

Carta del Lic^do Tejada. Mexico, May 23, 1544.

Carta de Gonzalo de Aranda al Rey. Mexico, May 30, 1544.

Carta al Rey del Presidente y oidores de la r^l audi^a de Mexico. Mexico, June 1, 1544.

Carta del oidor Lorenzo de Tejada sobre la residencia q se mande tomar en la Nueba Galicia. Mexico, March 12, 1545.

Carta del Virrey y Oydores del Rl Audiencia de Mexico. Mexico, March 17, 1545.

Carta al rey del Presidente e oydores de Mexico. Mexico, March 17, 1545.

Carta del Licenciado tejada oydor de la audiencia Real de la Nueva España. Mexico, March 12, 1545.

Carta del Licenciado Tello de Sandoval, visitador de Nueva España al Principe Don Felipe. Mexico, September 19, 1545.

Consulta de la Audiencia de la Nueba España de XX de Hebrero de 1548.

Carta de los Oydores del Real Abdia de Mexico sobre los enfermedades del virrey. Mexico, March 30, 1549.

Carta del Oidor Gomez de Santillan. Mexico, January 20, 1551.

58-5-9

Carta de la Audiencia de Mexico sobre hordenanças para descubrimientos de los minas y metales de plata oro. Mexico, December 10, 1577.

Carta de Lope de Samaniego al Rey. Mexico, December 1, 1537.

Carta de Gonzalo de Aranda al rey. Mexico, May 30, 1544.

58-6-10

Cartas al Rey de Geronimo Lopez. Mexico, February 25, 1545; March 1, 1545; September 10, 1545; March 1, 1547.

Rl orden a los individuos q componen dha Audiencia de Mexico q entienden ni armadas ni descubrimientos ni q tengan granjerias de ganados mayores ni menores labranzas ni mercaderias. Pregonado en Mexico, 1549.

59-6-23

Informaciones de oficio y parte. Baltazar de Obregon, Informacion de Servicios. Mexico, April 12, 1584.

60-2-16

Carta a S. M. de los religiosos Augustinos de Nueba España dandole cuenta de una cofradia q fundaban y de los estatuos o reglas de ella. Mexico, December 15, 1537.

Parecer de los frayles de San Domingo. Mexico, May 4, 1544.

Carta del Obispo de la Nueva Galicia Gomez de Maraver. Compostela, June 1, 1544.

Carta de Joan de Zarate obispo de Antequera al Rey.

Antequera, December 26, 1547.

60-3-17

Cabildo secular de Mexico, supplicacion que se de cedula para q se puedan meter a trabajar en la casa de moneda de Mexico los negros q fueron necesarios para labrar la plata. April 15, 1537.

60-3-23

Cartas de los oficiales de la Nueva España. February 16, 1537; September 20, 1538.

Ordenes del virrey Don Antonio de Mendoza sobre la casa de Moneda. Mexico, May 9, 1541.

Carta del cabildo secular de Mexico visto en el consejo. Mexico, January 20, 1543.

Cartas de Thesorero Juo de la Sosa y de los oficiales Rls de Nueva España. Mexico, March 12, 1545; March 15, 1545; September 6, 1545.

Abtos hechos ante los juezes de las cuentas del hazienda Rl de la Nueba España cerca de las dichas cuentas. Mexico, May 7, 1547.

Carta del contador Gonzalo de Aranda al Rey. Mexico, February 7, 1548.

Cartas de los offs Res de Nueva Espa. Mexico, February 20, 1548; July 24, 1548; October 29, 1548; December 30, 1548.

Los fondos existente en tesoreria de la Nueba España. Mexico, November 12, 1549.

Cartas de los officiales Res de la Nueva España. Mexico, July 5, 1549; February 20, 1550.

66-5-14

rrelacion sacada en suma de vesita general hecha por el señor licenciado hernan martinez de la marcha oydor allcalde mayor en la Real Abdiencia que Reside en la cibdad de Compostela ffechas por las partes probincias e pueblos en la dicha vesita.

67-1-18-No. 2a

Carta al rey de los oydores y Alldes Mayores. Compostela, November 28, 1549.

No. 3a. Carta a S.Mt. de la Justicia y rregimio de Compostela. November 1, 1549.

No. 4a. Carta de los oficiales de V. Mt. de Nueva Galicia. December 20, 1549.

No. 5a. Carta de Juan de Cespedes. Guadaljara, August 25, 1550.

No. 6a. Carta al rey de la Justicia y Regimio desta Cibdad de Guadalajara. September 1, 1550.

67-1-18

Libro en pergamino contiene varios cartas escritos al Rey por la Audiencia obispo y oficiales reales y otros personas de la Nueva Galicia. 1569-1571.

87-6-1

Registros de oficio y partes, Reales Ordenes dirigidas a las autoridades y particulares de Nueba España. 1529-1539.

87-6-2

Registros de oficio y parte, Reales ordenes dirigidas a las autoridades y particulares de Nueba España. 1548-1569.

87-7-6

Reales cedulas dirigidas al virrey y otras autoridades. 1546-1548.

88-6-2

Hordenanças hechas por el muy illmo Sr Don Anto de Mendoça Visorrey y gobernador por su Mt en la Nueba España para la buena Gobernacion della y el buen recabdo de la Real haciendo de S. Mt. Mexico, August 30, 1539.

Hordenanças hechas por el vissorey Dn Anto de Mendoza. Mexico, October 4, 1540.

Hordenanças hechas por parte del virrey Dn Anto de Mendoza. Mexico, March 20, 1542.

91-1-9

Poder dado al doctor Anto Rodriguez Quesada y Juo y Sebastian Rodriquez por los oydores del Real Audiencia de Mexico. Mexico, October 24, 1550.

D. Indiferente General.

139-1-3

Registros:—reales ordenes y capitulaciones sobre la expedicion de Alvarado y venta de su armada 1538-1540.

139-7-14

Registros:—Reales decretos y ordenes Generales. La jornada de Monzon desde 30 agosto de 1537 hasta 8 de Febrero de 1538.

Diferente jornadas de Monzon desde 6 de Junio de 1542 hasta 22 de Diziembre de 1542.

140-3-9

Real cedula sobre el pagar de los diezmos por los q en Nueva España cogen seda. El principe, Valladolid, 1543.

144-1-10

Informacion sobre el desacato q cometio el P. Frano Juan de Zumarraga con la Audiencia de Mexico estando esta en la carcel haciendo ciertas diligencias. Mexico, March 5, 1530.

144-1-11

Probanza hecha en la cibdad de Mechuacan a 15 de otubre de Myll quinientos y treynta y tres anos para haber informacion de las minas de cobre q ay en esta provincia.

144-1-12

Informacion sobre la villa de San Miguel a la provincia de Culiacan y Ynformacion q sobre ello se hize. Guadalajara, November 22, 1538.

144-1-13

Oficio de Tesorero de la armada a Anto de Almaguer. Don Anto de Mendoza y Pedro de Alvarado. En la villa de Autlan, Provincia de Colima. February 8, 1541.

145-1-10

Merced a Andres de Dorantes. Madrid, December 15, 1539.

Peticion de los mercaderes y otras persones q tratan en la Nueba Espa. Recibido en Sevilla. March 22, 1538.

E. Archivo Nacional, Madrid.

No. 1049

Libro tercero de cartas de la Inqon de la Nueva España desde el año 1595, hasta 1603. Poblacion.

F. Ayer Collection of the Newberry Library, Chicago.

Ordenanças hechas por el Sr Vissorey don Antonio de Mendoça sobre las minas de la Nueva Spaña. Mexico, January 14, 1550.

G. Bancroft Library, University of California.

Cronica commentario o narracion de los descubrimientos antiguos y modernos en la Nueva España y Nueva Mexico. Baltasar Obregón. April 17 and 26, 1548, letters dedicating the work to the king. A transcript from the Archives of the Indies in the Bolton Collection. (Patronato Real, No. 7, 1-1-3/22).

H. Biblioteca de la Real Academia de la Historia. Muñoz Collection. Copy of the Juan Páez diary of the Cabrillo-Ferrelo voyage. (36-13.)

Printed Materials

Academia de la historia.

Boletín de la real Academia de la historia, Madrid, 1877.

Memorias de la real academia de la historia, Madrid, 1796.

Memorial histórico Español, Madrid, 1851, referred to as M. H. E. in the text.

A. S. Aiton and J. L. Mecham, "The Archivo General de Indias," *The Hispanic American Historical Review*, IV. 533-568.

A. S. Aiton, "The later career of Coronado," *The American Historical Review*, XXX. 298-305.

A. S. Aiton, "The first American mining code," *The Michigan Law Review*, XXIII. 105-114.

L. Alamán, *Disertaciones sobre la Historia de la República Megicana desde la Época de la Conquista que los Españoles hicieron à Fines del Siglo XV y Principios del XVI de las Islas y Continente Americano hasta la Independencia*, 3 vols., Mexico, 1844-49.

Cayetano Alcázar, *Historia del Correo en America*, Madrid, 1920. (Editada por la Sociedad de Historia Hispano-Americana. Reviewed in "Boletin de la Real Academia de la Historia." Tomo LXXVIII—Cuaderno II. Febrero 1921, p. 107.)

Rafael Altamira y Crevea, *Historia de España y de la Civilización Española*, 4 vols., Barcelona, 1913-14.

Elias Amador, *Bosquejo Historico de Zacatecas*, Zacatecas, 1892.

José María Antequera, *Historia de la Legislación Española*, Madrid, 1884.

Argentina, Biblioteca del Congreso, *Audiencia de Lima, Correspondencia de Presidentes y Oidores*. Madrid, 1922.

Edward Armstrong, *The Emperor Charles V.*, 2 vols., London, 1902.

Antonio Ballesteros y Beretta, *Historia de España y su influencia en la historia universal*. Barcelona, 1919, 3 vols. to date.

Hubert Howe Bancroft, *History of California*, 7 vols., San Francisco, 1884-90.

Hubert Howe Bancroft, *History of Central America*, 3 vols., San Francisco, 1882-87.

HUBERT HOWE BANCROFT, *History of Mexico*, 6 vols., San Francisco, 1883-87.

HUBERT HOWE BANCROFT, *History of the North Mexican States and Texas*, 2 vols., San Francisco, 1884-89.

HUBERT HOWE BANCROFT, *History of Arizona and New Mexico*, San Francisco, 1884-88.

ADOLPH FRANCIS [ALPHONSE] BANDELIER, "Contributions to the History of the Southwestern portion of the United States," *Papers of the Archaeological Institute of America*, V. Cambridge, 1890.

JAMES N. BASKETT, "A study of the Route of Coronado between the Rio Grande and Missouri Rivers," *Kansas State Historical Society Collections*, XII. 219-252.

PABLO DE LA PURÍSIMA CONCEPCIÓN BEAUMONT, *Crónica de la Provincia de los Santos Apostoles S. Pedro y S. Pablo de Michoacan*, Mexico, 1874.

FRANK WILSON BLACKMAR, *Spanish Institutions of the Southwest*, Baltimore, 1891.

HERBERT EUGENE BOLTON and THOMAS M. MARSHALL, *The Colonization of North America, 1492-1783*, New York, 1921.

H. E. BOLTON, *Guide to Materials for the History of the United States in the Principal Archives of Mexico*, Washington, 1913.

H. E. BOLTON, *The Spanish Borderlands, a Chronicle of Old Florida and the Southwest*, New Haven, 1921.

H. E. BOLTON, *Spanish Exploration in the Southwest, 1592-1706*, New York, 1916.

EDWARD GAYLORD BOURNE, *Spain in America, 1450-1580*, New York, 1904.

KONRAD BURGER, *Die Drucker und Verleger in Spanien und Portugal von 1501 bis 1536*, Leipzig, 1913.

JAMES BURNEY, *A Chronological History of the Discoveries in the South Sea*, 4 vols., London, 1803.

ALVAR NUÑEZ CABEZA DE VACA, "The Narrative of Alvar Nuñez Cabeza de Vaca," *Spanish Explorers in the Southern United States, 1538-1543* (Frederick W. Hodge, ed.), New York, 1907.

Cartas de Indias. Ministerio de Fomento, Madrid, 1877.

ANDRÉS CAVO, *Los Tres Siglos de Méjico durante el Gobierno Español hasta la Entrada del Ejercito Trigarante; Obra escrita en Roma por el Padre D. Andrés Cavo de la Com-*

pañia de Jesús, Publicada con Notas y Suplemento en 1836 por el Licenciado D. Carlos Maria de Bustamente, Jalapa, 1870.

CHARLES EDWARD CHAPMAN, *A History of California: the Spanish Period,* New York, 1921.

CHARLES EDWARD CHAPMAN, *Catalogue of Materials in the Archivo General de Indias,* Berkeley, 1919.

Colección de documentos inéditos para la historia de España, 113 vols., Madrid, 1864-1886, with continuation of 6 vols.

Colección de Documentos Inéditos, relativos al Descubrimiento, Conquista y Colonización de las Antiguas Posesiones Españolas en América y Oceania. (Edited by Joaquin F. Pacheco, Francisco de Cárdenas, Luis Torres de Mendoza), 42 vols., Madrid, 1864-84. Referred to as Pacheco y Cárdenas in the text.

Colección de Documentos Inéditos de Ultramar, segunda série, 13 vols., Madrid, 1885-1900.

MANUEL COLMEIRO, *Historia de la Economía Política en España,* 2 vols., Madrid, 1863.

HERNÁN CORTÉS, *Escritos Sueltos,* Mexico, 1871.

(Mariano Cuevas, ed.), *Cartas y otros documentos de Hernán Cortés novisimamente descubiertos en el Archivo General de Indias,* Sevilla, 1915.

MARIANO CUEVAS, *Documentos inéditos del siglo XVI para la historia de México,* Mexico, 1914.

CHARLES HENRY CUNNINGHAM, "The Institutional Background of Spanish-American history," *The Hispanic American Historical Review,* I. 24-39. Washington, 1918.

CHARLES HENRY CUNNINGHAM, *The Audiencia in the Spanish Colonies,* Berkeley, 1919.

MANUEL DANVILA, "Historia crítica y documentada de las communidades de Castilla," *Memorial Histórico Español,* XXXV-XXXIX.

MANUEL DANVILA Y COLLADO, *El Poder Civil en España,* 6 vols., Madrid, 1885-86.

GEORGE DAVIDSON, "An examination of some of the early voyages of discovery," *Report of the Superintendent of the United States Coast and Geodetic Survey,* appendix 7, 1893.

GIL GONZÁLEZ DÁVILA, *Teatro Eclesiastico de la primativa Iglesia de las Indias Occidentales,* Madrid, 1649.

Juan De la Torre, *Bosquejo Histórico y Estadistico de la Ciudad de Morelia*, Mexico, 1883.

Gaston Desdevises du Desert, *L' Espagne de l' Ancien Régime: Les Institutions*, Paris, 1899.

Gaston Desdevises du Desert, "Vice-Rois et Capitaines-Généraux des Indes Espagnoles à la Fin du XVIIIe Siècle," in *Revue Historique*, CXXV, 249; CXXVI, 250.

Bernal Diaz del Castillo, *The True History of the Conquest of New Spain* (Alfred Percival Maudslay, trns.), Hakluyt Society Publications, London, 1916.

Emmanuel Domenech, *Histoire du Méxique*, Paris, 1868.

Joaquín Escriche, *Diccionario Razonado de Legislación y Jurisprudencia*, 3 vols., Madrid, 1847-51.

Francisco Escudero y Perossa, *Tipografía hispalense*, Madrid, 1894.

John Fiske, *The Discovery of America with some account of Ancient America and the Spanish Conquest*, Cambridge, 1892.

Fabian Fonseca and Carlos de Urrutia, *Historia General de Real Hacienda*, 6 vols., Mexico, 1845-53.

Antonio Martín Gamero, *Historia de la ciudad de Toledo*, Toledo, 1862.

Francisco Monterde García Icazbalceta, "El primer Torneo habido en la Nueva España," *The Hispanic American Historical Review*, V. 742.

(Joaquín García Icazbalceta, ed.), *Colección de Documentos Para la Historia de México*, 2 vols., Mexco, 1858-66.

(Joaquín García Icazbalceta, ed.), *Nueva Colección de Documentos para la Historia de México*, 5 vols., Mexico, 1886-1892.

(Joaquín García Icazbalceta, ed.), *Don Fray Juan de Zumárraga*, Mexico, 1881.

(Joaquín García Icazbalceta, ed.), *Bibliografía Méxicana del Siglo XVI*, Mexico, 1886.

Gentleman of Elvas, "The Narrative of the Expedition of Hernando de Soto" (Theodore H. Lewis, ed.) *Spanish Explorers in the Southern United States, 1528-1543* (Frederick W. Hodge, ed.), New York, 1917.

Francisco López de Gómara, *Annals of the Emperor Charles V* (Roger Bigelow Merriman, trns.), Oxford, 1912.

Luís Gonzalez Obregón, *México Viejo*, Mexico, 1900.

Konrad Haebler, *Bibliografía Ibérica del Siglo XV*, La Haya, 1903-17.

Great Britain: Public Record Office, *Calendar of Letters, Despatches, and State Papers, Relating to the Negotiations between England and Spain*. Pascual de Gayangos, ed., 11 vols., London, 1862-1916.

Charles Wilson Hackett, "Delimitation of Political Jurisdictions in Spanish North America to 1535," *The Hispanic American Historical Review,*" I. 40-69. Washington, 1918.

Charles Wilson Hackett, *Historical documents relating to New Mexico*, (ed. for Adolph Bandelier) Introduction, Washington, 1923.

Richard Hakluyt, *The Principal Navigations, Voiages, Traffics and Discoveries of the English Nation . . . devided into three several volumes*, London, 1598.

Clarence Henry Haring, "American Gold and Silver production in the first half of the Sixteenth Century," *The Quarterly Journal of Economics*, XXIX. 433-479.

Clarence Henry Haring, "Ledgers of the Royal Treasurers in Spanish America," *The Hispanic American Historical Review*, II. 173-188.

Clarence Henry Haring, *Trade and Navigation between Spain and the Indies in the time of the Hapsburgs*, Cambridge, 1918.

Joaquín Hazana y la Rua, *La Imprenta en Sevilla*, Seville, 1892.

Sir Arthur Helps, *The Spanish Conquest in America and its Relation to the History of Slavery and to the Government of Colonies*, 4 vols., New York, 1900-1904.

Antonio de Hererra y Tordesillas, *Historia General de los Hechos de los Castellanos en las Islas i Tierra Firme del Mar Oceano*, 4 vols., Madrid, 1601-1615.

Roscoe R. Hill, "The Office of Adelantado," *The Political Science Quarterly*, XXVIII. 646-669.

Alexander Humboldt, *Political Essay on the Kingdom of New Spain*, 4 vols., London, 1814.

Icazbalceta, see—Garcia.

Instrucciones que los Virreyes de Nueva España dejaron à sus Sucesores, Mexico, 1867.

Albert Galloway Keller, *Colonization; a Study of the Founding of New Societies*, Boston, 1908.

EDWARD, VISCOUNT LORD KINGSBOROUGH KING, *Antiquities of Mexico*, 9 vols., London, 1830-48.

JULIUS KLEIN, *The Mesta, a Study in Spanish Economic History*, Cambridge, 1921.

MIGUEL LA FUENTE-ALCÁNTARA, *Historia de Granada* . . . Paris, 1852.

CHARLES DE LANNOY and HERMAN VANDER LINDEN, *Histoire de l' Expansion Coloniale des Peuples Européens, Portugal et Espagne*, Brussels, 1907.

PIERRE PAUL LEROY-BEAULIEU, *De la Colonisation chez les Peuples Modernes*, 2 vols., Paris, 1908.

GEORGE CORNEWALL LEWIS, *An Essay on the Government of Dependencies* (C. P. Lucas, ed.), Oxford, 1891.

FRANCISCO ANTONIO LORENZANA, *Historia de Nueva España*, Mexico, 1770.

WOODBURY LOWERY, *The Spanish Settlements within the Present Limits of the United States, 1513-1561*, New York, 1901.

GERÓNIMO DE MENDIETA, *Historia Eclesiástica Indiana*, Mexico, 1870.

ANTONIO DE MENDOZA, Carta de D. Antonio de Mendoza á la Emperatriz participando que vienen à España Cabeza de Vaca y Francisco Dorantes, que se escaparon de la armada de Pánfilo de Nárvaez. Mexico, February 11, 1537. Pacheco y Cárdenas, XIV. 235-236.

ANTONIO DE MENDOZA, Provision dada por el virey don Antonio de Mendoza al reverendo y magnifico señor Don Vasco de Quiroga para contar los Vasallos del Marques del Valle, Don Hernando Cortés. Mexico, November 30, 1537. Pacheco y Cárdenas, XII. 314-318.

ANTONIO DE MENDOZA, Carta de D. Antonio de Mendoza, virey de Nueva España, al Emperador, dándole cuenta de varios asuntos de su Gobierno. Mexico, December 10, 1537. Pacheco y Cárdenas, II. 119-139.

ANTONIO DE MENDOZA, Relacion del virrey de Nueva España . . . sobre los servycios personales. . . . Pacheco y Cárdenas, XLI. 149-161.

ANTONIO DE MENDOZA, Instruccion de don Antonio de Mendoza, visorey de Nueva España (al Fray Marcos de Niza). Pacheco y Cárdenas, III. 325-338.

ANTONIO DE MENDOZA, Lettere scritte dal' illustrissimo signor don Antonio di Mendozza vice rè della nuoua Spagna alla maesta dell' imperatore. Ramusio, III. fol., 355 (1556 ed.). Antonio de Mendoza, Carta del virey don Antonio de Mendoza al Emperador. Jacona, April 17, 1540. Pacheco y Cárdenas, II. 356-362.

Antonio de Mendoza, Instruccion que debia observar el capitan Hernando de Alarcon en la expedicion à la California que iba à emprender de orden del virrey D. Antonio de Mendoza. Mexico, May 31, 1541. Smith, *Florida*, pp. 1-6.

Antonio de Mendoza, Carta de D. Antonio de Mendoza virey de la Nueva España à Juan de Aguilar, pidiendole se la autorizase para avenirse con los portugueses sobre la posesion de territorios . . . Pacheco y Cárdenas, III. 506-511.

Antonio de Mendoza, Carta de Don Antonio de Mendoza virey de la Nueva España al comendador mayor de Leon, participándole la muerte del adelantado de Guatemala y Honduras, y el estado de otros varios asuntos. Mexico, March 10, 1542. *Cartas de Indias,* pp. 253-255.

Antonio de Mendoza, Carta del virey Don Antonio de Mendoza, dando Cuenta al principe Don Filipe de haber hecho reparto de la tierra de Nueva España, y exponiendo la necesidad que tenia de pasar à Castilla . . . Mexico, October 30, 1548. *Cartas de Indias,* pp. 256-257.

Antonio de Mendoza, Carta del virey Don Antonio de Mendoza Al Emperador Don Carlos . . . Guastepeque, June 10, 1549.

Antonio de Mendoza, Fragmenta de la visita hecha à don Antonio de Mendoza. Interrogatorio por el cual han de ser examinados los testigos presente por su parte don Antonio de Mendoza. Mexico, January 8, 1547. Icazbalceta, *Colección,* II. 72-140.

Antonio de Mendoza, Relacion, Apuntamientos y avisos que por mandado de S. M. dí al Sr. D. Luís de Velasco. *Instrucciones que los Vireyes de Nueva España dejaron à sus Sucesores,* 238.

Roger Bigelow Merriman, *The Rise of the Spanish Empire in the Old World and the New,* 4 vols., New York, 1918-1925. 3 vols. published.

Andrés Molina Enríquez, *Las grandes problemas nacionales,* Mexico, 1909.

(Alfred Morel-Fatio, ed.), *L' Espagne au XVIe et au XVIIe siècle*, Heilbronn, 1878.

HENRY CRITTENDEN MORRIS, *The History of Colonization from the Earliest Times to the Present Day*, 2 vols., New York, 1904.

BERNARD MOSES, *The Establishment of Spanish Rule in America*, New York, 1898.

MATIAS DE LA MOTA PADILLA, *Historia de la Conquista de la Provincia de la Nueva Galicia, escrita en 1742*, Mexico, 1870.

FRAY TORIBIO DE BENAVENTE ó MOTOLINÍA, *Historia de los Indios de la Nueva España*, Icazbalceta, *Colección*, I. 249.

MARTIN FERNANDEZ DE NAVARRETE, *Colección de los viages y descubrimientos que hicieron por mar los Españoles desde fines del Siglo XV.*, 5 vols., Madrid, 1825-1837.

MARTIN FERNANDEZ DE NAVARRETE, *Disertacion sobre la historia de la Náutica*, Madrid, 1846.

JUAN N. NAVARRO, *D. Antonio de Mendoza, I, Virey de la Nueva España. El Liceo Mexicano*, Mexico, 1844.

PACHECO Y CÁRDENAS, see under COLECCIÓN.

JUAN PÁEZ, Relacion del descubrimiento que hizo Juan Rodriquez Navegando por la contracosta del Mar del Sur. al Norte, hecha por Juan Paez. Pacheco y Cárdenas, XIV. 165-191.

ANTONIO PEÑAFIEL, *Ciudades Coloniales y Capitales de la República Méxicana*, 5 vols., Mexico, 1908-14.

WILLIAM HICKLING PRESCOTT, *History of the Conquest of Mexico*, Philadelphia, 1890.

WILLIAM HICKLING PRESCOTT, *History of the Reign of Ferdinand and Isabella the Catholic*, Philadelphia, 1864.

HERBERT INGRAM PRIESTLEY, *José de Gálvez: Visitor-General of New Spain, 1765-1771*, Berkeley, 1916.

H. I. PRIESTLEY, "The Old University of Mexico," *University of California Chronicle*, XXI. 369-385.

H. I. PRIESTLEY, *The Mexican Nation: A History*, New York, 1923.

VASCO DE PUGA, *Provisiones, Cédulas, Instrucciones de Su Magestad . . . para la Administration y Governacion de esta Nueva España . . . desde el ano 1525 hasta . . . 1563*, 2 vols., Mexico (1563), 1878.

HERNANDO DEL PULGAR, *Crónica de los señores reyes Cató-*

licas, Biblioteca de autores Españoles, LXX. Madrid, 1875-1878.

José María Quadrado, and Vicente de la Fuente, *Castilla La Nueva, España sus Monumentos y Artes,* Barcelona, 1886.

Giovanni Battista Ramusio, *Terzo volvme delle navigationi et viaggi,* Venice, 1556.

Recopilación de Leyes de los Reinos de las Indias, 4 vols., Madrid, 1841.

"Relaciones Geográficas de Nueva España," *Boletin del Centro de Estudios Americanistas de Sevilla,* Sevilla, 1920, pp. 36, 37.

W. E. Richey, "Early Spanish Explorations and Indian implements in Kansas," *Kansas State Historical Society Collections,* VIII. 152-168.

(Vicente Riva Palacio, ed.), *México à través de los Siglos,* 5 vols., Barcelona, 1888-89.

Agustín Rivera, *Principios Críticos sobre el Vireinato de la Nueva España,* San Juan de los Lagos, 1884-88.

Manuel Rivera Cambas, *Los Gobernantes de México,* 2 vols., Mexico, 1872-73.

William Robertson, *The History of America,* 2 vols., London, 1777.

Wilhelm Georg Friedrich Roscher, *The Spanish Colonial System* (E. G. Bourne, trns.), New York, 1904.

Pedro de Salazar y de Mendoza, "Crónica del gran cardenal de España Don Pedro González de Mendoza." *Memorial Histórico Español . . . Real Academia de de la Historia,* Tom. VI.

Alonso de Santa Cruz, *Crónica del Emperador Carlos V. Real Academia de la Historia,* 3 vols., Madrid, 1920.

Mario Schiff, "La Bibliothèque du Marquis de Santillane," *École des Hautes Études,* vol. 153. Paris, 1905.

Samuel Parsons Scott, *History of the Moorish Empire in Europe,* 4 vols., Philadelphia, 1904.

(Justo Sierra, ed.), *Mexico, its Social Evolution,* 3 vols., Mexico, 1900-1904.

Donald Eugene Smith, *The Viceroy of New Spain,* Berkeley, 1913.

Juan de Solórzano y Pereyra, *Política Indiana* (Francisco Ramiro de Valenzuela, ed.). 2 vols., Madrid (1629-39), 1776.

JOAN SUÁREZ DE PERALTA, *Tratado del descubrimiento de las Yndias y su conquista . . . Noticias históricas de la Nueva España* (Justo Zaragoza, ed.), Madrid, 1878.

JOAN SUÁREZ DE PERALTA, *Traduccion Paleográfica del Libro Cuarto de Actas de Cabildo de la Ciudad de Mexico* (Manuel Orozco y Berra, ed., with continuations), Mexico, 1859.

HENRI TERNAUX-COMPANS, *Voyages, Relations et Mémoires Originaux pour servir à l'histoire de la Découverte de l'Amérique*, 20 vols., Paris, 1837-41.

GEORGE TICKNOR, *History of Spanish Literature*, 3 vols., Boston, 1882.

JUAN DE TORQUEMADA, *Primera Parte de los veinte i un libros Rituales i Monarchia Indiana*, 3 vols., Madrid, 1723.

HERMAN VANDER LINDEN and CHARLES DE LANNOY, *Histoire de L'Expansion Coloniale des Peuples Européens, Portugal et Espagne*, Brussels, 1907.

JOSEPH DE VEITIA LINAJE, *Norte de la Contratacion de las Indias Occidentales*, Sevilla, 1672.

AUGUSTIN DE VETANCURT, *Teatro Mexicano descripción breve de los sucesos exemplares, históricos, políticos, militares y religiosos del nuevo mundo*, Mexico, 1698.

VILAR Y PASCUAL, *Diccionario histórico genealógico y heráldico de las familias ilustres de la monarquia española*, Madrid, 1859-66.

ANTONIO RODRÍGUEZ VILLA, *El Emperador Carlos V y su corte segun las cartas de Don Martín de Salinas embajador del Infante Don Fernando, 1522-1529*, Madrid, 1903.

HENRY R. WAGNER, *The Spanish Southwest, 1542-1794*, Berkeley, 1924.

HENRY R. WAGNER, "California voyages, 1539-1541," *Quarterly of the California Historical Society*, III. no. 4.

GEORGE PARKER WINSHIP, "The Coronado Expedition, 1540-1542," *Fourteenth Annual Report Bureau of Ethnology*, Washington, 1896.

(Justin Winsor, ed.), *A Narrative and Critical History of America* (vol. II), Boston and New York, 1886.

NICETO DE ZAMACOIS, *Historia de Mejico desde sus Tiempos Mas remotos hasta Nuestros Dias*, 18 vols., Mexico, 1877-82.

D. JUSTO ZARAGOZA, *Noticias Históricas de la Nueva España*, Madrid, 1878.

INDEX

Nuestra Señora de Zacatecas, founded, 75; see also Zacatecas.
Nueva Galicia, see New Galicia.
Nueva Vizcaya, 173.
Nuevo Reino, 96.
Núñez de la Marcha, oidor, 181: visitation of, 184 f.
Núñez Vela, Blasco, viceroy of Peru, 96, 175.

Oajaca, 45; see also Oaxaca.
Oaxaca, 91, 102 f., 174, 175.
Obregón, Baltasar de, 15.
Ocaña, Spain, 25.
Ocampo, Diego de, 176.
Ocharte, Pedro, printer, 108.
Ocoraritarco, viceroy's ranch, 48.
Offices, 55, 86.
Officials, various, 17 f., 47, 68, 69-73, 75-77, 79-82, 110, 112, 114, 163, 164, 178, 185.
Oidores, in New Spain, arrival of, 19; conflict with Church, 20; new appointed, 22 f.; salaries of, 23, 59; arrival at Vera Cruz of, 24; small number of, 47, 56; orders concerning, 49; harmony with viceroy of, 61 f.; in private business, 64, 184; residencias and visitas conducted by, 65; restricted residence of, 65; in cabildo, 67; counsel delay, 97; distribute charity, 98; in New Galicia, 181, 184; of Peru, rashness of, 192; see also Audiencia.
Olmedo, battle of, 5.
Oñate, Cristóbal de, lieutenant of Guzmán, 25; discovers mines, 75; government of, 138; narrative of, 142; at junta, 146; expedition of, 147 f.; aid to Alvarado of, 149 f.; with Mendoza, 151 f., 154; maestro de campo, 176: visita of, 178-81; mines of, 184.
Oñate, Juan de, 173.
Oporto, Cathedral of, 10.
Order of Santiago, 6.
Oregon, Rogue River of, 132.
Ortiz de Matienzo, Juan, oidor, 19 f., 23, 27.
Ortiz de Zuñiga, Alonso, 167.
Ordinances, local, 53; mining, 79, 185; sheep, 110 f.; silk, 112; see also Laws.
Oronato, lay brother with Fray Marcos, 120.

Oropeso, Conde de, declined viceroyship, 22.
Orozco, María de, 5 f.; see also López.
Osorno, Conde de, 21.
Otomi, Indians, 173, 177 f., 182.
Otumba, Indians of, 93.
Ozumba, viceroy's ranch, 48.

Pablos, Juan, Italian printer, 107-10.
Pacheco, Francisco, viceroy's mother, 9.
Pacheco, Juan, Marqués de Villena, 9.
Pacheco, María de, viceroy's sister, 10; widow of Juan de Padilla, 10; flight to Portugal and death there, 10.
Padilla, Juan de, leader of consumers, 10.
Páez, Juan, diary of, 132 f.; cronista, Juan Páez de Castro, 133.
Pánuco, 19, 28, 43, 45, 102.
Paper, for printing, 107 f.
Parada, Alonso de, member of first audiencia, 19, 23.
Paria, Gulf of, 96.
Patzcuaro, 4, 179.
Pay-rolls, 92 f.
Pedazco, defined, 53.
Peña Vallejo, Juan de la, 55.
Peñafiel, Spain, 14, 188.
Penalties, 73, 76, 80.
Peons, Mexican, 91.
Peralta, Martín de, 86.
Peralta, Suarez de, sees Coronado return, 127.
Pérez, Hernan, Doctor, 170.
Pérez, de la Torre, Diego, governor of New Galicia, 26, 118, 137.
Periods, of Mendoza's rule, 172.
Petaçal, chief of Jalpa, 141.
Peru, 13 f., 35, 83, 96, 133 f., 157 f., 170, 172, 175 f., 181, 190-93.
Philip, Prince, later Philip II of Spain, 14, 165 f., 186.
Philippines, 131, 134, 136.
Pirates, in American waters, 81.
Pioneers, discover mines, 74.
Pizarro, Francisco, conqueror of Peru, 13, 136, 157, 192.
Pizarro, Gonzalo, revolt of, 175 f.
Placencia, Pedro de, 178.
Policy, of Spain in New World, 32-34, of viceroy, 193-96.